PRAISE FOR *LEG*

"A strange, smutty, hilarious, beautiful, compassionate, provoking, big-hearted, sharp-tongued, original, brilliant memoir. It's about a very particular coming-of-age that will nevertheless remind readers of what it is to be young and to want everything. I hated to see it end."
—ELIZABETH MCCRACKEN, NATIONAL BOOK AWARD FINALIST AND AUTHOR OF *THE HERO OF THIS BOOK*

"*Leg* is a laugh-out-loud funny memoir that will hit you squarely in the heart and leave you with tears in your eyes. Tears of joy and tears of heartache, sure—but most of all tears of gratitude for this incredible tale of marvelous resilience, tremendous love, a larger-than-life family, and boner pills. Greg Marshall is one helluva storyteller, taking hilarity and emotional resonance and putting them in a paint mixer set to high until he creates an astonishingly bright, bold, and beautiful new color that is uniquely his own." **—ISAAC FITZGERALD, *NEW YORK TIMES* BESTSELLING AUTHOR OF *DIRTBAG, MASSACHUSETTS***

"*Leg* has all the ingredients of an addictive memoir. But what separates this book from the pack is Marshall's rich and rare perspective navigating the world as a queer disabled person. Marshall is one of the most exciting new voices in nonfiction. I could get lost in his brilliant brain forever."
—RYAN O'CONNELL, AUTHOR OF *JUST BY LOOKING AT HIM*

"In the struggles of his body, his family, and his own exploration of his identities, Marshall finds a mirror and a prism for life in America now. This is a funny, smart, and loving memoir, and I learned perhaps more about myself reading *Leg* than I did about Marshall." **—ALEXANDER CHEE, AUTHOR OF *HOW TO WRITE AN AUTOBIOGRAPHICAL NOVEL***

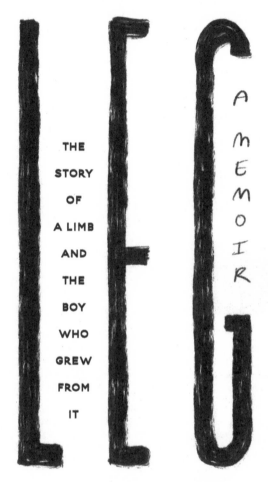

LEG

THE
STORY
OF
A LIMB
AND
THE
BOY
WHO
GREW
FROM
IT

A MEMOIR

Greg Marshall

TRAPEZE

First published in the United States in 2023 by Abrams Press, New York,
an imprint of ABRAMS,
First published in Great Britain in 2023 by Trapeze,
an imprint of The Orion Publishing Group Ltd
Carmelite House, 50 Victoria Embankment
London EC4Y 0DZ

An Hachette UK Company

1 3 5 7 9 10 8 6 4 2

A CIP catalogue record for this book is
available from the British Library.

ISBN (Hardback) 978 1 3987 1634 6
ISBN (Export Trade Paperback) 978 1 3987 1635 3
ISBN (eBook) 978 1 3987 1637 7
ISBN (Audio) 978 1 3987 1636 0

Typeset by Born Group
Printed and bound in Great Britain by Clays Ltd, Elcograf S.p.A.

MIX
Paper from
responsible sources
FSC® C104740

www.orionbooks.co.uk

To Dad, who said I could do it.
To Mom, who drove me to it.

Eleven doctors said he'd never walk. A few predicted a life of incontinence and wheelchairs. Physical therapists and pediatricians recommended a "special" school for the little baby born too early.

Medical professionals tried to comfort me with words like, "We're sure his IQ is normal," and "If he's ever able to express himself he may, one day, be able to be integrated in public schools."

They made diagnoses like polio, cerebral palsy, retardation, and in my usual headstrong way of dealing with life, I threw their words into the trash. I refused to listen. I don't believe in labels.

—DEBI MARSHALL, "SILVER LININGS," *MARYSVILLE GLOBE*, JUNE 25, 1997

CONTENTS

The Marshall family, 1993.
The author (top row, second from right) pretends he is an only child.

AUTHOR'S NOTES

Leg is a true story. Some names and details have been changed and some characters rendered in the composite. Dialogue has been recreated from memory. Though faithfully portrayed to the best of my abilities, my leg may have its own version of events.

Some of the chapters in this book originally appeared, in different forms or with different titles, in the following publications: "Next Week: Debi Fights for Her Life" in *Tahoma Literary Review,* "Marshall Family Vibrator" in *Nude Bruce Review,* "If I Only Had a Leg" in *Electric Literature,* "Never Get AIDS" in *Barely South Review,* "Suck Ray Blue" in *Tampa Review,* "The John" in *Fourth Genre,* "Melk" in *Off Assignment,* "Seksi" in *Foglifter,* "Heal Thy Angels" in *Green Mountains Review,* "An Unusual Event for Your Social Calendar" in *Narratively,* "More Ham" in *Joyland,* "Corey" in *Southwest Review,* and "Our Camelot, with Chickens" in *Transformations.*

Material was also adapted from "Revirgination," which appeared in *Hobart* and "Our Longest Point," which appeared in *Plenitude.*

My mom's extraordinary column, "Silver Linings," was instrumental in the creation of *Leg.* The column ran from 1997 to 2002 in many of the eight community newspapers and business journals my dad co-owned as part of his small publishing empire, Sun News. Those papers included the *Marysville Globe,* the *Arlington Times,* and the *Preston Citizen.*

I AM SPASTICUS!

Philip Roth once wrote that there aren't many words less abstruse than "leg," but it's taken me a lifetime to understand mine. I wish I could say my leg fought in a war, or had a drug problem, or escaped a polygamist cult, or smoked cigarettes with Gertrude Stein in Paris in the twenties, perhaps while wearing a beret and writing poetry. That leg would be worthy of a memoir!

"You can't call your book *Leg*," my mom told me when I brought up the idea. We were walking under the stars in Costa Rica, on the same beach where my big sister, Tiffany, would be married the next afternoon. The sand under my feet felt therapeutic in a vaguely menacing way, like walking on ball bearings and lug nuts. I have very sensitive feet.

"Who would want to read a book called *Leg*?" Mom asked.

"I would," said my mom's partner, Alice. "I think it sounds intriguing." She was drawing what looked like vaginas in the surf with her big toe, calmly avoiding scuttling crabs that left my little sister Mona and me squealing. Alice made jazz hands at the crabs. "*Leg!*"

"Don't agree with him, Alice. That's not your job."

Keeping Mom alive, that was Alice's job. Getting Mom, a sixty-year-old cancer patient, to this exclusive peninsular hideaway, that was Alice's job.

The journey from Utah had required, among other things, flying over a Neverland of sparkling ocean in a tiny propeller plane and then cramming into an off-roading Jeep. We all knew that Alice, my mom's doctor-turned-lover-turned-perpetual-fiancée, was the only person on the planet with the skill and will to do it, the only person who could *Weekend at Bernie's* Mom down the aisle on Tiff's big day, if it came to that. Plus, Alice would know what to do with my mom's body if she died in Central America. If it were up to us, we would just take her out in a snorkeling boat and roll her into the ocean. We might even do that before she died.

Having a mom who's been battling cancer since I was in the second grade has turned me into a morbid bastard, and my four siblings are no better. When your mom is always dying, you think she never will.

"I could call it *The Kid with the Limp*," I said.

"Jesus!" Mom said. "That's even worse."

We walked for a while in silence, listening to waves crash against the shore while taking in the distant flicker of tiki torches at Tiffany's rehearsal dinner farther up the beach.

Alice was squinting up at the sky through her nerdy rectangular glasses, trying to point out some constellations, when my mom interrupted her. "You know what's a great story? *It's a Wonderful Life*." I was almost positive my mom had never sat through *It's a Wonderful Life*—she hates black-and-white movies—but I let her continue for argument's sake. "Why don't people tell stories like that anymore? *It's a Wonderful Leg*. That's what you should call your book. *It's a Wonderful Leg and There's Absolutely Nothing Wrong with It and My Mother Did the Best She Could in Spite of Having Cancer and Five Kids and a Husband Who Died of Fucking ALS*."

Well, there you have it.

I was almost thirty when I discovered, quite by accident, that I have cerebral palsy. No one had ever told me about my diagnosis, not my physical therapists or my orthopedic surgeon, and certainly not my parents.

I've always walked with a limp and I spent a good portion of my childhood in casts, leg braces, and physical therapy, learning how to hop on one foot, skip, and touch my shins (my toes being forever out of reach). But as the middle child of five kids in a rowdy family where someone was always almost dying or OD-ing, I didn't ask too many questions, or, rather, the questions I did ask had nothing to do with my leg and were mostly muttered to myself: Was it possible to get an STD from a Brookstone back massager? Did my voice sound too nasally? How much would ass and calf implants run me, ballpark?

The thing is, I didn't ask about my leg because I thought I already knew everything there was to know about it. It was just a leg.

Imagine that.

I was born among the Sisters of the Third Order of St. Francis of East Peoria, Illinois, in a red-turreted hospital off Interstate 74. Scheduled to pop out vaginally the week after Thanksgiving, I was instead evicted by Cesarean in the predawn of an October morning in 1984, not more than eight hours after Mom started leaking amniotic fluid mid-frame at her monthly Entre Nous bowling tournament.

On my birthday, she liked to retell the tale of my traumatic birth. It involved her doing a headstand in her hospital bed to get me off the umbilical cord and concluded with me spending sixteen days in infant intensive care. At nine months, when I tried to pull myself up to the coffee table or couch, I sprang to the ball of my right foot, my tippy toes, and limped so badly I wore out the tops of shoes rather than the bottoms.

The brusque orthopedic specialist who diagnosed me with cerebral palsy at eighteen months didn't appreciate the fact that I peed on the floor of the exam room. "He's incontinent, too?" he allegedly said. Trying to lighten the mood, Mom noted my stifled, shuffling trot by quipping, "My son walks like Herman Munster."

My leg was what brought us to Salt Lake City. Before my fourth birthday, we moved from our small town in Illinois for my first surgery: an Achilles tendon release on my right side. It would be the first of a handful of operations over the course of my childhood to relieve contractures in my heel and hamstrings, bringing me off my toes and freeing my gait.

As I got older, my parents simply told me I had "tight tendons" and left it at that, making it sound like I suffered from a vaguely Homeric physical ailment rather than a neurological one. My leg was nothing serious. Those pesky tight tendons, they just needed a little loosening up!

I can understand their flawed logic: My folks didn't want me to feel crappy about myself, didn't want me to stare down a lifetime of diminished expectations. They made the inherently ableist and probably correct-given-the-time-and-place calculation that it was safer for me to try to pass as an everyday, *Wizard of Oz*–loving, acne-riddled, thinks-he-can-actually-speak-French dork with a trophy case in his room full of collectible Barbies rather than as a kid living with a disability.

And so, my childhood continued apace, filled with Nerf wars, school musicals, tennis lessons, pretend news broadcasts from the living room, and my mom's never-ending battle with non-Hodgkin's lymphoma. You know, typical kid shit.

Mom and Dad were both born and bred in southern Idaho, so moving back to the Mountain West was a sort of homecoming. We have Mormon relatives on my dad's side but because of my mom's Basque upbringing—the result of adoption, not genetics—we were raised Catholic. I suppose being outcasts on religious grounds in a pre-dominantly Mormon neighborhood provided a kind of pre-education for being gay and disabled. Our training in the ways of the Beehive State was what you'd call practical rather than theological and it would continue, in one way or another, for my entire childhood. Whether you want it or not, when you live in Utah you get the dirt on polygamy and missionaries and baptism for the dead, black magic, and golden tablets. As a general rule, Mormons can't stop talking about being related to Brigham Young and non-Mormons can't stop bitching about the state's restrictive liquor laws.

Our suburb, Holladay, didn't have a seedy underbelly. It had an *undergarment*. If you didn't know what to look for, you would think Holladay was like anywhere else, the ghostly outline of its strangeness just visible under the most ordinary clothes.

Like many other houses in Holladay, our big redbrick 1980s family home had been built with a plethora of walk-in pantries to stockpile nonperishables for the End Times. Picture a place where salvation is served like a warm plate of cookies left on a doorstep. A seminary building or ward—with its needlepoint steeple and satellite dish tuned to the signal coming from Temple Square—was conveniently within walking distance of every public junior high and high school so kids could receive religious instruction as part of their school day. The Church owned, and still owns, the local NBC affiliate. When I was a teenager, they didn't air *Conan* until past midnight and they didn't air *Saturday Night Live* at all. These were grave affronts. Who wants to sit through reruns of *Suddenly Susan* and *Mad About You* when you're in the mood for Camel Toe Annie and the Masturbating Bear?

In this von Trapp world, the Marshalls stuck out.

I'd like to think I'm not the sort of aging gay man who plops down at lunch and comes at you with a hundred crazy stories, but of course I am. I have one of those families. I once overheard someone at a party describe us as a bunch of unlikable assholes who happened to have a great dad—and that was coming from a *friend*. We've been through a lot and none of it seems to have made us better people. It's just made us more *us*.

Every day growing up was like an *ABC Afterschool Special* in which no lessons were learned, no wisdom gleaned, and I think at some point it started to annoy people, or just exhaust them.

My mom, Debi, was a local cancer celebrity with an inspirational newspaper column who would turn to prescription drugs to treat her bone pain and grief once my dad got sick.

Tiffany, the eldest of the five of us kids, bore the brunt of my mom's failing health and became the classic rebellious teenager, a vegetarian snowboarder sluffing school and disappearing up the mountain. She was either royally pissed off at the world or pissing her pants laughing, nothing in between. Mom named Tiffany after her childhood dog. In those years she liked to say, "The bitch is implied."

My brother, Danny—DJ—was the wisecracking big brother. He bit his hand whenever he was keyed up and terrorized my friends and made a fart joke every other word.

Michelle, or Mitch, is half Kiowa and half Navajo in an otherwise white family related by blood. Upon hearing my sister-to-be was an Indian (still the word we used), I, a towheaded six-year-old, lobbied to name her Sacagawea and hoped aloud to our pediatrician that she would be able to speak our language. Mitch was just a few days old

when she arrived at our house in January 1990, sporting what I took
to be a mohawk. Well-intentioned but misguided, racist but kind of
cute about it, I wore dreamcatcher necklaces and collected arrowheads
in her honor and showed up to school in one of my mom's long black
chemo wigs and a buckskin jacket with fringe for my third-grade report
on Geronimo. Planning her escape from an early age, Mitch collected
backpacks, wandered around the house conspicuously reading *A Child
Called "It,"* and hid the Book of Mormon under her mattress.

My youngest sister, Mona, aka Moe, aka Moeham, was the late-
arriving whoopsie baby who Han Solo-ed out of my mom's lymphoma-
filled uterus just before cancer shut things down for good. Starting
life with a pink bow stuck to her scalp with Vaseline and a mustache
of tape under her microscopic nose, Moe soon leapt out of her crib,
karate-kicked her ventilator, and began running around the house
like a nut. We called her Monster Moe because calling her a little shit
wasn't going to fly in Utah.

You'll hang out with all of the Marshalls but for now we can excuse
them for a coffee break. Take five, fam! Seriously, fuck off for a minute!
It's my turn.

A writer may appear to be writing about other people but he's only
ever really writing about himself. What are siblings and parents if not
alternate versions of ourselves, understudies who occasionally steal
the scene? If I'm throwing everyone else under the short bus with my
admittedly reductive frame, we may as well get back to the member of
my family most likely to appear in an *Afterschool Special*: Hello again.
I'm Greg, a gay guy with a limp, a dick that sometimes doesn't work,
and an adolescent addiction to Accutane.

About that limp . . . It wasn't until I left Utah for college in Chicago
that my secret case of cerebral palsy started catching up with me, a
stalker lurking in the shadows of my every thumping step or spastic
gesture. In that era of great reinvention, I was paralyzed—sometimes
literally—at the prospect of having to make so many first impressions.
A lot of the time when I tried to talk to someone my leg muscles would
tighten up, my toes writhing in my shoe. People would ask me why I

was wincing and I wouldn't be able to explain, not really. Nor would I be able to get away. I spent every bit of my social energy making sure no one saw me walk or move awkwardly. It was futile. "Do you have cerebral palsy?" an acquaintance asked when he saw me try to put on my coat. "What? No? My jacket's just a little small."

Even now, I'm not sure if he was being intuitive or bitchy. The guy had two thumbs on one hand and a crush on me, so I'll go with the former. Just recently, it got back to me that the first dude I hooked up with at Northwestern called me Peg Leg Greg to his roommates. Now that I'm on more than a nodding acquaintance with my weakest appendage—my dear leg turning, over the years, from stalker to fellow traveler—I find it sort of funny that my first name should rhyme with the biggest mystery of my life, but had I known of this little sobriquet at the time I would have been devastated. I remember asking my mom if it would be easier if I did just have a fake leg, something I could explain with knock-on-wood swagger.

If anyone asked if I was limping, I'd tell them it was just the old tight tendons, attempting to field queries in an unconcerned midwestern fashion that was the opposite of how I felt. I also didn't have another answer because the real answer, the truth, had never been shared with me.

I uncovered my secret case of CP in 2014 while applying for health insurance. I'll get into that shortly. For now, let's just say I found myself, at almost thirty, skipping past the need to forgive and going straight to feeling ravenous for more information. For weeks afterward, I alternated between a state of woundedness and acceptance as I jerked myself around town by my hair, pointing out the world's unfairness: cracked sidewalks, uneven stairs. Google taught me addictive new catchphrases like "spastic" and "ableism."

"That's ableism!" I told my then-boyfriend Lucas. (I'd later convert him to Husband, top him for the first time after a Renaissance fest, and write about it for the internet—you really should keep reading this book.) I made Lucas film me walking in our parking lot, seeing how I moved from the outside for the first time. I cringed the way you do when listening to a recording of your voice, not because it's so awful but because it's yours: the scraping toe, the bent knees, the hitch in my step that suggested the way people hoof it in old films, smiling self-consciously. I re-watched the episode of *Breaking Bad* where Walter teaches Walt Jr. to drive, this time teary-eyed. I looked up Geri Jewell, the first actor with CP to have a recurring role on TV, and fantasized about showing up to the Planet Fitness where I pounded away on the treadmill in one of her famous pink T-shirts, the kind she'd worn on *The Facts of Life*: I DON'T HAVE CEREBRAL PALSY I'M DRUNK.

"Think about it, Lucas," I'd say. "Some hot, normal person walks into the gym wearing that shirt? Everyone's mind would be *blown*!"

"Or maybe they'll finally get why you almost die every time you run on the treadmill," Lucas posited, trying to shake me out of three decades of denial.

It was like that for a lot of my body's foibles: I shimmy my shoulders when I have to poop; my hands and feet are always freezing and yet at outdoor concerts I get so overheated I have to wear a cooling vest like a distraught rescue dog; prone to panicked forgetfulness, I constantly slap my pockets whenever I'm out of the house to make sure I didn't forget my wallet or phone; anytime I'm nervous or out of sorts, my limbs start shaking hard enough that I can barely fire off a text.

The "spastic" of spastic cerebral palsy comes from the Greek *spastikos* and means "pulling," i.e., the "pulled" muscles in my legs that restrict my movement. "Pulled muscles!" I proclaimed. "Like tight tendons!" I contemplated giving myself the Twitter handle Spasticus. Like Spartacus, get it? Fortunately, Lucas intervened.

Spastic as a noun is an out-of-date slur for a person with CP. By the time I was a teenager, we'd shortened it to the much catchier *spaz*, a slight so common you can find it in the first entry of my seventh-grade journal, where I describe my brother as a "blast" and "overly energetic." "He is a spaz, but that makes him both hilarious and rude/mean."

So, what does it make me?

Anyone who has ever had to come out of any closet knows how twisty the path can be, and I suppose that's partly what this story is about: prickly questions about passing and privilege, obsession and denial, the parts of our identities we hide and those we claim and what it means to transform when there are things about ourselves we can't change.

For now, let's just say discovering the fact of my cerebral palsy has made me see my life, and my leg, with renewed appreciation.

My leg.

Contrary to college gossip, it never sailed the high seas in search of a whale, the prelude to a captain's wooden appendage. It didn't graduate summa cum laude or hike the fjords of Norway, or fight Nazis, or win a gold medal in rhythmic gymnastics—catching a ribbon between its spazoid toes—but it has swung and lifted and climbed. It's trotted along in theater tights and stood contrapposto at concerts. It's survived surgeries and trembled beneath first kisses and fucked its way through the former Yugoslavia and bent in prayer. It's dragged after me on the tennis court and even hobbled down the aisle toward a man with a mustache whom I'd topped after a Renaissance fest—in case you missed that part.

Leg is like a French farce about my body: the secret devotions, the fumbling intimacies, the tawdry jokes, the half-truths told in the name of love, and the family of unlikable assholes who stuck together through it all. This is a story about that little thing that has always bugged you about yourself, that thing you try to ignore that turns out to be the key to your entire existence. If Nora Ephron wrote this book, it would be about her neck. Because I've written it, it's about my leg. It's a wonderful leg and there's absolutely nothing wrong with it and my mother did the best she could in spite of having five kids and cancer and a husband who died of fucking ALS.

I mean, a leg—nothing could be less abstruse.

NEXT WEEK: DEBI FIGHTS FOR HER LIFE

The community newspapers my dad owned in Utah, Idaho, and Washington covered stories so local you couldn't find them anywhere else. This included news about my extremely nonlocal family. Mom published her weekly feature column among horoscopes and crossword puzzles, the school lunch schedule, new arrivals at the library, missionary announcements, who had sung what at sacrament meetings, even who had gone to whose house for Christmas dinner.

Life and death were the staples of her "Silver Linings" column, ordinary folks battling hard-to-pronounce illnesses with a steady diet of hope, joy, and a belief that the human spirit could overcome any obstacle. But the survivor Mom wrote about most often, the one who slowly came to dominate her coverage, was herself.

Shortly after my mom started writing the column, after nearly four years in remission from stage IV non-Hodgkin's lymphoma, an enlarged lymph node popped up on her jaw below her ear, where she held her brick of a cell phone. Mom went in for a checkup with her oncologist, hoping she might have an infected wisdom tooth. After what turned out to be unnecessary dental surgery, she and Dad came home to tell us what she later described in "Silver Linings" as "the most dreaded word in the English language for a cancer survivor: recurrence."

The enlarged lymph node was, in fact, a tumor in her parotid gland that made her cheek salivate when she was hungry or eating a particularly delicious Caesar salad. "Sorry, guys, but this dressing is to die for," she'd say, dabbing at the yellow discharge with a napkin.

That Mom's cancer should make its comeback about a month after she started writing the column was perversely perfect timing. "Silver Linings" was itself a silver lining, a place where she vented and told funny stories—and harrowing ones, too. She discussed biopsies, cancer-related root canals, Hickman lines, pulmonary embolisms, infected toenails, and drained tumors. "If you got it, use it," Mom liked to say. A cute wooden sign nailed over the dining room table bore her Churchillian slogan: NEVER, NEVER, NEVER GIVE UP.

Mom was a former daily newspaper reporter with a master's degree in journalism from Northwestern and a filing cabinet full of clips about rape trials and sudden infant death syndrome, but she avoided hard news in "Silver Linings." She wasn't only a journalist. She was a cancer survivor and the mother of five children. It said so in italics at the bottom of each column.

The picture of Mom that accompanied "Silver Linings" changed a few times over the years. The one I remember best was a glamour shot taken at Fashion Place Mall days before she started chemo that was soft-filtered so even in grayscale she glowed, jean jacket popped open, hair flowing over one shoulder. She was both too dressed up and too dressed down to resemble my animal-print-loving mom. In the context of the newspapers' rural readerships, it was like she was trying to prove her hick credentials, implying that after she finished the column she might work the land instead of the baseline of the tennis court that sat in our backyard.

Particularly because Mom was the boss's wife, the column could sometimes read like a family bulletin. Did subscribers in farm towns hundreds of miles away really care about *us*? All moms take liberties with the truth. The difference was my mom's liberties were in the newspaper. Eight of them. In towns where we didn't live.

Mom had a way of piling it on, of one-upping fate. One of the charms of "Silver Linings" was that every week was a fresh disaster, a new bad thing, another wrinkle in the fabric of our family. When these mini epics couldn't be squeezed into a single column, like when my dad fractured two cervical vertebrae diving into the ocean in Hawaii, they turned into cliffhangers and were "to be continued." *Next week: Bob's tragic injury threatens his life . . .*

A typical column featured my mom going through tests to determine if she was a candidate for a bone marrow transplant, my preemie sister, Mona, flipping over the handlebars of her bike, and me sustaining a concussion during a misguided attempt at ice skating in Sun Valley. If major medical tests and two sporting accidents weren't enough for one day of vacation, Mom sent the stakes soaring by writing that the night concluded with us witnessing a serious collision in which she cradled a teenage boy whose head had gone through the windshield. (In my memory, we'd only been rubberneckers told politely but firmly to move along.)

If the gussied-up headshot didn't look like her, then the mushy articles didn't always sound like her either. Despite her claims, Mom didn't cry during Mother's Day programs, thankful for the privilege of being alive, or seek the true meaning of Christmas in the beguiling words of little Mona, or find solace in crocuses poking bravely from the snow in the darkest of night. Though her wig had flown off on a rollercoaster at Knott's Berry Farm, it hadn't also fallen into a walrus tank at SeaWorld, leading her and Tiffany to take a stage bow to scattered applause.

Still, Mom made over-the-top inspiring. Her way of rendering life large put cancer in its place, making it part of our daily routine. It helped that Dad was always at her side, holding her hand through every doctor's appointment, blood transfusion, and chemo, but that was Dad's job: he toiled behind the scenes so Mom could bring sugar cookies to her chemo nurses, light luminaries, dedicate park benches to her fellow cancer survivors, and drive carpools wearing her NO HAIR DAY hat and then come home and conduct hours of phone interviews for her column at the foot of her bed.

On treatment days, my parents would push through the door after dark, a rumpled fortune teller in a bright headscarf and the good Samaritan who was kind enough to carry her purse. Dad would get to work on my math homework and Mom would crawl under their floral comforter and conk out for a day or two. I knew she was starting to feel better when her yellow legal pad returned to her nightstand followed by the clank of keys. Mom typed the way she played the *Batman* theme song on the piano in the living room, feet tapping, tennis bracelets jumping down her wrists. When she made a mistake, she deleted the entire sentence and started over.

Because of my gimpy leg, Mom pegged me as her apprentice from the start. I wasn't a scuzzy jock (her words) like Tiffany or Danny, out there snowboarding and playing basketball and doing drugs. My limp was my gift to the world, or at least my gift to her column.

I loved having a writer in the family, almost more than I would have loved having a famous talk-show host. In my eagerness to prove myself, I'd interrupt with suggestions, employing vocabulary words I'd learned while dictionary surfing that rarely made sense. My prose tended to be flowery, even for Mom's purposes, but she always made a point of trying it my way. "You're going to change the world with your words, Greg," Mom would say. "Now remind me again. What the hell does *mollify* mean?"

Much of what I'd come to understand about my mom's first battle with cancer in 1992 is based on reading her column when I was a teenager. I was eight at the time she was diagnosed and mostly recalled insignificant scraps that didn't warrant being written down: staying up late eating potato chips in my parents' bed as I waited for them to come home from the hospital, never brushing my teeth, drinking four Cokes a day.

Mom purposely got an ugly haircut so she wouldn't be sad to see it go. Then, a few weeks into treatment, she started shedding all over the house, like our Lhasa Apso, Annie. The night before Thanksgiving Mom and Dad invited us all into their bedroom. Seated on the carpeted steps to the tub, she told us to pull out her hair. Each strand represented a million dead cancer cells. The more we yanked, the more we killed. Years later in her column, Mom would portray this as a joyful moment but I remember being terrified. Once we'd gotten all but a few patches, Mom eased onto a candy-cane-striped chair, nervously flapping her legs as Dad drew a shaving cream *D* for Deb onto her scalp and went at her with a razor until her head shined.

Thanks to my second-grade teacher, a Germanic woman who would go on to work in women's prisons, I was obsessed with Roald Dahl's *The*

Witches and thought my mom might be one. Mom was hurt when she modeled one of her new wigs for me and I told her it made her look like the Grand High Witch. It was a compliment!

Mom wrote about it all for her readers—cancer past and present—packing as much as she could into eight hundred words.

The first time she devoted a "Silver Linings" to me—and the only time I remember coming across the term "cerebral palsy" as a kid—was after my graduation from sixth grade, when I won a leadership award called the Hope of America. I say the award was for "leadership," but I suspect it was for my colorful reading of the morning announcements over the school intercom.

When the principal called my name, my family bum-rushed the stage, my dad filming me trundling up to them in my giant Planet Hollywood polo shirt and baggy Mossimo shorts, the kind that happened to be in style and conveniently hid much of my scrawny right leg.

"As my son strode to the front of the auditorium of the 'normal' elementary school today, I thought my heart would burst from my chest, sprout wings, and fly around the room propelled by pride," Mom wrote. "The boy who was supposed to spend his life in diapers, in a wheelchair, wore a grin which spread from ear to ear as he accepted the framed certificate."

My childhood would have played out differently if my mom had come right out in her column and written that I had spastic cerebral palsy related to prematurity. *That* was why doctors thought I might not talk or walk or use the toilet. Instead, Mom brought up this diagnosis along with polio and retardation only to dismiss them all. Incontinence? Wheelchairs? A merely normal IQ? That wasn't my life—I just had tight tendons. (Also, to linger for just a moment longer on this . . . *polio*? In the mid-1980s?)

Rereading the column now is a study in maternal deflection and misdirection. Like a carnival psychic, Mom highlights super specific details like my birth weight, four-and-a-half pounds, only to get foggy when it comes to other foundational medical facts. She mentions CP right up top to refute that I have it, not to disclose that I do. A few paragraphs later, you can feel her edging up to the point of revelation and turning away:

> The early struggles associated with low birth weight seemed paramount, until he attempted to walk. Relentlessly we dragged him from doctor to doctor, looking for someone who would tell us everything was fine. When that diagnosis never arrived, we decided to fight.
>
> "Everyone has some kind of challenge, Greg," we'd tell him. "There isn't a person alive who doesn't have some kind of obstacle to overcome. You can spend your life feeling sorry for yourself, or you can work with all your heart and all your soul and learn to walk. You can become someone the world looks up to."

That was the truth as I understood it, the lines I heard whenever I asked about my leg.

The story Mom told her readers about the callous doctors who predicted I'd never be able to walk or express myself verbally, who said all sorts of horrible things about me, was as familiar as my own memory. So was the part where I proved them all wrong. The part where Mom and I learned to harmonize to Beach Boys songs on the drive to physical therapy twice a week. The part where Dad strapped me into casts at night. The part where I braved the surgical table to stretch my tight hamstrings and Achilles tendon so I didn't walk on my toes. "Instead of a child with a disability," Mom wrote, "he became a child with a quick wit and an incredible sense of humor."

I read the last paragraph of the column so many times I developed an eye twitch:

> Greg is my hero. He could have chosen to go through life concentrating on all the things he can't do. Instead he focuses on what he CAN do. His worries don't include walking with a limp. His concerns are those of any 12-year-old kid: the first hint of acne, a lousy score on a math quiz, and hoping the girls notice

him some day. He hasn't given his "challenge" in life the power
to become a problem.

The *girls*? Apparently, there were limits to maternal intuition.

In any case, her words often made me believe what I felt: that I'd
overcome my challenges. The little boy who was not supposed to walk
was the Hope of America.

Like my mom, I would throw on a jean jacket, mousse my hair up
big, and become a writer.

Maybe it was the shorter word count that attracted me to poems. At first
I stuck with abstract ideas like freedom and liberty, broken shackles,
that sort of thing. It didn't take long for me to work up to cancer since
my idol and mentor made mention of it often. Soon I was declaring war
on non-Hodgkin's lymphoma with alliteration and capital letters in a
poem titled "Survivor's Spirit." "You must wield the Shield of Support,"
I urged, borrowing the lexicon of my favorite fantasy novels, a series
about talking mice and badgers who live in an abbey. "Carry the Sword
on which Glory is told / Stay in the Haven of Hope and be touched by
the Lance of Love."

Mom was silent after I finished reciting. Then, after a beat, she said
wow and told me to start from the beginning.

Before long she was typing my poem for inclusion in the next
installment of "Silver Linings," suggesting minor edits. "I'm going to
change spears to shears," she said. "Shears are like scissors, so they
would go better with the line about cutting off my hair."

The newspaper arrived a few days later. There on B5 was my mom's
picture. The part I'd waited for came a ways into her article about getting
a port installed near her heart. "As we were leaving for the hospital the
morning of the surgery, our son, Greg, pulled me into a fierce hug and
handed me the following poem."

Its title was in bold, its single long stanza in italics.

I thought my drama queen of a leg, tense with excitement, might
dance out of its socket and jitterbug around the kitchen counter. Mom

came up from behind and hugged me so hard her diamond earring indented my cheek. Ceremonially pulling me into the office, she cut me a check for fifty dollars, her full weekly fee. "It's important for writers to get paid," she said. "That's how you know you're a professional."

So there I was: a professional writer at twelve.

Driven by nepotism, the modest achievement of appearing in a column my mom wrote, in a newspaper my dad owned, was enough to encourage me to crank out heartwarming fare almost daily, always with the hope that during a week when my mom needed filler, she might turn to me.

"You strode up that mountain just as gracefully and resiliently as you have embarrassed the likes of cancer," I wrote to my mom after a Survivors at the Summit hike. "In truth, you are not simply a survivor but a hero to those who do not have your same triumph, for I know there's only one give 'em hell girl like you."

My parents flew us up to Seattle the summer I was thirteen and dumped us on Camano Island for a few days with my dad's mom, Grandma Barbie, so they could meet with doctors in the city. With the recurrence of her cancer, Mom was talking about harvesting her own bone marrow for a future transplant.

While my siblings poked jellyfish with sticks, dug for clams, and caught crab, I scribbled tributes to my mom on the back of envelopes and airsick bags left over from the flight. When that got old, I scoured the moody gray shore for poetry-worthy shells, the kind with smooth undersides that could handle a little marker. As Mom packed a beach bag for the hospital the next morning, I limped up and presented her with my humble, rainbow-colored gift from the sea, blushing with pride as I read the splotchy words of my shell poem. I was a little embarrassed.

"That's cool how you wrote around the barnacle," Tiffany tried.

"Cool?" Mom cried. "It's remarkable! It's the most remarkable, amazing thing I've ever heard. Start over. And this time go slower."

At a time when no one else saw me as particularly talented, my mom was making copies of my poems about raging seas, cruel nightmares, majestic passions, and icy hells and, with her Christmas-card list in hand, mailing them to her Basque aunts and uncles and cousins. The lady at McDonald's even got a poem or two, handed off at the drive-thru window. I'd go to the hospital and chemo nurses I hardly recognized would silence alarms to say, "You must be the writer." The tears cried over my poems formed a humble pond / Then a river / Then a mighty ocean that washed away sadness.

By eighth grade, I had started telling kids at school I limped because of knee problems. I was tentative in PE and shy about making new friends. I tried to either walk behind my classmates or catapult in front of them, hurrying through the halls to avoid getting slammed against a locker and called Marsha Marshall by a kid on the wrestling team who was a good six inches shorter than I was. At the annual Fun Run, a big-boned guy named Ronnie called me a cripple when I jogged past him. A smart guy with a stutter named Dustin referred to me as C-C-C-Cleg, a combination of my shameful appendage and the first letter of what he thought my name was, Craig. That one hurt more. I was so not a Craig.

"To me the limp isn't a big issue. I figure everyone has some challenge in their life and if this is mine I got off way easy," I wrote in my floppy leather journal, echoing my mom. "My leg does make me concentrate, which is a good skill. As for not telling kids the exact truth I don't want them to think of me as handicapped or whatever. Who would understand what a tight tendon is anyway?" *Including you, buddy.* I was hiding a truth that wasn't exactly the truth after all.

It speaks to the gentleness of my upbringing that the most traumatic leg-related incident from junior high came during an audition for the school musical in the ninth grade. After my best attempt at dancing, the middle-aged choreographer pulled me aside to ask if my limp would be getting better in time for the show. I had to admit it wouldn't.

In the months to come, my mom and I gnawed at this scene again and again: the discriminatory choreographer, the less capable classmates who landed lead roles. Griping was one thing, but Mom took things a step further. In her column, she claimed to have been in the back of

the auditorium the whole time, crossing her fingers and holding her
breath when my name was called and I walked *as gracefully as I could*
onto center stage. In her version, there was no choreographer and my
humiliation, at the hands of the drama teacher, was much more public:

> "Is that limp permanent?" the teacher asked harshly.
>
> Greg's blue eyes, which had sparkled with such hope and
> promise just moments earlier, dropped shamefully to the stage.
> The whispers amongst other students fell silent.
>
> Then, looking straight at this woman, his voice bold and
> strong, he said, "Mrs. Little, you had me in drama for two years
> now. Is this the first time you've noticed I walk with a limp?"
>
> Then, downtrodden and dejected, he exited the stage, stalked
> angrily up the aisle to where I was sitting, and, close to tears, said,
> "Come on, Mom. Let's get out of here."

You can't blame a mother with a terminal illness and a newspaper column for trying to make her kid look good, but I'd be lying if I
claimed her embellishment didn't bug me. The low point of my existence
wasn't just another one of her columns. It was my life!

"You just didn't see me there," Mom told me, clicking shut her laptop like she had prepared for this conversation. "Regardless, if I teach
you kids one thing before I die, it's to stand up for yourselves. You're
too damn nice, just like your dad. And you know what happens to nice
guys?" I didn't. "They end up with bitches like *me*."

From then on, the poems I left on her pillow came with notes:
ONLY FOR YOU. DO NOT SHARE WITH A SOUL. I'd read her my screenplays about Mormon missionaries falling in love and Black women
rising in the ranks of the military, all while swearing her to secrecy.
Basque relatives stopped saying I had a knack for the written word.
Medical alarms went unsilenced at Mom's IVIG infusions. These
treatments, undergone every three weeks, bolstered her damaged
immune system with antibodies from the blood of healthy donors
and were a constant in our lives. Mom treated them almost like spa

days. "He's still writing," she would tell her nurses, looking pale except for the bright red lipstick that had made its way onto her teeth, like a vampire. "He's just not sharing. It's all a big conspiracy. His mother is proud of him. Isn't that terrible?"

By the time I was learning to drive, I had begun to outgrow the childish explanation that I had tight tendons. It was more than just my flimsy right foot getting trapped under the gas pedal or having to perform a million motor functions at once, none of which came naturally to me. It was also a total absence of any sense of direction. An honors student more determined than gifted, I considered myself smart. Why did I get lost driving down the street? And why couldn't I wrap my mind around backing up?

It was one thing to suck at opening my locker or to always be the last one to turn in a test, but that was kid stuff. This was the real world. A driver's license was on the line.

On one of our white-knuckle excursions, with me behind the wheel of Mom's red Expedition, which we dubbed Big Dog, I finally caved and asked what you called my tight tendons, technically. It's probably not a coincidence I brought up this sensitive subject when my mom was cinched into the seat next to me, a rosary balled in her fist. Still, she stonewalled, shrieking at other cars, grabbing the wheel. Knowing it would piss her off, I experimented with using one foot for each pedal: left foot for the gas, right foot for the brake. It wasn't long before I accidentally stomped down on both pedals at the same time, causing the tires to smoke and the car to skid, so I switched tactics and tried driving just with my left foot.

"Quit being ridiculous," Mom erupted when I almost rammed through the front of a Barbacoa Mexican Grill. "You're driving with your right foot, same as everyone else. I don't want you in some special car with hand controls. If I thought you needed all that extra crap, I'd get it for you. I'm telling you, you're a naturally bad driver. It doesn't have anything to do with your leg."

"Never mind," I said. "Let's just get home."

"Your leg is the last thing people notice about you," Mom said. "Believe me, you're lucky. It could have been a lot worse. I'm talking it could have affected your whole right side."

"In some ways it has," I said, realizing with a pang that it was true. I was even left-handed. Trying to make light of my ineptitude at pulling and toggling the lever on the right side of the steering wheel, I added, "It's definitely affected my windshield wiper pinkie."

When we finally made it home, Mom had to unbuckle her seatbelt and pull in her side-view mirror so I could inch into the garage without swiping it off. The tennis ball we used as a car-stop thudded reassuringly against the windshield. "*Hemiplegia*," she blurted out. "That's what your tight tendons are called." I squeezed the brake, bringing Big Dog to a head-bobbing halt. Mom was already pressing the power locks, opening her door. "Now don't go feeling sorry for yourself. Cancer is way, way worse."

Hemiplegia is one of a million different subcategories of cerebral palsy. Each corresponds to different areas of the brain and different symptoms: stiff or tight muscles, shaky or involuntary movements, poor balance or sense of positioning in space. It's easy to get lost in the jargon, and apparently Mom did: though hemiplegia is a kind of cerebral palsy, it's not the kind I have. The word doesn't come up in my medical charts. I'd find out years later she cribbed it from a childhood friend of hers whose son *does* have hemiplegic cerebral palsy.

To be fair, in my teens my orthopedic surgeon used a related term, hemiparesis, to describe the muscular weakness caused by nerve damage on the right side of my body. It's a less severe form of hemiplegia, which essentially means paralysis on one side. For what it's worth, my primary diagnosis is cerebral palsy with spastic diplegia, meaning that my legs are mostly what's affected, and what my pal Iris calls my all-American upper half has mostly been spared. But what matters in understanding my story is only this: my parents swapped a stigma-laden term for ones no one had ever heard of. Mom and Dad talked about the symptoms of cerebral palsy while conveniently never pointing out their underlining cause. It was like being told you have lymphoma but not that lymphoma is a kind of cancer.

In all those years thinking I had hemiplegia, I only remember being questioned about it once. When I was twenty-eight, I went to a friend's house for dinner with her Army doctor boyfriend. Sunburned and sore from a day of riding waterslides at Schlitterbahn, I explained my pained movements with my usual line.

"Hemiplegia?" the doctor said. "You don't have hemiplegia."

I don't know if my orthopedic surgeon was in on the cover-up with my parents, purposely not using the big, scary diagnosis in front of me, or if he was simply opting for as much specificity and precision as possible—being surgical, in other words. Our appointments tended to be quick and efficient, Dr. Stevens like a dentist popping in after a hygienist has completed a routine cleaning. He'd measure the lengths and angles of my legs, test my flexibility, watch me walk, maybe write a prescription for physical therapy, and send us on our way.

My dad explained my condition in simpler terms than all that, anyway: the signals my brain sent to my leg didn't always get through, which is why I had to stretch and concentrate to walk flat. He was careful not to use the expression "brain damage." It was more that my brain had to work around things, which is probably why I was so creative, and maybe, I wondered to myself, why I wanted to bone the Utah Jazz's backcourt. I figured liking guys and having tight tendons had to be related.

To the surprise of everyone in our house, especially me, I passed my driving test on the first try even though my leg was basically convulsing. Utah driver's licenses in those days were laminated cardstock, so easy to counterfeit kids made fakes in the graphics lab at school. It gave me a boost just the same to know I could drive (and run into things) like any normal kid my age. I could roll into surgery the day after Christmas for a pair of scheduled hamstring releases knowing that a temporary handicap pass would soon be dangling from the family station wagon. *Temporary* being the key word.

In "Silver Linings," Mom documented my rocky emergence from anesthesia during which I dry-heaved into a pink emesis basin for ten hours and my body temperature dipped to a cool ninety-three degrees. Though she made sure to pile on the medical drama in other ways, how the nurses had to bury me in blankets and put a heated sandbag on my chest, I was grateful she left out my catheter and the fact that my withered penis rested on a sponge stuck to my abdomen, this with an attending physician handsome enough to play a doctor on TV.

Feeling light-headed from the epidural, paralyzed but not, I got teary when the nurse made me stand for the first time. "You're hurting him!" Tiffany sobbed, and I thought this nurse might kill both of us. It was beyond moronic being sixteen and in a pediatric hospital. When I laid back down, my feet nearly hung over the edge of the child-size bed. Dad joked the surgery had been too successful: I had been stretched into a giant.

"There are moments I blame myself for his problems," Mom wrote in her column. "Why couldn't I carry him the full nine months? Why did this have to happen?"

Her remorse was wretched enough that I couldn't help but be touched. When she asked to publish some of my poetry later that January, I told her to go for it.

The worst part of poetic clichés is that they are insidious. Every hackneyed innovation feels like the real thing at the time. Skewering inspiration, by tenth grade I'd begun to write about despair. "Give 'Em Hell, Girl" was part of my past. Now I was delving into intense shit about dying infantrymen, stillness, and cocoons icing over before they hatched. Could the "Silver Linings" crowd handle "Crying in the Wind"?

"I'll use my best judgment," Mom promised, collecting a stack of loose pages.

That Wednesday's column updated readers on the seasonal maladies plaguing my brother and sisters—viral pneumonia, croup, strep and scarlatina, a nasty flu bug—and my progress in physical therapy. "Because of his inability to participate in school athletics, Greg has learned to express himself in another way: through his writing. Today I would like to share with you a few of his poems, for it is in these words that I feel I can leave the mortal plane and for a brief moment reach out and touch the very hand of God."

The very hand of God, I thought. *Not bad.*

The beret-wearing kids on the high school literary magazine did not, alas, see me as a deity. Of the dozen poems I strategically scattered in submission boxes around the school, they accepted only one for publication, about a crippled boy on a park bench who teaches a bird to sing. They also turned down my application to be on staff the next year until declining enrollment forced them to reluctantly reconsider.

The magazine was called *Satorian* after the Zen concept of satori, or sudden enlightenment, as was haughtily explained on my first day. Rhyming was out. Lowercase letters were in. Also in: suicide, ponytails on guys, and vomiting into jars and hiding them in the closet, like Calista Flockhart did in a movie about bulimia we'd watched in Health. "This is really different from your other stuff," Mrs. Stone said when I read my first assignment to the class, a trippy meditation on driving called "25 Miles to Eternity."

"Yeah," one of the vomit-jar girls said, "it's not about your mom."

Salt Lake played host to the Winter Olympics the January after 9/11. Months before the terrorist attacks, Mona had auditioned to perform in the Opening and Closing Ceremonies as a Child of Light, a role that consisted of being herded around in an Eskimo costume with hundreds of other kids, each holding a fake lantern. It was a nervous time for stadium acts and Mom was quick to sign up to be a chaperone. "This way if we go out, we'll go out together," she said.

With this same macabre logic, Mom spent thousands of dollars on tickets to the show so the rest of us could enter the suicide pact, freezing our asses off in the stands. I can't speak to what it was like in big cities at the time, but the terrorist threat was almost a competition in Salt Lake. Anytime Mom heard Mormons fretting about the Temple downtown, she'd say, "You think a terrorist would choose that godforsaken Temple over the Opening Ceremony of the Olympics? I mean, hello? This is the *Olympics* we're talking about. A global event. People from all over the world will be watching. The president will be there."

"And Michelle Kwan," Mona would say.

"And Michelle *fricking* Kwan."

Rehearsals ramped up that fall and winter and Mom took an extended break from her column. She even stopped making us dinner. We were stuck eating pizza for months.

The final time her byline appeared in any of my dad's papers was in a short, wistful note saying she'd be back at it the next fall, though I think we all knew she wouldn't be. It bugged me Mom would so readily give up on my dream of having a writer in the family. I wanted her to do a book, something that didn't smudge your fingers. Mom wanted to dress like a yeti and shake hands with George W. Bush in the bowels of a stadium and have a few health crises—basal cell carcinomas on her scalp, tissue expanders, more infected toenails, more chemo—without having to write about them. Five years of consistently producing a weekly column is a long time.

Mom may have been finished with "Silver Linings," but "Silver Linings" wasn't finished with her. In our lives, as in her column, there was a devastating medical twist toward the end. I was a senior in college, in late 2006, when Dad noticed a twitch in his shoulder while training for the Boston Marathon. He thought it was nothing, maybe a potassium deficiency, only to find out he was suffering from a rare neurological disorder named after a famous baseball player. For most of my childhood we'd been planning for Mom's death, celebrating last Christmases, saying goodbye just in case. Lou Gehrig's disease had other plans: Dad was going to go first.

Given the global recession that was about to hit, we were lucky to sell the newspapers when we did. It was still sad to help Dad pack up his office, his professional life reduced to a couple pens rattling around a desk drawer, some paper clips, and a legal pad. Dad had made a list of life advice when he could still write. No. 1 was *You don't have to make the last dollar on the deal.* No. 5 was *Get over it.*

Of course, tragedy doesn't make a silver lining. Resilience does. As winter became spring and Dad lost the ability to tie his shoes and zip his fly, Mom made collages of a wheelchair-bound Christopher Reeve and told Dad we weren't going to give up. When Dad's weak diaphragm made lovemaking too strenuous, she started giving him regular morning blowjobs: she wanted him to feel something good, physically, every day. "Everything else is broken," she confided to me. "But that part still works."

Mom hadn't published a column in half a decade, but she knew a good feature story when she saw one: two terminally ill parents and a marathon, mortality wrapped in the foil blanket of a national sporting event. She started making calls to the *Tribune* and *Deseret News*. An article here or there would have been one thing. Mom made the story go national.

If you caught *CBS Evening News with Katie Couric* a few nights after the marathon, you would have seen my mom and dad chatting about their own deaths at our kitchen table, Mom holding just Dad's thumb, and then footage of my dad walking across the rainy finish line in Boston, a running buddy on each arm as the race timer ticked well past six hours.

All morning Mom and Danny and I had ridden with cameramen in the news van, cheering Dad on, and we were there to hug him at the end, my backwards Boston cap matching his forward-facing one. I'm glad someone was there to film the scene. I didn't see much of it myself at the time, being blinded by fat tears of joy, the kind of joy that made suffering small by comparison. That was my mom for you: a shrinker of sorrow, a maker of moments you could later fold against yourself for protection, like a pair of wings.

Six years after Dad's death, as we were packing up the house, I came across a stack of Mom's columns in a clear plastic storage container in the office. Judging from the dry turds on top, it had been used as a litter box for as far back as two cats ago. As overzealous garage-salers picked through our belongings and angled our kitchen table out the front door, muttering about how the other half lived, I started digging around for the columns about me, knowing that if they went into one of the pods in the driveway they'd probably never come back out.

That summer, newly out of graduate school, I applied for private health insurance on my own for the first time in my life. Thinking nothing of it, I noted hemiplegia/hemiparesis on my application and tried to offer a fair accounting of my now-distant history of leg surgeries and physical therapy. I hadn't had a checkup with Dr. Stevens since the summer after freshman year of college. The trouble with my leg felt like part of the distant past, if you didn't count the fact that I could burn through a pair of running shoes in about a month. Backaches and sore hips, knee and shoulder pain, and tumbles down the stairs—that was just part of everyday life, not a reason to see a doctor. I still stretched and exercised to make sure I could safely move around, but I hadn't gone to physical therapy since recovering from my final leg surgery when I was sixteen.

My friend from graduate school, Mary, was also applying for health insurance. Her application was approved within hours; mine was put on hold pending a follow-up interview over the phone. The insurance representative politely posed questions that had never occurred to me. What was the source of my traumatic brain injury? Had I suffered a stroke? Was there any cognitive impairment?

"Cognitive impairment?" I yelped, already short of breath, sweating through my shirt. "I have a graduate degree!" As if to heighten the insult, I watched out my window as a squirrel effortlessly dashed across the swaying branch of a crepe myrtle, exhibiting the kind of balance I never could. I told the insurance rep I was born two months premature and had never known life without tight tendons. He explained that I'd need to send along my childhood medical records before the insurance company could decide whether to cover me or not.

More than a little curious, I had the records unearthed from a medical warehouse in Salt Lake and faxed to an Office Depot near me in Austin. Whatever was in there I wanted to see for myself. It was a muggy day in September, three weeks before my thirtieth birthday, and I watched as the machine spat out sixty-two pages of charts, pre- and post-surgical checkups, and physical therapy evaluations. No wonder the insurance company had flagged my application. The all-too-obvious missing link in my medical history was everywhere. "To Whom It May Concern," read a memo from Dr. Stevens excusing me from high school PE. "Greg Marshall has spastic cerebral palsy related to prematurity."

Back at my condo, I went through page by page with a shaky red pen and highlighter, the way I read Dostoyevsky in high school, keeping a list of all the words and terms I didn't know. There were seven on the first page alone. *His ankle can be dorsiflexed past neutral on the right. No torsional ranula deformities on the right. Foot is plantigrade and relatively supple.*

The pages had arrived in reverse chronological order. This was the story of my leg told backwards to a doctor's Dictaphone. And yet, dry as our Mormon neighbors' food storage back home, there it was: a gorgeous novella of straight leg raises, flexed knees, and hiked hips.

Soon I was pacing around the living room, the charts a jumble covered in fresh coffee stains. The leg and his boy grew younger at every turn, hopping down and up on one foot, flying backwards onto a balance beam, sticking a sawed-off cast back on, reaching for crutches, and rowing out of the room ass-first. I went back and back, the font getting blurrier and more typewriter-like on every page, until I found a naked toddler vacuuming up a puddle of urine from the floor of a doctor's office with his tiny uncircumcised penis.

I had to call three or four times in a row to get Mom to answer that night. Her voice sounded bright, if annoyed. She was helping Alice prepare for her oral boards by giving her a makeover. (By then, they had been together for years.) All week, Mom had texted me pictures of Alice getting her split ends snipped at a trendy salon and squeezing into Spanx. "The plastic surgery people are all about the superficial," Mom said, jumping in before I could tell her why I was calling. "You can't go in there looking like a big lesbian, no offense, Alice."

"No, I agree," Alice said.

My phone dinged with a picture of Alice in a classy black dress and pearls. I'd never seen her without a baseball cap and fanny pack, let alone sporting curves.

Once we'd gotten the pleasantries out of the way, it was time to get down to business.

"Goddamn that man, leaving me to deal with this," Mom said when I told her what I'd found in my charts. She was talking about my dad, of course. He was always "that man" when she was upset with him, even though he was just cremains in a cloud urn. "I was hoping I'd be dead for this conversation. Seriously. I thought if you found out you'd go kill yourself. Are you? Going to kill yourself, I mean?"

Mom's panic spiraled into sobs as we talked for the next two hours. Even hearing how much she was hurting, it was hard to quell a teenage sense of indignity. Once someone has administered medication to you rectally, you'd think there wouldn't be any mysteries left.

Before obscuring my diagnosis, Mom had to get one in the first place. She described how the doctors at St. Francis in Peoria blew her off, telling her to give it more time. I couldn't get up from sitting sideways on the ground, a warning sign for CP, but I passed other diagnostic tests of strength and coordination.

"You were right on the borderline," Mom told me on the phone. "You didn't exactly fit anywhere, physically, so they said you probably just had tight tendons." Still, they put Mom in touch with doctors in St. Louis and Chicago and eventually referred us to the orthopedic bigshot in Salt Lake who confirmed Mom's fears.

The tone shifted with CP in the picture. It went from "Maybe everything's fine!" to the specter of special schools and the possibility that I wouldn't be able to walk as I grew, that I'd spit words out the side of my mouth. The label brought help—physical therapy and eventually surgeries—but not always liberation. School officials conflated my physical weakness with mental deficiency. They took one look at the brace bloating my right shoe and lumped me with the other slow learners. I spent first grade languishing in remedial classes, learning to read the time on the clock, before my mom raised hell and got me put into the reading and math groups for the average kids.

This scenario, my in-betweenness, would play out again and again in my childhood: I was too disabled to run with the normies, but not disabled enough for what Mom called the "perks." I couldn't ride a bike without training wheels—in an era of kids having Spielbergian adventures around the neighborhood, I was stuck at the end of the driveway—yet the organization in town that handed out adaptive tricycles for kids with movement disorders turned me down after I excitedly went for a test ride: I rode, and walked, too well. Same deal with the adaptive ski team in Park City and the custom-made boots they provided.

"Nothing wrong with him?" Mom shouted at the instructor after I slowly plowed into a stranger on the bunny slopes. I could make a ski pizza but only half. "Are we talking about the same kid? You think I'm making this up for shits? I don't even *like* to ski. What, do I need to slit both his Achilles tendons for him to get help?"

At some point, the battles weren't worth it. It was easier to tell people I just had tight tendons. "I have never believed in labels, Greg," Mom said, her voice going hard, suggesting a defensiveness that belied her certainty. "I didn't want you to be the spaz down the street. Like, 'Look, there goes Cheetah of the Apes.' It's like, no, he's going to be on top of the world."

Only after we hung up did I notice my leg tingling with exhaustion and, I'd think later, intuition. I thought I remembered coming across "cerebral palsy" in "Silver Linings," maybe even asking what it meant. How, then, had I not figured out my tight tendons were the result of cerebral palsy at twelve? Was this a case of denial or deception? How dumb was I?

Of the hundreds of "Silver Linings" Mom had managed to copy at Kinko's with no problem, and that I'd swiped from the house as we'd moved out, only the one from sixth grade about my traumatic birth had its headline and first few paragraphs cut off. My answer was in those cut-off paragraphs. I just had to find them.

My Hope of America award from sixth grade happens to be prominently displayed in my office, and it happens to have a date on it. Knowing my mom's column about me had come out around the time I won the award, in June 1997, I called the paper (no luck), a local university, and finally the Washington State Archives. Thanks to a friendly librarian, a copy of the incriminating column, reproduced from microfilm, arrived in my inbox the following afternoon. The ninety-nine words Mom had tried to Xerox out of existence proved to be the Watergate tapes of my childhood, revealing both crime and cover-up. When Mom wrote in her column that she threw my doctors' words in the trash, she meant it literally.

This is how I found myself, at thirty, waking up to a disability I've had my whole life. Go figure. I'd been out of the closet as gay for more than a decade, but it was strange to contemplate embracing a new identity that, like my sexuality, has been a part of me since birth. It struck me as funny that in a childhood filled with cancer and catastrophe, cerebral palsy was one of the only things that was verboten. I saw how I'd been complicit in the lie, too. It was easier to call myself a ditzy blond when I got lost going to a friend's house or backed Big Dog into a wall than to have an honest conversation about, say, brain damage and spatial reasoning. Sorting through the contradictions in my life made me want to grab my reporter's notebook, throw on a jean jacket, and mousse my hair up big, like Mom.

To have to dig up a basic fact about my body like an investigative reporter was jarring, not unlike the realization in my teens that wanting to have sex with Jazz point guard John Stockton made me "gay" or typing up poems for my mom didn't, on its own, make me a "writer." It has been empowering, and a little scary, to have a term that demystifies my body, one that doesn't make me feel like I'm whining about a pulled hamstring. There are other people like me. I am part of a movement. Who knew?

The "Silver Linings" about my ill-fated audition for the school musical in the ninth grade, the one where Mom claimed to be watching from the back of the auditorium, is called "The Mother of Oz."

The Wizard of Oz has come up a weird amount in my life. It's an apt analogy for us. Behind a not-so-Great and not-so-Powerful kid with cerebral palsy was a greater and still more powerful mom—a Wonderful woman concealed in the curtains. Even in my dull medical charts you can spot glimpses of her, a fortune teller juggling a newspaper column, chemo, and five kids, making Dr. Stevens note when I didn't perform up to expectations or that I participated in both swimming *and* dance lessons. Sometimes she wore a turban and waved her hands over a crystal ball, and other times she was nothing more than smoke and mirrors, a bellowing green head taking up most of the stage, always one move ahead of me until she wasn't. Until she was just a mom on the phone trying to explain.

MARSHALL FAMILY VIBRATOR

Long before the discovery of my hidden diagnosis in a storage container covered in cat feces in the office, the Marshalls were no strangers to life's curveballs. Unlike other families, we leaned into them. The rigmarole of the everyday we weren't good at, but it was easy to draw close in times of crisis. Fortunately, we had a lot of them. *A good family*, we called ourselves, which meant, as far as I could tell, that we were members of a country club. Nothing bad was supposed to happen to good families, and mostly nothing did, but there were problems even money couldn't keep out.

When I was six, my Basque grandparents' brand-new electric blanket caught fire one night and nearly burned their house to the ground. Instead of fleeing, Grandma Rosie dialed the fire department from the living room. We drove up to Idaho after the flames had been doused to find her heating a can of beans in the ash heap that used to be their kitchen as Grandpa Joe kicked up his feet in his destroyed Barcalounger. For the rest of their time in that house, they lived among trinkets warped in the fire.

Later, visiting Grandma Rosie in the psych ward after she'd undergone shock therapy, I'd watch her roar with laughter as urine darkened her sweatpants. After-hours in the cafeteria, I'd feed her dollops of a strawberry milkshake from McDonald's—her favorite—only to realize with dawning horror that her gold and gray teeth were clamped around the spoon in a futile attempt to swallow it. "Let it go Rosangela," Mom would sigh, digging in her purse for gum. "You're not killing yourself today."

During my mom's first round of chemo when I was eight, she coaxed our teenage nanny out of polygamy by offering to buy her a new car if she left her fiancé, a mustachioed man in a wifebeater and camouflage pants. At first gallant, Mom's meddling got weird when she said she'd throw in a tennis bracelet if the nanny agreed to marry my dad and raise us kids as her own should Mom kick the bucket.

After a summer of belting out *Jesus Christ Superstar* with me at the mall, my favorite babysitter, not the polyg, tearfully confessed at the food court that she had gay parents: her mom liked women and her dad liked men. It wasn't chance that brought these two observant Mormons together, but a shrewd bishop. They had stuck it out for years before splitting up. "My mom and dad couldn't live a lie anymore," the babysitter told us, shyly playing with her straw. I didn't know if I could live a lie anymore either but before I could come out to her, she busted Tiffany for smoking weed in the backyard. In retribution, my big sister claimed the babysitter had tried to molest her and got her fired.

"What?" Tiffany said. "It has to be the weird, creepy uncle for it to be wrong?"

Of all the oddball occurrences in my oddball family, Danny's campaign for a pet monkey probably doesn't sound like much. It began in the spring of 1994 when my mom took us to see the movie *Monkey Trouble*. Danny, then around twelve, waltzed out of the theater nursing a serious boner for both young Thora Birch and her co-star, a capuchin in a backwards baseball cap named Finster. My brother's desire for a simian partner-in-crime lasted about as long as the car ride home, the amount of time it took my mom to imagine aloud what it would be like to wrestle a primate into a diaper. With surprising ease, Danny pivoted to other exotic pets.

By dinner, he had decided on an iguana.

To hear my brother at PetSmart the following day, you'd think the scaly, bored reptile before us was just a monkey with a removable tail. "It'll be pretty cool to have this little guy on my shoulder as I do my homework," Danny said, poking his finger through the cat cage that contained Oozy.

Oozy got his name not from the semiautomatic weapon, the Uzi, but because he looked like dried slime. Oozy was well into his adolescence and already more than a foot long, not including his tail. He didn't blink and if you tried to stare back at him, he would scamper under your shirt and sink his curved nails into your flesh. He made love to a Utah Jazz sweat towel and attacked anything green: the diamond on an argyle sweater, a sock.

The main difference between my fish and Danny's new iguana was that if I got sick of my fish all I had to do was feed them flakes until their fins sagged and they went belly up. Fish were more or less plants with tails. Even when I tried I couldn't keep them alive. The only thing I'd ever been able to grow was mold on a slice of cantaloupe in the freezer room. Oozy you couldn't contain. Once he erupted out of his enclosure, he took over Danny's room, depositing his plant-filled scat on the windowsill and making my brother's tidy double bed smell like a terrarium. "You thought a monkey was bad? Just try to put a diaper on that thing," Mom laughed.

Snaggletoothed Annie and all our cats were terrified. Even our plus-size golden retriever, Moose, who'd lick anything and generally acted like the whole world was his personal ham hock, reared back and barked at Oozy.

Our Polish cleaning lady, Stana, was the only one brave enough to venture into Danny's room amid the hostile takeover. She packed the dresser drawers with laundry each Tuesday, leaving us no choice but to forage for stray socks and underwear.

I don't know if all brothers share underwear growing up or if it was just us. We couldn't have stopped if we'd wanted to. Mom would buy us matching boxers—they were usually boxers, this being the era before chafing—and it became impossible to tell whose was whose once they were in the laundry chute. We shared all our clothes, to the point that when my brother left for college years later, it was like I'd gone through a divorce and lost the better half of everything.

But back in the Oozy days, our boy butts clad in interchangeable billowy boxers, we studied our new pet's every painstaking move.

"Daaaaaad," we'd say. "Oozy just took a shit."

"Go annoy someone else," Mom would shout back. "Your dad can't do everything for you."

"But it was a big one."

"Listen, when we have time to take a shit ourselves we'll go take care of your pet iguana instead," Mom would say. "Tell them, Bob."

"Guys? Mom's right," Dad would say. "You're on your own with this one."

Rightly scared to enter his own room, let alone sleep there, Danny crawled into bed with me. I enjoyed our school-night slumber parties, both of us sipping Sprites. One of these nights, in iguana exile, Danny brought in my mom's Brookstone back massager. It was nothing fancy: a standard model with a flat, round head and a long white handle, like a back scratcher, presumably so Danny could rub his shoulders without needing me to do it for him. While I wasn't sure what he was up to as he uncoiled the cord and plugged it into the outlet next to my bed, testing the settings against his palm, I believed his intentions were honorable at first. He really did love having his back rubbed.

Now that I'm nearly forty, the idea that a Brookstone back massager is actually a sex toy is so common as to be cliché. At the time, I puzzled over how Danny had figured out how to turn an otherwise innocent gadget into a rapturous advancement. Had he dozed? Had the massager skidded down his basketball shorts? However you figured it, my brother was a genius. He had invented masturbation, and I do mean invent. Besides humping the Looney Tunes pillow on my bed and getting fresh with the occasional hot tub jet, the massager was *the* gateway to pleasure.

My brother was a bold architect of boyhood fun. Give Danny one of the little girls' tricycles and a tennis ball and he'd come up with a new sport. Give him a household appliance from Brookstone and in a few minutes you'd be wiggling it against your dick and balls, wondering what you'd say if Dad shouldered through the door. *Oozy made me do it!*

When you're ten years old and a little brother, you sign a kind of anti-Hippocratic Oath: First, do self-harm. Ask questions later. Without Danny, I would have spent my days staging plays in the dusty sunlight of my room, my shirt bunched through a T-shirt clip. Instead, we passed summer nights consulting our neighbor Paul's Ouija board and playing kick the can, dirty words flying out of our mouths between screeches. (I did most of the screeching.)

I was always complicit in my brother's crimes, or at least in on the joke. Because of Danny, I was never the bottom of the totem pole. My friends were. My brother and Paul and another neighbor boy, Raf, once staged a home burglary in gorilla costumes to try to scare my stinky, easygoing friend Chip during a sleepover. The shtick included cap guns, stage blood, and a death scene. My own role was straightforward: all I had to do was drop a shoe down the laundry chute to let them know we were coming downstairs.

Danny wasn't a bully as much as an insult comic, pointing out Chip's BO or our pal Robin Harris's large head. Rory Shuman's tan baseball-cap-with-a-neck-flap made him look like a camel. Quinn Halliday had hair like Lisa Simpson. Maren Hall always appeared to have just smelled a fart, probably because around us she had. Mom said that if anyone else were as obnoxious as Danny, he would have had no friends. My brother was an oddly charismatic antagonist. My classmates, even Chip, not only tolerated being humiliated, they basked in it. They begged to come over to play kick the can or dynamite or have a butt war on the trampoline. If Danny tricked them into smacking their tailbones on the trampoline's hard edge, so be it. They were always game for more.

My brother could get any guy he wanted. And he did.

Danny and I pursued activities only brothers can: we stayed up on weekends to catch *Real Sex* on HBO and peruse the swimsuit issue of *Sports Illustrated*, dog-earring the pages we liked best. I would compliment a model's eyes or lips, the lacework of her bikini bottom, and Danny would dry-swallow and pass me the massager. "Oh, by the way, have you tried it on your butt?" I'd ask, thinking of the hot tub jets. "It feels really good on your butt."

Danny would consider for a moment. "I think I'll stick with my dick."

The feeling was different from humping, like being gently assaulted with an eggbeater. It felt good and then it felt great and then I could feel my heartbeat in the blue vein along the underside of my penis. My right leg shot out. My hands went numb. I hadn't hit puberty yet, not really, so there wasn't any mess. It was like swinging a mallet at a carnival game, trying to push a puck up a tower, not quite ringing the bell.

Like most great inventions, the back massager was too incredible to keep secret. After we'd used it together a dozen times, Danny taught Paul and Raf the ways of the massager. What made the vibrator the high point of my sex life was not just the full-body numbness it caused, my right leg becoming inelastic. It was the sense of camaraderie, of being in a club. It was a different story for Tiffany, who had achy knees and cramps and awful skin, but early puberty was a box of wonders for the boys of Briarcreek Drive. Danny, Paul, Raf, and I spent hours in the basement firing Nerf guns, playing pinball and ping-pong, and retiring to the guest room to use the vibrator one last time.

It was cool and dark back there, decorated to look like a bed-and-breakfast. The only light came in through leaf-filled window wells, and the closet was full of dead-people clothes and retired winter coats. My great uncle John's son had died in a motorcycle accident after coming home from Vietnam, where he'd lost his left testicle. I'd slip on his leather jacket before climbing into the guest bed. It was way too big on me but I liked how it smelled. I liked to pretend it was the jacket he'd died in.

None of us ever got under the sheets, treating each time like a cat-nap that left the bed rumpled, the pillows in need of a good fluffing. The vibrator canceled out neighborhood noises: the thud of flat basketballs, dogs, the scratch of stools against the kitchen floor upstairs. Those thirty seconds, lying atop the messy comforter, my ball sack basking in a warm, electric dance, were exquisite and lonely.

Once I was doubled over, fighting through the postcoital stupor to find the off switch before my nails shook free of their nail beds, I liked striding back out into the basement living room, back to boxelder bugs in the lights, games of Double Shot and air hockey and the family portrait we'd taken at Fashion Place of the seven of us in denim mounted above the chunky rock fireplace. I couldn't have put the feeling into words, but it was a kind of instant nostalgia. After my brush with adult sexuality, I got to be a kid again.

"Just wait until you can jizz," Raf said one day during a round of pinball. That was our word: jizz. We weren't trying to be gross, or maybe we were, but just a little bit. "It's like the feeling you get after you throw up," Raf said.

"It's like your dick throwing up," Danny corrected.

"Don't tell him that," sensitive Paul said. "You're going to freak him out."

"What's it like then?" Raf asked.

"It's like hitting your funny bone really hard," Paul said.

My brother bit his hand, getting himself worked up, and shouted over his fist, "It's like that feeling you get during the drop in a roller-coaster but just in your *dick*."

The pinball took an unlucky bounce and Raf waggled his hips before the machine, a human tilt. "It feels good," Raf said. "Trust me. It's the best feeling in the world. Just don't hold it on there too long or it can hurt."

By the time I'd started using the vibrator, I had left behind my old physical therapy studio, K2D2, with its balance beams and beanbag tic-tac-toe, in favor of an orthopedic gym called the Back Institute. I was the only kid there. The other patients were middle-aged, meaning any age over twenty, and had been busted up in car accidents or injured on the job. A lot of them worked out in jeans. The term "workman's comp" got thrown around. I had no idea what it meant, but I liked the sound of it.

My physical therapist, Bill, stretched me on a massage table in the back and talked about white-water rafting, maneuvering my legs like they were paddles. I'd never been handled by a man before, and I wondered if he could see up my shorts, if I wanted him to. He went at me so hard that first day I almost cried out in pain.

I slid off the table, my hair askew, and floated through my workout, walking backwards on the treadmill, working the thigh press, doing toe lifts.

God made men, and then he snapped off a tight hamstring and made me to admire them. Even the receptionist was coarsely, beautifully male. With slick hair and bearish forearms, he looked not unlike the actor who played Superman on *Lois and Clark*.

It's not like my family was all that Catholic, but I felt guilty when I daydreamed of Clark Kent, the mild-mannered secretary, answering the massager like a phone and then pressing it to his crotch, his eyes rolling to the back of his head. I was superstitious rather than religious. I said an "Our Father" and a "Hail Mary" every night and erected a force field around my bed by using my hands and feet to touch each corner of my mattress at the same time.

As far as church went, though, we only attended the children's Mass at St. Vincent's on Christmas Eve so we could shake hands with the Jazz's backcourt when the priest told us to turn to our neighbors. John Stockton and Jeff "Horny" Hornacek were both observant Catholics whose fit wives and abundant offspring flanked them in the pews. In their own way, they were also heartthrobs. Hornacek always rubbed the side of his sweaty face three times before shooting a free throw, and I think my brother and I both hoped some of the magic from that shooting hand would rub off on us. "Peace be with you, Horny."

"What if Stockton and Horny are gay?" I asked my dad as I pulled myself to my feet during one Mass. When I wasn't shaking their hands, I liked to hang back and stare at their clean-shaven necks. I'd heard my mom say it was the sexiest part of a man.

"That would sure explain Horny's bad knees," Dad said, bending the way people do to keep from fainting.

I tried to work girls into my tree-house fantasies, but the vibrator was the real star of the show. It buzzed through every muscle and tight tendon like a kind of omniscience. Horny and John wouldn't stand a chance. They'd be as helpless to its charms as Clark Kent, as anyone. "Just don't hold it on there too long or it can hurt," I'd warn them.

Afterward, I'd tell myself never again, but a few hours later I'd be in the guest room, pulling back the bed skirt and rooting around for the vibrator once more, hauling it out from under the bed by its cord.

Having a sex life as a kid is a strange thing, even if what you're having sex with is a Brookstone back massager. I was still young enough to dress up for Halloween and talk seriously about becoming a famous actor, but I also had, for the first time, a real need to be alone: I started planning my life around the massager. I'd wait for Mom and Dad to take the little girls up to bed or fake sick and stay home from family outings so I could sneak down to the basement and become as untamed as our pet iguana. I was not alone in my addiction. My brother was usually slumped at the bar in the basement, sipping a Mountain Dew. "It's my fourth time today, Gregor," he'd say. "I just hope I can lay off it once school starts."

"You're about to be in junior high. You'll be so busy you won't have time for this stuff," I said, hoping it wasn't true.

I could tell Danny was getting sick of basement games. He played competitive basketball now and was not shy about reminding me that I was a waste of height, two inches taller than him even when I stood on my shorter leg. I envied Danny's hairy, muscular calves and ankles, the way he didn't instinctively stare down at them with every step, certain they'd wobble away like a lopsided basketball. The way his shoelaces stayed tied. No matter how big a lead he gave me, I'd always lose. Danny didn't have to go to a gym to be a real boy and this was somehow related to all the rest of it: the phone that never stopped ringing for him, the fact that even teachers called him Marshall, like he was on their team. He had a fro and a funny two-handed jump shot that never looked like it was going in until it did. The coach on his super league team called him an asset, the next John Stockton. My mom compared him to Muggsy Bogues. "If that little peanut can dunk, so can my little Danny Boy," she'd say.

Toward the end of that summer, I saw Rory Shuman naked in the locker room after swim team practice on a frigid morning at the club and came home raving about it to Danny, Paul, and Raf. Rory had taken off his wet Speedo and was holding a towel in front of him, shouting and horsing around with the other guys, when I came out of the stall where I'd been changing and caught a glimpse: circumcised, shrimp-curled, as hairless as a statue. It was a fluke, like spotting a tropical fish in the club's murky duck pond, and because it was a fluke a feeling of providence came over me, my tongue tripping in amazement at the amazing *thing* I'd just seen.

Still hanging out the morning after a sleepover, Danny was preparing to serve a ping-pong ball into Paul's quivering bare back, eight lashes for the eight points by which Paul had lost. It was a game we called bareback. "Come on, QB," Danny scolded. Queer Bait was one of his nicknames for me. It was a slur disguised as a safe word, or vice versa, affectionately muttered whenever I'd taken things too far. Neither of us had much idea what it meant. "You can't go around talking about another guy's penis. That's very, very gay."

Of course. How had I been so stupid? I'd learned about Paul Revere in school. Well, here I was being Penis Revere, telling my brother a fag was coming, and that fag was me. The fact that Rory went to school with Chip and me had the potential to make things so much worse.

The irony of my turn as Penis Revere is that being in the company of penises made me nervous. I always changed under a towel or in a stall. Forget being naked in front of other guys. I couldn't stand anyone seeing my underwear, even when it was shoved in a shoe at the pool. What I was worried about—tire tracks or pee stains—I couldn't say. I suppose it was an old-fashioned case of body shame. Paul had used my swim trunks to sit in the hot tub a couple days earlier and I'd been seriously peeved. "I don't know why you care," he'd said. "It's not like my guys were swimming with your guys."

I didn't know why I cared either.

Danny began his junior high career by running for elected office: seventh-grade vice president. As if to illustrate his athletic superiority, he mutilated a Superman poster of mine with an X-acto knife. Cutting out the Man of Steel's face, he glued his yearbook picture in its place. *Vote for Super Dan!*

The vibrator became a secret selling point of Danny's candidacy. Kids I'd never met before turned up in the basement and didn't go home for most of the weekend: math nerds, Greeks, the Mormon kids on whose ward ball team Danny hoped to be a ringer. (Every church team was allowed two nonbelievers. Preference was given to good passers.) This being the mid-nineties, there was also a crowd of cool kids who wore multiple knee-high socks and said "Yo" a lot.

"Yo yo yo," they'd say when I came downstairs. "It's Marshall's bro bro bro."

What united these disparate groups of guys was the buzzing appliance from Brookstone with the flat round head. It wasn't just my brother and Paul and Raf and me retiring to the guest room anymore. There was a line.

The Back Massager Club didn't last long. My inchoate sex life was not to be one of boys clasping sticky hands as their bodies contorted in ecstasy. Still, for a few months, the basement became a jungle of jocks in basketball shorts playing pinball or whacking ping-pong balls at each other's bare backs as they waited their turn to get off.

Chip was grounded from our house for two weeks after his mom spotted fat, round welts going from his shoulders to just above his toweled butt when he came out of the shower. Considering that he would go on to describe barebacking an entire junior high worth of seventh graders, it was a light punishment.

There's a time, as boys, when we're all in the closet: sneaking, sniffing, logging on, trying it with Icy Hot. It's a closet not because it has anything to do with being gay but because it's made out of a shared secret. The question is how long you stay there. How long before you venture out or get caught.

In spite of getting grilled about the debauchery going on in the Marshall basement, Chip remained mum on the vibrator and even found one of his own among the Coca-Cola memorabilia at his grandparents' house. It had a red handle and looked like a curling iron from the eighties, but Chip swore it worked.

For those two weeks, I felt Chip's malodorous exile more acutely than I would have thought. Even if I couldn't quite put my finger on it, I must have known that my brother's friends, or guys like them, would come to reject me one day or, worse, not acknowledge me at all. If you want to find a person who had almost no homosexual experiences growing up, find a gay guy who was a kid in the nineties. Double points if he's disabled. If he's lucky, he'll tell you what I'm about to, that he was a bystander and not a victim, that no one ever humped him like a dog or pantsed him, that he never woke up with colorful dicks drawn on his face.

A musky boy-mist hung beneath the basement's fluorescent lights, airborne puberty. I'd come down to find five or six guys roughhousing in the guest room. Once they reached a certain level of arousal, they had no choice but to keep going. It didn't matter what they were thinking or who else happened to be around—it was automatic, like an eggbeater. That's what I liked about it. Nothing to figure out or screw up, no physical test unsteady hands could fail. Just an on switch to bliss. "Dude, Brandon is using it bare dick!" I'd hear. "He doesn't even have underwear on."

And silently, from the bottom of the stairs, I'd thank God.

My elementary school held a maturation program for the fifth grade that fall. Since I had an older brother, and a vibrator, I'd been looking forward to snarking my way through this charade. When it came to sex, I had the answers in the back of the book.

That sense of casual superiority evaporated when I learned that the maturation program was not coed. We arrived at school that evening, congregating near the front office, and were divided. The girls, my natural foils and allies, went off with their moms to learn about pubic hair and tampons, and the boys were marched with our dads into a small classroom off the multipurpose room that doubled as a PE supply closet.

Squirming in a folding chair next to Dad, among cages of kickballs, bats, and clubs, we pondered our dads' Adam's apples and were asked to describe how they smelled when they came in from working in the yard. We learned about deodorant and that it was called a scrotum, not a ball sack. "Is that where jizz comes from?" Chip asked courteously. I knew he was up to no good. He'd slicked his hair down with water from the drinking fountain to try to look older and he was wearing a clean shirt. Even when he didn't smell, he smelled like his house.

Just when I thought the evening couldn't become more mortifying, Rory Shuman was called to the front to demonstrate the small differences between the sexes, like how boys carry books at our sides whereas girls cradle them on their hips like babies. If one of our friends "experienced" an erection, we should ignore it. If we got one, we should think of our mothers or baseball. "When I was your age our anatomy was a *toolbox*. That's it. That's what we called it," the doctor concluded. "I hope if nothing else we can be more mature than that."

I clutched my stomach and rocked in my chair, letting out a stream of giggles. If I didn't know better, I would have thought I had cramps.

Dad told me to cool it, Greggo. Just cool it.

Not long after maturation, Oozy attempted to escape. He scampered into the hallway, took a chunk out of Danny's index finger, and scuttled over the banister at the top of the stairs. Ricocheting discordantly off the piano a story below, he hit the carpet like a dropped toy.

True to his demon nature, Oozy survived the fall. What he couldn't survive was the subsequent blow to his reputation, not with Danny sobbing as he held his bloody finger at the top of the stairs. Mom took him in for a tetanus shot and then she swept Oozy into his cat cage with a dustbin and returned him to PetSmart for no refund.

For as imperfect as Oozy may have been for a couple of massager-obsessed boys, I was sorry to see Stana and Dad haul the UVB light and heated rock and glass enclosure to the trash cans in the driveway. It meant Danny and I weren't going to share a bed anymore. With Oozy out of the picture, my brother had his room back and I was the one in exile, stuck with a tankful of dead fish. No more sleepovers or passing the massager back and forth, talking about the swimsuit issue.

"But you can have your poster back," Danny said. He'd lost the election to a Mormon kid. Even the vibrator had its limits.

"Wow. Thanks," I said.

Somehow, bullets bouncing off Superman's bulging pecs weren't a turn-on with my brother's yearbook picture on top. For as much as I would've liked to rip it out, how could I without hurting Danny's feelings? Super Dan went up right over my bed. When that proved untenable after a day or two, I rolled up the poster and stuck it in the closet with my old shoes, the ones that had holes in the toes.

The first time a sticky, clear substance squirted out of me was during a humping session that summer. I didn't bother to hide my boxers under my dresser, like Danny did, and let the stain stay there on my Looney Tunes pillow, daring Stana to ask about it as she changed my sheets.

Week after week, she made my bed and arranged my pillows without ever bothering the stain. It stayed right where it was, on Tweety Bird's cheek.

How's that for boyhood? We built a closet in the basement with a Brookstone back massager. Eventually, as we got older, we each came out of it. Even me.

IF I ONLY HAD A LEG

Up With Kids started as an unofficial offshoot of Up With People, the 1970s show choir now notorious for its ties to an evangelical cult, the Nixon administration, and Halliburton.

Our director Bonnie's salad days were touring with the group, which she referred to simply as People. It took a real insider to drop two prepositions. So much projecting over the years had left her vocal cords frayed and full of benign polyps. Now in her forties, an Up With Kids T-shirt plunging from her chest and a wad of nicotine gum in one cheek, she suffered from a permanent case of laryngitis. Looking back, this was probably due to her having been a smoker, but as Bonnie reenacted long-lost Super Bowl halftime shows in the Presbyterian church where we rehearsed, squeezing out notes like the debarked corgi on our block, it was like music itself had worn her out. I couldn't imagine a better life.

I could still remember the bleak afternoon of yore when Bonnie had burst into Mrs. Gardner's first-grade classroom with a neon flyer for her Musical Theatre and Motion Picture Academy: TRAINING YOUNG ACTORS FOR STAGE AND FILM. AGES 4–15. *NO AUDITIONS. It's hard to say if it was her white jean shorts and matching Payless shoes or her big, white teeth, but I knew from the moment I saw her that I'd found my People. It took courage to be that overcaffeinated in front of children.

I suspect it was different elsewhere, but in Utah there was only one reason to introduce young people to the performing arts, and that was because they couldn't play sports. Thus, perhaps unsurprisingly, my Up With Kids crew turned out to be in no better shape than the population I hung out with at physical therapy. Bonnie's daughter, for one, had Down syndrome. Another boy pushed a walker around stage. Most of us Kids were damaged in more minor but no less noticeable ways:

chronic pink eye, early-onset facial hair. One girl with the last name Wood insisted we call her *Holly* Wood even though her real name was something like Sarah.

My own eccentricities were enough to leave my parents scratching their heads. Imagination was survival mode. For me, there was no place like home, and no place but home to express my essential weirdness. I routinely broke into song, wore a witch hat recreationally around the house, and instead of calling my mom "mom," I invented monikers for her—Kiss of Africa, Ariel of Sun Ray, Duke of Chutney—that my older siblings would only have conceived after whiffing rubber cement.

That's where Bonnie came in. She set my every whim to music.

With her, we were *encouraged* to act out, unclasp our prim choir hands, and beatbox our way through record-scratching remixes of "Zip-A-Dee-Doo-Dah." Bonnie gave us free rein to affect accents and devise fictional alter egos. My raspy-voiced friend Maren arrived each week in the sophisticated tartan skirt and beret her mom had carefully laid out for her that morning. She morphed into a horse the moment she stepped through the door and spent the hour galloping around the room, neighing. The older kids in class spoke assuredly of future careers in movies when all they had to look forward to was acne and, after that, acne scars.

Soon enough, my preemie sister, Moe, joined our ranks and we went on tour.

Every summer my family took a trip with Up With Kids and patiently watched me scream "Supercalifragilisticexpialidocious" into a microphone on the boardwalk outside Universal Studios or snap and twirl through a Beach Boys medley, a plastic lei flying around my ears. Outside a tank of honking sea lions, we beamed that SeaWorld (not the more traditional choice, Disneyland) was the happiest place in the U-S-A, and at an America Sings Summit in Washington, D.C., Moe and I didn't worry that we weren't good enough for anyone else to hear, we just sang, sang a song, like the Carpenters.

"Do *you* want to tell Bonnie about the massager or should I?" Danny asked when I came off our small side stage on the National

Mall. We'd just finished our D.C. run in style with a rendition of our almost-eponymous showstopper "Up With People." ("If more people were for people . . ."). Bonnie claimed it was so good it gave her goose-bumps. Never mind that we were only singing along to a track we'd pre-recorded at her house.

Refusing to let my brother's perverted question burst my squeaky-clean bubble, I assured him I didn't have a clue what a massager was, this as the color rose in my face and the faucets in my pits turned on again. If my earnest public persona was at odds with masturbating in the basement, I never showed it. My brother scratched at his smile. "Gregor, no offense, but you are the worst actor alive."

Dragged to all of our cheesy performances, Danny called Up With Kids the Special Olympics of acting, which was fine with me. Sparkling in a loose-fitting gold lamé shirt while Moe was trapped in a puckering leotard of the same material, I was the actor among social rejects. If any-thing, my brother's mockery made me feel superior to my castmates. I honestly couldn't see that I had much in common with them. Self-hatred would have been one thing, but this was closer to full-blown denial, the way I could disappear into a TV show or play. I was in Up With Kids because I was a rising star, not because something was wrong with me.

My leg presented mild challenges in terms of choreography (it could be like waltzing with a small, invisible dresser), but I was still oblivious to the fact of my diagnosable disability. As was Danny. He might imitate my thwacking footfall to remind me to walk flat after a long day of seeing the sights, but my loud chew at breakfast bugged him far more than my limp.

If, on my most inquisitive days, I wondered aloud how my dancing compared to, say, that of Christian, the boy with the walker, Mom would threaten to beat me with the wooden spoon she kept on the dashboard of the Suburban. "You stop that kind of talk right now, you hear me?" she'd say. "That is not how a star behaves. To think your tight tendons are in the same league as what that little handicapped boy has to deal with is just terrible. If I hear you talk like that again, I'm going to have Bonnie give him your lines."

It was all just an act: the wooden spoon, my mom's scolding. She'd never have me give up lines. She wanted me to be a celebrity as much as I did. In reality, she was only doing what any manager might, telling me exactly what I wanted to hear.

"What do we always say, Greg?" she'd ask. I'd aim the air-conditioning vent at my face, hoping to preempt any tears, and softly tender our creed. "True talent rises to the top."

"Damn right it does. And don't you go forgetting it, kid."

I wonder if my leg let me get away with being a ham. For most kids, *acting* was shorthand for acting gay. Christian and I were exceptions. Anyone who saw me lip-sync an Elvis tune as I did my labored version of his hip-shake probably assumed I was there because of brain damage. My *outlet*, they would have called it. Rather than an abomination, I was an inspiration. It's the kind of camouflage my leg provides to this day: people assume I'm more wholesome than I am. Years before I had any conception of my disability as such, I felt responsible for shaping how others saw me, which is, essentially, the job description of an actor.

That didn't always mean hiding my leg onstage, not when I could use it as a prop. I may not have uttered the words "cerebral palsy" back then, but as I gained experience as a performer I didn't downplay my condition, either. In Up With Kids I found not just a fun after-school activity but also a place where dragging my right foot and having my right arm creep up my side when I wasn't paying attention were not necessarily detrimental. It would be an overstatement to say I used my limp to get plum roles, just that, in retrospect, they all fell into a certain pattern. I sat on thrones or made pronouncements from center stage, blowing kisses and doing small claps. No one could stand quite like I could. Pelvis thrust forward, my right foot dangled off my slender ankle so that my legs, in princely tights, formed a jaunty lowercase *k*.

By far my best role with Up With Kids was also, fittingly, my last. In the fifth grade, when I was twelve, Bonnie cast me as Scarecrow in *The Wizard of Oz*. It was my best role, I should say, because I had always loved *Oz*. This was my excuse, with the help of the hobby shop in the basement of Cottonwood Mall, to live over the rainbow. Before I'd even highlighted my lines, the merch began pouring in: an Emerald City snow globe, an accent pillow of Scarecrow's face, a Toto stuffed animal. While my brother bought the latest Beckett in the card shop upstairs, tracking the value of his Shaq and Michael Jordan rookie cards like they were blue-chip stocks, I hauled out to the parking lot a life-size cardboard cutout of Scarecrow, the Wizard, and Tin Man and propped it at the foot of my bed to block out the sports wallpaper.

For a kid with a limp, it was easy to see Dorothy's plight as orthopedic. She had to navigate all kinds of uneven terrain: brick roads, poppy fields, hot air balloon platforms, stairs—and in sequined kitten heels. Skipping as best I could, I'd struck out on the replica of the Yellow Brick Road at MGM Grand in Las Vegas. Waiting in line for the Great Movie Ride in Orlando, I'd saluted those uncomfortable-looking ruby slippers by trying to click the heels of my own battered sneakers. The way they shimmered in their glass case gave me new insight into their allure. Through my toddler years, I'd preferred, like Dorothy, never to take off my shoes, even when I slept. It felt better to keep my feet encased in a little magic. (This magic did not extend to the ankle-foot orthosis shoved *into* my shoe, but with socks on I could survive the rubbing.)

Following surgeries in the third grade, I made sure my cast was as close to emerald as fiberglass could get. Even the braces and elastics in my mouth were green. My parents drew the line at green sunglasses, saying they would attract the wrong kind of people.

Sure, I knew that if Glinda could have popped onto the pilled carpet of Cottonwood Presbyterian she would have told me, in her airheaded way, I needed look no farther than my own two feet. This had never stopped me from daydreaming. Tin Man needed a heart, Cowardly Lion needed some nerve, and I needed a new leg, one that wasn't short and small in circumference around the calf and ankle; one that wasn't zipped up the back with scars; one that didn't need to be taught how to skip.

Whether in a cast or not, I never stopped thinking about my leg. Part of my brain was always sending stray signals to the tips of my toes, making me feel mildly electrocuted. What I loved about the stage was

that self-consciousness was a given and it was against the rules to walk
and talk at the same time, which I can't do anyway. It wasn't a matter of
forgetting about how my knee pointed inward or my right heel floated
off the ground. It was about all of us feeling awkward together.

As our first *Oz* extravaganza neared, Bonnie crowded the stage with as
many farmhands, crows, talking trees, flying monkeys, winkies, and
munchkins as there were cleared checks. She threw emerald smocks
over the denizens of Oz and a gold tiara on the busty blonde giant playing Glinda. Mona and the other munchkins wore ruffled sleeves and
scrunchies that even I had to admit were pretty cute. Being a munchkin
was perfect for my little sister. She leapt around the stage like a replace-
able idiot while I carried the show with my natural stage presence.

The same show business philosophy that led Bonnie to book our
summer stock at amusement parks led her to schedule one early *Oz*
performance in a homeless shelter in downtown Salt Lake, Bonnie's
philosophy being that a captive audience is better than one composed
exclusively of parents and relatives. Only those too sick or stoned stayed
for the duration, their faces dirty and drawn, a bunch of Aunt Ems
and Uncle Henrys doing their best to ignore the spectacle of Bonnie
crouched in the center aisle, mouthing along to the action onstage,
fleeing an invisible twister.

Sweat rolled down the back of my neck and dripped under my gold
lamé as soon as the overture to "If I Only Had a Brain" blasted through
the shoddy sound system and I hobbled to my mark, a masking tape
X. My leg wouldn't stop shaking as I swung it around. Nerves were a
good thing, Mom said. They meant you gave a shit. I was a natural
singer. I sang, naturally, all over the house. Sounding good in front of
a crowd was an order of magnitude beyond me. And dancing—how to
put this? Dancing was, if not my secret power, my secret joy. I wasn't
silly enough to think I was good at it, but it sure did get a rise out of
people. I was only a little worried about what my brother would say.

Since I couldn't hide my chicken leg no matter how large my
quilted poncho from the Costume Closet or how high I pulled my

socks, I tried to turn it into part of the act, jerking around like a real-life man of straw, wincing animatedly when my jean shorts rubbed against the incision scar on my hamstring. Seesawing into scenery, my clumsy right foot mashed crows' feet and sent plastic apples spiraling into the first row seconds after bitchy trees lobbed them at us. There were genuine gasps when I fell and genuine applause when I got up again. Stuck for ages with a pole up my back, I was finally free to dance.

It wasn't until our last curtain call, when Bonnie presented me, Mona, and every other cast member with hollow plastic Oscar statues, that she revealed the big surprise: we were going to meet one of the last surviving munchkins from *The Wizard of Oz*. It must have been a chore to track down Margaret Pellegrini in those dial-up days of the internet. In any case, this chance encounter had the ring of fate as it represented the next logical step in my progression as an actor. I was about to be discovered. Margaret would know agents and producers. All I had to do was sing for her and I'd have it made.

"But *I'm* a munchkin," Mona said.

"No, you're a weirdo in a gold leotard," Danny said, biting his hand.

Margaret is on-screen a lot if you know who to look for, a flyspecked grain of color lost in some paddy cake choreography—as gape-mouthed and adorable as Mona had been in the same role and, from the look of it, not much older. There she is on a footbridge, a flowerpot tipped on her head, as Judy Garland begins to sing "It Really Was No Miracle." Later, as the chorus cheeps, "Wake up you sleepy head," Margaret stretches from an egg in a pink nightgown and bonnet. When I paused the rented videotape, Mona squealed and kissed the screen, flying back when a branch of static shocked her.

"You idiot," Tiffany said from the couch, skater shoes tucked under her.

"Yeah, idiot," Mitch echoed from the other couch, her smaller skater shoes also tucked under her in perfect mimicry of our big sister. Unlike Moe and me, Mitch really could act, but she only ever wanted to act like Tiffany.

I pressed PLAY on the VCR and Margaret churned back to life. Mom came over from the kitchen, drying her hands. "Look at that little thing rub her eyes. That woman really knows how to wake up."

Mom wasn't being sarcastic. She saw real talent in the Munchkin Pellegrini. Like the pope, a munchkin didn't have to do anything special to win Mom's affection. She just had to *be*. "I bet she taught Judy a thing or two."

"Look at what she's wearing," Tiffany objected. "A pink nightgown? In the afternoon? And she doesn't even know the steps."

Protest as my siblings might, when the time came we all piled into the Suburban to meet Margaret's plane. On the way to swim meets and basketball games, Mom blasted "Make It Big" by the Beach Boys. For the munchkin drive, we were in rehearsal mode, practicing being ourselves in front of a celebrity. Danny sang his version of "The Lollipop Guild," a finger thrumming his small Adam's apple, and Mom kept cackling, "I'll get you my pretty" as I mugged in the mirror up front, preparing my toniest smile for little Margaret. "Brains? I don't have any brains."

"*Brains?*" Mom repeated, emoting to the nth degree. "*I don't have any brains. Only straw.*"

"*Only straw,*" I screamed back.

"This better be the smile I see at the airport," Mom said, leveling a finger at me. "I'm telling you. I want you to be this obnoxious. Ham it up for her, Greg. Ham it up!"

Airport security was considerably more lax in those days and children's musical theater companies could storm the terminal, shouting renditions of "The Munchkinland Song." As I glided along the moving walkway, too tense to bend my knee, Tiffany speed-walked beside me, Mitch half a step behind her as usual. Even in their baggy pants they moved better than I did, like they were floating. "Don't worry, Googers," Tiff said. "You're going to do great."

More than fifty years after the release of the film, a munchkin's visit was still a big enough deal to attract local news crews and a reporter or two. Passengers began wearily filing out, picking at the seats of their pants and searching for signs to baggage claim. My mom pulled Mona and me to the front of the crowd, beeping, "Scarecrow, coming through," and gave me an encouraging swat on the ass in my straw-stuffed jeans. "You can out-sing these spazzes. Make her think you're the only one in the room."

When Margaret stepped off the plane, our ensemble devolved into a rancid cult of celebrity. "The munchkin!" Mona cried. "Munchkin lady!"

We gave Margaret the kind of at-the-gate welcome usually reserved for boys returning from Mormon missions. Kids shook autograph books, snapped pictures, and clutched cutesy posters. I DON'T THINK YOU'RE IN KANSAS ANYMORE!!! In their minds, Margaret hadn't flown coach; she'd fallen from a star. Bonnie's hands flew into motion and we began dinging and donging, singing high and singing low to let *Margaret* know the Wicked Witch was dead.

Even before our song petered out, I noticed how strange Margaret looked, like she really had come from Munchkinland. Her hands were spotted like Tostitos. Her dress was trimmed with feathers where it shouldn't have been and so long she couldn't walk without tripping on it. She'd given up on the war with peach fuzz, and the hair on her head looked like it had been dyed with whatever they use to turn cotton candy pink. Parted in the middle, it sat in two fluffy mounds on either side of a very small hat.

"Is she wearing a costume?" I asked as we followed Margaret back through the terminal to the escalator.

"She probably can't find stuff that fits," Tiffany said.

"Not that you can either, skater girl," Danny said.

"Honestly, you kids," Mom said. "I couldn't even hear you back there and now you won't shut up."

At the luggage carousel, Mona weaseled her way to the front of the seething crowd of gold lamé and handed Margaret her Tinker Bell wand. Instead of calling security, Margaret began casting spells. At the talk she gave at a local high school later that day, Margaret humored requests to rub her eyes and sing, "Wake up you sleepy head." She posed for photos, signed people's crap, and told every child they were beautiful. The word *star* was used liberally. "Maybe you'll be a big star one day," she said, "or a little one like me."

It's hard to say exactly when it occurred to me, like the first twinge of a developing cavity, that all this was a little sad.

It could have been when Margaret told the crowd, to an uproar of delight, that Toto made twice as much as she did because the dog had a better agent. It could have been when she projected the promotional poster onstage of Henry Kramer's Hollywood Midgets, the acting company that had given her her big break, or when my mom elbowed me in the middle of Margaret's talk to say she sounded just like a kazoo. "Isn't her little voice just *precious*?"

Most likely, though, the revelation that Margaret was being exploited for her short stature came months later, on one of those death-by-errand summer afternoons, when Bonnie called my mom to offer me the star role in the new Up With Kids musical. They were doing *The Hunchback of Notre Dame*. Some of that old theater electricity shot from the phone through my body and I didn't know how to control it. I struggled to keep my smile glued in place, worried what might replace it. Mona, who slept whenever we drove anywhere, yawned awake from the backseat. "What's going on?"

Mitch calmly slugged a Coke beside her. "Greg's going to be Hunchback."

"Greg's going to be the *star*," Mom amended.

The muscles in my leg rippled and I tried to hide a grimace. "Like the Disney movie?" I asked into Mom's cell. Maybe there was another hunchback, one who wasn't a deformed monster whose only friends were priests and singing gargoyles.

"You don't have to decide right now," Bonnie growled softly, chewing her nicotine gum. "Just think about it, OK? Like I said, no one could play it like you. You were born for this."

I went to bed that night with a stomachache, the life-size cardboard cutout of Scarecrow, the Wizard, and Tin Man a monstrous silhouette at the foot of my bed. Gouty old men were a specialty of mine, those chair-bound sovereigns with slumping crowns. I'd been a Shakespearean player in a donkey head, a Trojan nobleman who took an unscripted tumble off the city wall (a picnic bench covered in a bedsheet), the Grinch on tiptoe, Santa Claus staggering under a heavy sack of toys. Losing myself in each role, I was acutely aware of my leg yet somehow certain the audience wasn't. The same wouldn't be possible for Quasimodo. I'd look down on my crooked leg and so would everyone else, each twisted step an exercise in stunt casting. My leg wouldn't be the prop. I would be.

In the dim hours of dawn, I concluded that I didn't want to be hired because of my disability, like Margaret had been. Duct tape a pillow to my shoulders and wheel in a particleboard bell tower and a stained-glass window made of tissue paper and the musical was pretty much my daily life. I wanted to be a star, not a groveling Hollywood hunchback.

It goes without saying that I didn't put it as eloquently as all that. Back then, I couldn't or wouldn't have thought to apply the term *disability* to my leg anymore than I would have thought to apply the term *gay* to my acting. The sleepless leap connecting my exceptional body to Margaret's was as accidental as evolution. It had taken the heightened reality of showbiz to expose an essential fact about my body. Margaret and I had more in common than I'd bargained for. Among the messy blast of emotions, one predominated: I was royally pissed.

At school that day, I thought about how I'd quit. Tiffany had ended her tumultuous relationship with the saxophone by pleading short fingers. Danny had put the kibosh on piano lessons by tearfully accusing Mom of trying to turn him into a girl.

That night I told Mom—informed her, really—that I was through with Up With Kids. I was too old and I wasn't a girl or a retard, no matter how much Bonnie or my mom wanted me to be.

In the middle of making tacos, Mom was unfazed by what she called my little performance. "They'll find another kid to play Quasimodo in two seconds," she sighed.

"Yeah, Bonnie's daughter," I said.

Mom gave me a look like *Really, kid?* and dumped four pounds of ground beef into a frying pan. I thought she might disappear in a cloud of smoke like the Wicked Witch but she was still behind the stove when it cleared. "Just drop it, OK?" she said. "If you don't want to have fun anymore, you don't want to have fun anymore."

A chance for redemption came in the ninth grade, when my drama teacher announced we would be putting on *The Wizard of Oz*. I promptly threw my hand into the air and volunteered the use of my replica 1939 shooting script. I'd grown a bunch since my Up With Kids days, though not as a performer. Sprouting to a gangly five-ten, I was proud to only be a few inches shorter than Dad. However, the growth spurt meant I badly needed my hamstrings surgically lengthened once again, this time on both sides. My walk was a crouch and a persistent hammertoe on my left foot bloodied my sock. I demanded to hold off on the operations until after the play. My school needed me.

At the audition, while my competitors struggled through tepid R&B songs and climbed on chairs à la Britney Spears, I crooned "If I Only Had a Brain" and trilled the scales. Leaving the auditorium that night, a goth kid in the back row slapped me high five. "Dude, you're totally going to get it."

I arrived late for the dancing portion of the audition the next day. A couple of girls walked me through the routine in the aisle, and soon I was shambling up on stage to the tune of "The Merry Old Land of Oz." With a *ha ha ha, ho ho ho* and a couple of *tra-la-la*s, I was skipping my way to the lead.

The middle-aged choreographer pulled me aside as I came off stage. This woman was not a teacher but one of the industry people my drama teacher had brought in to help with the production.

I expected the choreographer to tell me I was a shoo-in for Scarecrow but instead she said, "What's wrong with your leg? It looked like you weren't rotating from the hip." She clutched one of her sharp shoulders, wheeling it around to illustrate her point, as if just watching me made her sore.

"Are you talking about my shoulder?" I asked, hopeful.

"No, your leg," she clarified.

I should have been flattered. She thought I was injured.

Ordinarily, I had an arsenal of excuses about my limp. Sometimes I told people it was knee pain from growing so fast. Sometimes I mentioned my legs were different lengths. I'd recently told a substitute tennis instructor at the country club that, yes, my tendons had been operated on but my orthopedic surgeon had screwed up and now it was a big mess. Who can say why the truth—at least the truth as I understood it—popped out of my mouth when a lie about twisting my ankle doing her idiotic choreography would have suited me better?

"I have tight tendons," I said.

"Oh," the choreographer said, not missing a beat. "Because it looked like your hip wasn't working right." Here again she worked her shoulder. The woman was as lean and elegant as a candlestick with her chignon and ballet flats, her cheekbones set at handsome angles. "Will it be getting better in time for the show?"

"No," I admitted. "It won't."

The woman offered a serenely understanding smile, as if I were a golden retriever, all blond hair and bad hips. "Well, you did really great."

Children are sad creatures, so full of hope and light and judgment. So sure of their place in the world. My first thoughts, as I waited for Mom to pick me up, were ones of anger: *Who was this haughty witch to tell me what I could do? If she was so special, why was she volunteering at a junior high instead of choreographing on Broadway?*

Of course, such thoughts denigrated the whole enterprise—the school, the play, my meager acting ability. Part of me wanted to tell her how *believable* I could be as Scarecrow. When I fell, the audience would gasp, and when I got up again they would cheer. It wouldn't have mattered.

In the choreographer's gentle rejection lay a deeper truth: I would never be a professional actor. The fantasy was over. Later, I'd call this my munchkin moment: the moment I realized I was window dressing along the Yellow Brick Road, not the one skipping down it. I was one of the little people some other, more charismatic teenager would pledge not to forget. That night, I took down the glittery star that had hung on my door for years and fondled Margaret's autograph in my replica *Oz* script as if she were a real celebrity. She'd signed it "Munchkin Love."

My drama teacher was clever. Outright shafting the kid with the limp would have been poor form and so, instead, she gave me the title role. I couldn't shrug off the fact that Professor Marvel prognosticated from a sitting position on a wooden crate and his over-the-rainbow alter ego, the Wizard, didn't sing or dance and bellowed most of his lines in the wings, behind a curtain. Being upstaged by a dog was one thing. It took a special actor to be upstaged by a plywood head and a member of stage crew wagging the chin for comedic effect. Great and powerful I was not. Given so little to do, I overacted every scene, shouting so loud the mic cut out, unleashing a low electrical drone as the house lights strobed.

I was a good man and a bad wizard, handing a diploma to Scarecrow, a medal to Cowardly Lion, and a ceramic heart to Tin Man. Like Dorothy, I knew there wasn't anything in that leather-fringed purse for me. I wouldn't be getting a new leg. I was stuck with the one I had.

During the curtain call of our final performance, I took my bow and retired to a rickety rainbow platform at the back of the stage. A moment later, the chorus parted and Scarecrow, Tin Man, and Lion skipped in to a standing ovation. There wasn't enough space on the rainbow platform to do anything more than sway to the music, to bob my head and arch my eyebrows to keep the spidery tears of self-pity from crawling down my cheeks. To someone in the audience, it might have looked like nothing at all: a kid worn out with happiness after a fulfilling run, and then, confused, making a premature exit stage left as Scarecrow and Dorothy presented my drama teacher with flowers.

It took a while to compose myself in the dressing room and turn in my costume. No matter how encouraging the rest of my family would be, my smart-ass brother was sure to put me down for running off stage in tears. When I made it back to the auditorium, covered in flop sweat and runny makeup, they were waiting for me like always, scattered over a few otherwise empty rows. The Wizard of Oz head scowled down at us from the stage, his chin now wagging open like he'd suffered a stroke.

"You're right. It was a nothing role. What can I say? You got totally, completely screwed," Mom said, swinging her gold purse on her shoulder.

"I'm proud of you for toughing it out, Greggo," Dad said.

"You certainly made the most of it," Mom went on. "Ask anybody. You were the only one I could hear."

I gave Tiffany a hug and tried to keep a neutral expression on my face as my brother shuffled toward me down the aisle, popping a pretzel into his mouth. To my surprise, he offered the only thing I'd ever really wanted from him: a positive review. "It was way less shitty than Up With Kids," he said, chewing. "You had a real dog play Toto this time and Dorothy was pretty hot." Putting a hand on my soaked head in an odd display of brotherly affection, his eyes lost that joking sparkle. "Seriously, Gregor. You were the best thing in the show."

This, it turned out, was my final bow.

Leg surgeries the next Christmas kept me from auditioning for my high school drama department's one-act play, a show about a monstrously deformed writer being held prisoner in a closet. As I was confined to a wheelchair at the time, encased in Ace bandages and knee immobilizers that went from my butt cheeks to my ankles, *Crippled: The Greg Marshall Story* would've been a fitting title. I could have tried out. If I'd only had the balls.

There were other things to fail at in high school: making the tennis team and convincing my friends I was straight. None of them were as fun as belting out "If I Only Had a Brain" to the homeless. Little home-video footage remains from my brief dramatic career. I suppose this is for the best as it allows me to remember my histrionics as scene stealing, my voice as blunt and captivating. If I didn't limp, I tell myself, I might really have made it.

For the next few weeks of that semester, as I graduated from wheelchair to walker, my teachers let me out five minutes early so I wouldn't be trampled. I think it was tipping through those empty halls that I

gained a begrudging respect for Margaret Pellegrini. If the opposite of
being typecast for having a disability is not being cast at all, being a
Hollywood Midget didn't sound so bad. At a time when nearly everyone
who had worked on *The Wizard of Oz* was dead, she was still signing
autographs, rubbing sleep from her eyes. Mom was right: the woman
knew how to wake up. Every *Oz* anniversary landed Margaret a spot on
the local news, where she repeated her famous line (or at least famous
to me) about Toto having a better agent.

History isn't told by the winners. It's told by the living. When you're
a kid, you're taught success depends on embracing who you are. It's
actually much simpler than that: to succeed, you have to stick around.
By marching around in a replica costume like the veteran of some
whimsical war, Margaret recast herself as an indelible part of the story.
Outlive the Coroner and you become the grand marshal of all things
Over the Rainbow. Sometimes, surviving is its own form of stardom.

NEVER GET AIDS

HIV started like a common cold: fever, chills, sore throat, muscle aches. You might suffer some fatigue or have swollen lymph nodes, but a week or so after primary infection your ailments would subside and your health return to normal. Rushing to the clinic wouldn't do any good as it could take six months after being infected, maybe longer, to test positive for the virus that causes AIDS. "The window period," Mrs. Palmer said, strolling the rows of my seventh-grade Life Science class. She kept her arms crossed and her gaze trained on some middle distance, the American flag or the TV bolted above the chalkboard. "Will you test positive during the window period?"

"No."

I chanted along with the rest of the class, trying to make sure my voice was not more ragged than those around me. Failing to hide my nerves, I ripped a corner of paper from my binder and tore it into smaller and smaller pieces, my good leg jiggling like I had to pee.

Mrs. Palmer moseyed by my desk, momentarily enveloping me in her lotion scent. The rare junior high teacher who had a genuine rapport with her students, Mrs. Palmer was more like a friend's mom, affectionate but quick to correct. The district pushed a strict no-touching policy—our teachers were supposed to be like actors in a haunted house, frightening us but never making bodily contact—but Mrs. Palmer had no problem brushing off dandruff or straightening a collar. I felt her linger over me, studying the mess I'd made with my scraps of paper, and for a second I worried she'd put a comforting hand on my distressed shoulder, singling me out as the one this was all directed toward. Did everyone know I was gay? Was this lesson for me? These other assholes weren't going to get AIDS, but I was. I kept my eyes fixed on my scraps of paper.

When Mrs. Palmer came to the end of my row she twirled around, lifting a prosecutorial finger as if she might finally stump us. "But can you get other people sick during the window period?"

"Yes," we said.

Mrs. Palmer had sensible dark hair that curled obligingly at her shoulders. Like our moms, she preferred pleated khakis, appliqué vests, and headbands. Unlike our moms, she could turn bland textbook passages into rhapsody. "That's right," she said. "Viral loads can be very high during this time. Viral loads can be what?"

"High during this time," we repeated.

A hand shot up. A girl asked, "Will this be on the test?"

Mrs. Palmer paused significantly before answering. "We're not having a test on HIV/AIDS." She always said the two together, like they were a package deal. "Life will be your test." Mrs. Palmer had told us this a hundred times before. The thought of getting out of an exam made the other kids in my class cheer. It made my heart flutter in my ears.

I was thirteen. Closeted. A virgin.

"Closeted" sounds strange to say as it implies I knew for sure I was gay, no question about it, and I'd chosen to hide. This is close enough to the truth, I suppose. My earliest memory is of undressing my Spider-Man doll at the age of two and my first boner came a few years later when, playing with my action figures, Superman and a cowboy named BraveStarr began torturing each other. My hang-up was not accepting I was gay but figuring out how this fact would apply to my life. It's possible both to like guys *and* to picture a woman on your arm when you daydream about walking the red carpet.

My tight tendons only compounded questions about my body. I was at a loss when trying to place myself in the framework of the larger world, trying to figure out where I fit: I walked with a limp, but so did Jeff Hornacek with his bad knee. Despite years of off-and-on physical therapy, I could still beat Chip in basketball. I wasn't the smartest kid in school by a long shot, but I'd long ago worked my way out of remedial classes.

My body was seriously messed up, though. For one, my boners expanded warmly against my stomach when, clearly, they were supposed to stand straight up at ninety-degree angles from my pelvis, even when I was lying down, hence the expression *tentpole*. The shaft of my penis curved a little. Nothing about me was straight. Not my dick, not my spine. I remember feeling amazed that I passed the scoliosis screening in gym, that I'd been allowed to slip back on my Wasatch Warriors shirt and rejoin the normal kids.

If I had one thing going for me, it was my large testicles. Mom claimed that the feather-haired nurses in neonatal intensive care told her I was so well endowed in the balls region they wanted my phone number when I turned eighteen. It didn't matter that I was a mess of wiring, gauze, and blue and red electrodes in an incubator with a recently reinflated right lung and what would turn out to be a spastic set of limbs, too premature to even be circumcised. According to Mom, I was a stud.

This is the story I grew up hearing and I can't say I gave it much thought. I just walked around with the secret knowledge that I had large testicles and, with them, an outsize empathy for creatures similarly afflicted, like Moose in his red rocket days. I think Mom figured if I ended up an angry question mark in a wheelchair I'd want something to show for myself, some physical trait to hang my hat on, so to speak. She gave me big balls because she knew I'd need them.

There were other suspected homosexuals in seventh grade, a baby-faced boy named Garth and a knock-kneed fop named Charlie, the only other kid on my third-grade basketball team to not score a single layup in an entire season. I fancied myself less obvious than these boys—less effeminate, less flitty—but I couldn't be sure. Suburban Salt Lake in the late 1990s was not especially cruel; it wasn't especially enlightened, either. Kids used the word *gay* in the same way they used the word *retarded*—to signify something they didn't like. You might not have gotten your ass kicked for openly liking guys, but it wouldn't have made you any friends. There was no incentive to come out, no queer world waiting to claim you. Being gay was a social death sentence as surely as AIDS was an actual death sentence.

Tiffany was obsessed with Drew Barrymore and had a poster from the movie *Mad Love* taped above her bed. When I pressed my mom's Brookstone back massager into my crotch, my right leg shooting out at the moment of climax, I thought not of Drew but of her co-star, Chris O'Donnell. After the Rory Shuman dick debacle, it would take me a few more years to fantasize about boys from my grade. Until then, I told myself I didn't like guys. I liked celebrities.

I can see now that my fear of AIDS kept me in the closet. I had never met an openly gay person or seen a gay character in the movies or on TV unless you counted the "Ambiguously Gay Duo" from *Saturday Night Live*. (This was before the Mormons took the show off the air in Utah.) *SNL* also exposed me to my first drag performers, not that I would have known to call them that: Adam Sandler, Chris Farley, and David Spade playing mall employees on lunchbreak at the food court. I realize that this sounds archaic and impossible, from another century, and it was. "You really grew up in the nineties?" my husband will ask me. "Are you sure it wasn't the fifties?" To be fair, *Will & Grace* would premiere that fall, but in the spring of 1998 *Veronica's Closet* was the gayest thing on Must See TV and there were no gay characters on it even though it was set at a lingerie company.

When gay people did come up on TV, it was usually on the news, and those stories were almost exclusively about AIDS. Gay guys weren't the *only* ones infected with the virus, but *all* gay guys were infected with the virus.

I couldn't earn better than a B-plus in pre-algebra, but the transitive logic was so simple even I could complete it: Greg is gay. Gay people have AIDS. Greg has AIDS.

I don't want to suggest I was the only seventh grader whose world was rocked by the disease. Anyone who was a kid in the late nineties will tell you it was quite the opposite. Mrs. Palmer made a point of saying the virus afflicted not just gay men, but Democrats in general: brown kids, goths, girls. AIDS, as they say, was catching. Magic Johnson had HIV. So did a nurse on *ER*. Ryan White, the hemophiliac who had been expelled from middle school for being HIV-positive, was now posthumously a national hero. There was the AIDS Quilt, *Rent*, Freddie Mercury. Chip, who was in Mrs. Palmer's class with me, was so terrified of AIDS he said if he ever got married and wanted kids he'd have his wife artificially inseminated. I wasn't planning on having sex with anyone's wife, let alone my own, but even I knew that was taking the fun out of it.

For the two weeks of our HIV/AIDS unit Mrs. Palmer packed the house. The skater boys, who were truant or checked out when we discussed DNA or mitosis or wetlands, came alive when we talked about AIDS. At full attendance, there was not a single spare seat in the room. Without a desk to sit in, Mrs. Palmer's dead-eyed ninth-grade teacher's assistant beached himself on the radiator. We could smell his oils simmering as surely as we could taste the Oreos on our breath from lunch a period earlier.

School policy when it came to sex ed was for kids to never have any, ever. Abstinence only. If anything, the tone from sources of authority had grown more strident and less forgiving since the maturation program in elementary school. Now that the changes were upon us, no one was taking any chances. We could start fucking at any time; the time for fucking around was done.

Besides Chip and me, most of the kids in Mrs. Palmer's class were Mormon. The girls weren't allowed to wear tank tops, let alone *reproduce*. The length of their skirts had to extend past their fingertips. Hairstyle was not protected speech. Hair color was not protected speech. You could dye your mop but only to a shade that existed naturally, no purples or blues. Wearing more than one pair of earrings was considered out there. And jacking off was a sin, not a hobby. So it was a small act of courage for Mrs. Palmer to teach us the word *prophylactic*. "The only one hundred percent safe sex is not having any," she would say. "But if you do choose to have sex, using condoms greatly reduces the risk. Using what?"

"Condoms," we would say in unison.

Mrs. Palmer had no illusions she was training the next generation of professors and pathologists. We were not Gifted and Talented. We had average test scores and average life prospects. Life Science covered everything from evolution to pasteurization. Squinting through microscopes, dissecting frogs, debating whether or not Pluto was a planet— the object of these lessons was as much civic as it was scientific. Mrs. Palmer endeavored to mold us into decent people, to prepare a bunch of sheltered kids for the world by arming us with facts, and, when that didn't work, by scaring the bejesus out of us.

The last day before spring break, Mrs. Palmer wheeled in a TV from the library. Before pressing PLAY, she excused the few kids whose parents wouldn't sign the permission slip she'd sent home weeks earlier.

Oprah introduced the movie and then a warning appeared on-screen: *The following film is about AIDS. Parents should discuss its content with their kids.* The peanut butter and jelly sandwich I'd eaten for lunch turned in my stomach, threatening to climb up my throat as the title splashed across the screen: *In the Shadow of Love: A Teen AIDS Story.*

Clocking in at about forty-five minutes without commercials, *Shadow of Love* tells the tale of a promising high school anchorwoman who, over the course of filing a report about teenagers living with HIV, discovers that her boyfriend has infected her with the virus.

It's the end of the movie I remember best. Katie is sitting dazed behind her anchor desk at school when her camerawoman, Lisa, runs in to tell her they have won a journalism contest. Their story will appear on Channel Three, where they are going to be summer interns. A deliberate silence settles over the almost-abandoned newsroom. Doing a report on AIDS was Lisa's idea to begin with, and now Katie resents her for it. "It's all your fault," Katie says. "This had nothing to do with me until I met you."

In a lesser production, things would have turned scene-chewy fast. It's a credit to the actresses that they underplay their lines. Soon, Katie has moved from accusing her friend to blaming herself. "Why did I do it, Lisa? Why did I sleep with him?"

"Because you loved him," Lisa consoles.

"Yeah, but now I'm going to die. I'm not going to be a reporter. I'm not going to be anything," Katie says before tumbling into Lisa's arms.

Shadow of Love is the kind of paint-by-numbers parable that made *ABC Afterschool Special* not just a long-running TV series, but also a catchphrase for the overwrought, arresting drama in our own lives. I've only ever been a tourist in the annals of television history, a kid with a Coke in hand, transfixed by hours of programming. Still, it's not hard to see what makes *Afterschool Special*s exceptional. They were one of the few places queer or disabled people were portrayed on TV, though often in instances of strife and suffering. Inseparable from our trauma, we were matinee martyrs, pitied and patronized yet routinely more interesting than the bland main characters to whom we taught lessons or imparted dying wishes. Maybe that's why this saccharine series would both win Daytime Emmys and go on to be parodied in our culture ruthlessly, and often hilariously, by shows I'd love in my twenties like Amy Sedaris's *Strangers with Candy*. Good intentions get campy with too many close-ups. Cliché slides into comedy. First comes Cousin Geri on *The Facts of Life* then comes Jerri Blank.

The message to kids like me was subliminal: my life, so ordinary in a million ways, would never be part of morning shows or game shows, cooking shows or prime time sitcoms. Regular programming was for regular people. The "special" kids at my junior high weren't the ones winning awards. They were the ones responsible for cleaning the lunchroom. "It's job training for them," a friend's mom once told me as we tried to get them to clear out so we could work on an extra-curricular project.

We may not have cared much for special people but special stories, even the most ham-fisted, could appeal broadly. Take *Shadow of Love*. By today's standards, the movie may be hokey, its scenes scored with jazz guitars and flutes, but on that April day in 1998, I was not the only one quietly weeping. You have to love a TV movie so earnest that the support group's leader, a woman with a head full of loose braids, gets away with mentioning you can catch HIV not just from semen and blood, but also from vaginal fluid. The show also gained points in my mind for casting Harvey Fierstein as an auntish AIDS counselor. I recognized Harvey as Robin Williams's brother in *Mrs. Doubtfire*, so on second thought I had seen a gay character in a movie.

Mrs. Palmer sauntered to the light switch, giving us just enough time to wipe snot onto our sleeves. Using my middle fingers, I pulled my lids taut to sluice away tears, like my mom did when she cried. It was hard not to wonder if my funeral would get anything near this outpouring. Dabbing her eyes, Mrs. Palmer told us to have a safe and wonderful spring break.

I wasn't sure how wonderful it would be. Mom's cancer was back. What had seemed like a permanent victory over non-Hodgkin's lymphoma had turned pyrrhic, nothing more than a three-year-plus break between rounds. Mom's epic rematch had so far taken place largely offstage, while I was worrying about selling tickets to the school musical and pledging in my floppy leather journal to masturbate less. The parts I did see of Mom's treatment were carefully curated comedy sketches.

On her way out the door to have bone marrow drawn out of her hip with a terrifying needle, Mom would moon me to reveal the words "Big Butt Jokes" on her ass slashed through with red marker. "I don't want my nurses getting any ideas," she'd say.

"Does it seem like Mom is . . . *enjoying* this?" Danny asked while we played ping-pong one night. I'd never seen him look more befuddled. It did seem like it.

I didn't remember her finding her cancer funny the first time, taking control in small ways to lighten the air in the room, like she did in round two. Maybe it was because we were older now and thus a better audience, or maybe it was because Mom had survived once before and believed she would again, but she started wearing funny shirts to the hospital, hula skirts, glasses with bug eyes on springs, treating cancer like it was a big laugh.

If humor helped humanize Mom to her doctors, it also made the rest of us minimize her illness. She turned our worries from chemo to carpools, from hospitals to homework, delivering such a commanding performance as an onery spitfire that we bought it. "I'm an old battle axe," she'd say, as if she were not forty-two but eighty-two.

It helped that Mom's chemo, Rituxan, was more sophisticated than her previous regimen. A targeted therapy, it killed cancer cells and mostly left hair and skin cells alone. She *looked* better than before, hot rollers singeing her already-fried mane. Another perk of Rituxan: Mom could usually make it to and from the toilet to be sick, an improvement over the last time. I would shoulder into my parents' room to watch Nick at Nite and discover her Pompeian form huddled next to the toilet and think, *Good for you.*

Chemo was on Tuesday. By Saturday, she would feel well enough to get dressed and by Sunday, when the Mormons were in church, she would go to the grocery store to do our shopping for the week, always making the same joke to the young cashier as the total reached into the hundreds: "There goes my Hawaiian vacation."

From what I could tell, there were some similarities between AIDS and non-Hodgkin's lymphoma. Both were chronic conditions that attacked the immune system and ended life as you knew it. I marveled at the differences, too. AIDS was shrouded in shame and secrecy, the kind of thing that cast a long shadow. Cancer, on the other hand, may not have always been comedy gold but it didn't scare anyone away. No one worried about drinking from your glass. People thought Mom was brave. They invited her to speak at Utah's first Cancer Survivor Day at the zoo. She even made the local news. "Brave? I don't feel brave," she'd say into microphones, holding Moe on her lap. "If I put on a chicken suit and clucked around the hospital, I'd feel appropriately dressed. I just didn't want my kids to grow up without a mom."

If ABC made an *Afterschool Special* of our life it would be called *In the Shadow of Mom: The Thing That Wouldn't Die.* My mom attended support groups filled with gutsy friends we'd come to know by the kinds of cancer they had (pancreatic, ovarian, glioblastoma), friends who were always getting last-minute facelifts so they would look good in their coffins and bequeathing us their terrible cats. Mom's social life was one of hospice vigils, bedside goodbyes, and soaring eulogies. She outlived *everyone*. "I met a really nice lady at group tonight," she'd say. "Boy, I'm going to feel lousy when she croaks."

The cancer show went on even when it wasn't fun anymore. We lived under a germophobic regime where handwashing was a form of prayer. Wringing our hands, we would beg, *Please don't let Mom get sick.* The pettiest of colds could give her pneumonia and, from what I understood, she didn't have two white blood cells to rub together, not unlike an advanced AIDS patient. If my brother or sisters or I brought home friends with runny noses, Mom would make them call their parents to come pick them up. We didn't blame her, exactly, but it was humiliating having her shut herself up in her room, shouting from behind her door. "Was that a sneeze? I heard a sneeze."

Because of Mom's cancer, all of us kids were real hypochondriacs. We'd go to the doctor for just about anything and generally feared death more than your average children.

I started coughing on the third or fourth day of spring break. By that weekend my voice was a strangle of vowels. Hitting tennis balls with my dad one afternoon, I started to worry. If it could happen to Katie, anchorwoman and journalistic luminary, it could happen to me. But it also was possible it was a false alarm. I just had to lay off the cigarettes I didn't smoke.

As the ball flew toward me, I told myself that if I missed this shot I had HIV. My sore muscles, swollen lymph nodes, and cough were symptoms not of a cold but of the disease we'd been studying in Mrs. Palmer's class. I was a goner. I couldn't stay in the house if I was sick, so I was bound for a squalid foster home where I would be forced to befriend spiders and mop toilet bowls with my tongue. Conversely, if I made the shot, I was negative and would be fine.

I lined up the forehand that would seal my fate. My rinky-dink shot cleared the net by seven feet and sailed over the fence, thudding on the lawn. It was out. I'd missed the shot. I had AIDS. Then I bargained. I told myself it was best of three shots, and then best of five, of seven, of eleven. I made some ground strokes and missed many more and walked off the court more anxious than ever. I had AIDS for sure. Or maybe not. Or maybe so. Who knew?

On some level, I knew what I was doing was illogical. Mrs. Palmer had taught me better; I didn't have HIV since I wasn't engaging in risky behavior—having sex or shooting juice (a phrase I'd picked up from one of the infected teens in *Shadow of Love*)—and I certainly wasn't exposing myself to vaginal fluid. The fear might have subsided if I'd been willing to tell my dad about it, but then he would start to ask questions. "Why should you be scared, Greggo?" he might wonder, tapping my chest with his white Wilson. "Is there something you need to tell us?"

The first day back from spring break, I woke up to find my shirt soaked in sweat. "You don't look good," my dad said when I came down for breakfast. I chugged the glass of OJ he poured me and went to the couch to die. Not wanting to worry my dad, who looked quite blissful flipping pancakes with his spatula, I kept my diagnosis to myself. *The Price Is Right* would be on soon. There were worse things than dying to the Showcase Showdown.

I missed school that day and the next. When I returned, Mrs. Palmer told us that her dear friend was coming the next day to talk to us about HIV/AIDS. She was intentionally vague, saying he might be a doctor, patient, or counselor and we were not to ask if he harbored the disease.

"He totally has it," Chip whispered.

Walking into science that day, I expected a woman in a lab coat to prick my finger and administer an HIV test on the spot. I took some relief in the fact that, seeing as how I was in the window period, I would test negative. The technician would need only massage my lymph nodes and feel my pasty forehead to detect my ravaged immune system, but for conclusive evidence we would have to wait. At least I wouldn't be hauled away on a gurney.

As I made my way to my desk, I was taken aback to find Mrs. Palmer gossiping with a surprisingly attractive guy at the front of the room. He whispered little insights that made her chortle.

A jean jacket hung on the back of Mrs. Palmer's chair, where there was usually a small, bright cardigan. The guy's shirt was rumpled and tucked into a smart pair of dark jeans. Though his status was supposed to be a secret, before the tardy bell rang he came right out and told us he had AIDS. Not HIV. Full-blown AIDS.

It says something that even after seeing the unflappable infected teens in *Shadow of Love*, I expected my first real-life AIDS patient to be hunched and skeletal, a lover of dark corners with a breathy voice.

We'd studied the virus from a polite distance for so long, learned all the right things to think and say, and yet I couldn't help but be electrified by the news. Here was someone from the real world, not a teacher but an actual adult with an actual first name, and for the rest of the period I was free to study him.

Dennis was cute, prissy, and self-righteous as truth-tellers can sometimes be, not a scare-'em-straight motivational speaker but a whistleblower from the corrupt company called Adulthood. He looked a little vexed standing before us. Hand planted on his hip, Dennis rested most of his weight on one tennis shoe while the toe of the other just barely scraped the ground, like Hornacek. Or me. Did Dennis have tight tendons? No, but that was fine. He had a nice smile, stiff and defiant, a mix of handsomeness and ruin. Maybe all I mean is that Dennis didn't repulse me, that I saw myself in him, and instead of being appalled I sat back and listened.

Years later, Mom would tell me that she had known so little about cancer treatment when she'd first started, in a room the size of a closet where they used to store brochures, that she thought the first drop of her first chemo might kill her, like arsenic. I thought the same thing about HIV: You don't become a reporter, à la Katie. You don't become anything. You get HIV and the image freezes and the credits roll. You get it and you die.

Dennis was living proof of the opposite. He was *living*—neither character nor corpse. No movie or TV show could have been as powerful to me as the real man standing at the front of class.

Before she retired to the windowsill, Mrs. Palmer squirted some Purell onto Dennis's palm and then onto her own, as if simply being in our presence required hand sanitizer. She wasn't wrong.

"Like we've talked about, class, because of Dennis's weakened immune system you're more of a risk to him than he is to you," she said, the aroma of rubbing alcohol wafting back over the rows. Purell was my mom's signature fragrance, too.

Dennis worked the clear gel between each finger, studying his shiny cuticles as he said, casually, "You really are. You could kill me."

Dennis began with an About Me section. "Like I said, I have AIDS, which sucks and is awful. I like long walks on the beach and riding my bike." He looked to Mrs. Palmer. "What else?"

She shrugged. "It's your class."

"I really freaked out the last group, so I think I'm just going to have fun with you guys," he said.

I remember being disappointed to hear Dennis was from Farmington, a village outside of Salt Lake, and not a big city. How did he contract HIV in Farmington? Maybe it was a case of animal-to-human transfer. A carnival had come to town and a gorilla or a sooty mangabey had snapped its leash and lovingly bitten him.

Dennis chalked two columns of monthly expenses on the board: Medical and Everything Else. The first column was for his drug cocktail and doctor's bills and the second, which he filled with our suggestions, was for expenses like rent, food, and movies. Mrs. Palmer called it a brainstorm, but it was really just a shouting match. "Milk," one girl cried. "Soda," said another. "Ba-loan-ya," said Chip, trying out a new persona as class clown. Everyone laughed.

"Keep it together, people," Mrs. Palmer warned.

Dennis was lithe, almost balletic, and so short he had to arabesque to reach the upper third of the board. I didn't participate in the discussion that day, not because I thought I was too good for the auction-like commerce of ideas but because I was holding in a cough. Several coughs. If I opened my mouth, I worried they'd go flying out like saliva-covered bats. Dennis would catch pneumonia and die and

I would be to blame. Mrs. Palmer would show up to school Monday wearing a black veil, maintaining composure until I walked into fifth period. "*You*," she would say. "Why didn't you listen?"

Dennis's handwriting was thrillingly messy and unteacherlike. The chalk clattered in his fingers and when he turned to us, wiping his mouth with his forearm, we saw that he had smudged his dark jeans and his billowy dress shirt.

Following up his baloney hit, Chip recommended Cheez Whiz.

"How do you spell that?" Dennis asked.

The laughter couldn't be contained.

"W-i-z," Chip said, as if in a spelling bee. He'd gotten it wrong but it didn't matter.

Dennis let us inspect his handiwork as a girl with a completely unnecessary TI-82 came up with totals for each column. Then he put another dollar amount on the board, his monthly budget, and drew frantic circles around it. The chalk might have even snapped as he did this.

Anyone could see the man's modest income wasn't nearly enough to cover both his medical expenses *and* his living expenses. He tossed what remained of the chalk playfully in the air and caught it, asking which he should choose: food and movies and an apartment, or his medicine.

Educators would have called this a teachable moment. Dennis and Mrs. Palmer had let the class go on and on, crafting an encyclopedic list of all the foods we loved and all the things we liked to do so that we'd get a sense of loss. This was all we *couldn't* have. Mrs. Palmer had taught us the scientific method, about making assumptions and coming up with a hypothesis, only to use it against us. We had assumed Dennis could afford to indulge his appetites. AIDS, it turned out, was pricey.

Dennis tossed what remained of the chalk into the tray and picked up the eraser. With several graceful strokes, he smeared away everything we'd come up with and dramatically wiped his hands before he settled on top of Mrs. Palmer's desk, his thumbs rapping on the metallic edge.

It was disquieting to have him sitting primly in front of us, legs crossed at the ankle and posture so perfect it had to be an act. He picked a spot on the floor and didn't look up from it. "Now I'd like to tell you about my friend Terrence," he said.

Dennis had no problem telling us he had AIDS, but it pained him to talk about this Terrence guy, who had died three years earlier of complications related to the disease. Dennis described delirious trips to the emergency room that turned into interminable hospital stays, and how frightened Terrence had been at the end. "I've lost my best friend. And now I'm all alone. Me and my bills," Dennis said.

He must have already told the story to Mrs. Palmer's other classes that day, but his voice became husky, as if he'd finally caught my cold. Grief made his features uneven. He squinted one eye and twisted his mouth from one side of his face to the other, straining not to cry until, all at once, he slapped his thighs and hopped up from the edge of the desk. Mrs. Palmer came over and put a hand on his back. "Give Dennis a round of applause," she said.

I'd like to say I knew Dennis was gay right away, but that would be an exaggeration. It would have been no different if he'd had bulging muscles and worn a mustache and a shirt that said SO MANY MEN, SO LITTLE TIME, the kind Mom would have strutted around in if she were a gay man, or even if she weren't. It's hard for any of us to comprehend just how naïve and unhip we were as kids, how lost in daily life, ignorant of the themes and events that shape us as they're shaping us. Only upon reflection at home would Dennis's sexual orientation become obvious to me: Terrence wasn't Dennis's friend but his *friend*. I wish now I would have given the guy a hug, germs be damned, but when the bell rang, I filed out with everyone else and, once in the hall, let out an ab-straining cough.

My family didn't believe in counseling, but if Harvey Fierstein could have sat me down, his voice crackling like a campfire, he could have helped me understand. "You have a crush on Dennis," he might have said. "That's why you're freaking out."

As a seventh grader, my greatest fear was dying of AIDS, though it may be just as accurate to say the opposite: As a seventh grader, my greatest fear was *not* dying of AIDS. Worse than AIDS was the prospect I might never find anyone to love me.

If my logic sounds tortured, perhaps even schizophrenic, it's because it was schizophrenic. I wanted to join my denim-on-denim-wearing brethren, maybe even take part in a fashionable support group, but I didn't want to die. As a kid who was probably gay with no gay people to confide in, I desperately wanted to belong even if I wasn't yet ready to name the place I belonged. I wanted a community, a pack of people like me, but that came with devastating knowledge: being gay meant having AIDS.

Mom offered a confusing example. She had found her people through illness and was most at home among her comrades in arms, her oncologist Saundra, her nurses, and fellow survivors. Cancer had given her a community but it was more than that. It had given her a purpose, a reason to fight. It sometimes felt like Mom's real life was up at the Huntsman Cancer Institute. Anywhere else, even on vacation at the beach, she didn't know quite what to do with herself. Rather than hobbies or close friends, she had a house full of dead ladies' cats and the promise of a crowded funeral. People enjoyed my mom, wrote her fan mail for her column, told us she was amazing. It's just that they didn't really know her. At thirteen, I'm not sure I did either. Mom filtered out a lot of her fear and anger. It would take me years to see through her act. I could hardly remember a time before she got sick. Mom's life began when she was diagnosed. Maybe mine would, too.

I saved any mention of Dennis for the end of my journal entry that night. The few sentences I managed were as much about fighting desire as they were about disease. *Make the right choices. Do not let AIDS take you in! Fight! Never get AIDS. Never!*

I remained a hypochondriac for the rest of my teens. Donating blood during a schoolwide drive in the tenth grade, I wondered if I would get a call from a counselor telling me I had the virus, never mind that

I was still a virgin. Superstitious bets were going on in my head any-time I shot a basket or swung a tennis racket—*If I make this, I'll stay negative. If I miss it, I'll get HIV*—but Mrs. Palmer's lesson diminished my ignorance. Anytime I lost my cool, I remembered that my personal life equation was not Greg equals AIDS but Greg plus condoms equals safe. I couldn't get rid of my fear, but I could put a prophylactic on it.

It took me until my freshman year of college to come out of the closet and another year to find someone who would have sex with me. Dennis became my stand-in fictional boyfriend on many nights when my only company was AOL Instant Messenger and porn.

I didn't know whether Dennis was dead or alive, but whenever I came home on school breaks I imagined running into him in the beer aisle on a Sunday while all the Mormons were in church. Despite the years that had elapsed, he would still look the same as he had that day in seventh grade, the cuffs of his rumpled shirt rolled almost to his elbows, his jean jacket tossed over one shoulder. When I saw him, I would squeeze his bicep and steal Katie's line from *Shadow of Love*. "It's all your fault," I'd say. "This had nothing to do with me until I met you." And then I would tumble into his arms.

SUCK RAY BLUE

I'd picked up a few things in two years of French. I couldn't speak the language, but I could tell you that life overseas cantered along at a slower pace. Women went topless and ate sensible portions supplemented with cheese. Salad came after the main course. Frenchmen smoked cigarettes without dropping dead and kissed each other on the cheek without being called faggots.

When my French teacher, Monsieur Arnaud, proposed a trip to Paris, the Loire Valley, Normandy, and Brittany the summer after eighth grade, I was one of the first to sign up. To walk among the cobblestone streets in soft-toed shoes, to talk with my hands and wear turtlenecks without fear of judgment—this was the life for me. I may not have been much in the classroom, but it would be a different story once I hit the Champs-Élysées. Travel is transformational. All I needed was a crash course in pastries and conversation. In Paris, as I palled around with schoolboys and fashioned my pants into culottes, I would become *Gregoire*.

Because I lack both a sense of direction and the ability to put on my shoes in a timely fashion, Mom was reticent about sending me abroad. My friend Robin was coming along, but with his giant head and hyperactive thyroid, he hardly counted as security. Mom would have gone with me but she required Valium to fly. And anyway, she had lymphoma and two little girls whose *perdis*, she said, still needed wiping.

After finishing Rituxan, Mom had spent the previous summer at a cancer hospital in Seattle, harvesting her stem cells for a future bone marrow transplant, the only potential cure on the horizon for a chronic cancer patient in her forties with no known siblings and therefore no stem-cell matches. We'd lived in a Marriott Residence Inn across the street from a Hooters while Mom underwent high-dose chemo and had her bones scraped out and the contents stored in a medical freezer. She returned to Salt Lake after the start of school that fall and took advantage of her cue-ball pate by going as Uncle Fester for Halloween, a lightbulb in her mouth. She'd run errands wearing a T-shirt proclaiming, I'M TOO SEXY FOR MY HAIR. THAT'S HOW COME IT ISN'T THERE, but some days, even nearly a year after the bone marrow harvest, she was too run-down to get out of bed.

When I really pressed her, she admitted that she'd never been to Europe and didn't trust the water. Her blood counts were still low, so she needed to avoid crowds and people with contagious illnesses, which in Mom's estimation was ninety percent of France.

That left my sweet, uncultured dad as a potential chaperone.

Dad spent a semester of college in Vienna, but he was an Idaho boy through and through. As a child, he hadn't worn underwear to bed in a household that forbade the use of more than three squares of toilet paper per sitting. This family tradition was painfully rehashed anytime we visited our cousins, whose naked bottoms smeared the couch cushions. Now that Dad was grown, he wore tighty whities and not even a good brand: Fruit of the Loom. Most days, he walked around with shaving-cream highlights in his sideburns, bloody toilet paper stuck to his cheek where he'd nicked himself.

Dad treated maladies with a glass of wine at dinner, and, if the weather was nice, a glass of wine and a jar of Planters Peanuts after dinner on the gazebo. Get him started on the price of Qualcomm and a few hours later, one hardened drop of Kirkland Merlot at the bottom of his glass, he'd be telling me about his summers on Flathead Lake or the ranch he worked at as a boy: picking up stones or lighting trash on fire or riding a runaway mare, Ribbons, to the edge of a ravine.

It had been five years since Dad fractured his top two cervical vertebrae, C1 and C2, diving into the ocean on vacation in Maui. For as frightening as the accident had been—I can still picture him crawling back to shore, swim trunks awry, head no longer screwed on right—his recovery from spinal fusion surgery could not have gone smoother. Hip bone had grafted to neck bones, titanium screws had dissolved. In a matter of months, he'd shaved the scraggly beard he'd grown while on blood thinners and jumped back into life, knocking down wasp nests, grilling steaks on the gazebo, and bounding back onto the tennis court.

Because of the location of the injured vertebrae, at the base of his skull, the fusion cost him nearly all the mobility in his neck. Dad stood ramrod straight, chin shoved into Adam's apple, neck and shoulders tight and frequently sore, pilloried into position. Because he couldn't rotate his head more than an inch to either side, his peripheral vision worked overtime, like a Kit-Cat Klock. Dad had to turn his whole torso to look at you and tilt his head the little he could to show he was listening. If Mom liked to say I'd walked like Herman Munster as a toddler, it's fair to say Dad was now a Munster, too. The Neckless Wonder, we called him.

"Just be grateful he can still walk," Mom said. "The doctors say he's the only person they've ever seen with this injury who wasn't instantly killed or paralyzed."

Instantly killed or paralyzed. How often did we hear that line over the years? It may have even been true.

We had inducted Dad back into everyday life the only way we knew how: by giving him shit. Now that he slept on his back, shifting uncomfortably on a bank of pillows, his snores roared through the top floor of the house. Rushing into her room the second it got dark, Tiffany would say, "I have to get to bed before Dad or I'll be up all night."

In a family with a sarcastic streak, such traits were largely absent in Dad. This I took as a sign of deficiency: Dad was a milquetoast. A doormat. How else could he be married to Mom? He watched what she watched, fell asleep to the mystery novels she passed on to him rather than finding books he might actually enjoy. Dad had gone to a no-name college in Iowa that he said sounded just enough like Duke to impress people. His solution to any problem was to tell us to go outside, spend time in nature. He insisted I ski. Butt frozen to the seat of the chairlift, I'd feel my hamstrings fray with the weight of the boots and skis hanging off them as Dad butchered a retelling of *Lord of the Rings* for the hundredth time. "And this is something people actually read?" I'd ask. "I mean, outside of Pocatello?"

What can I say? Dad was a good sport. Whatever we were interested in, Dad was interested in. He took a winter sports conditioning course with Tiffany in the off-season, played tennis with me, cheered with Danny at Jazz games, coached the little girls' softball teams, and carried demented Grandma Rosie and her wheelchair up the front stairs to the house on holidays. On weeknights, you'd find him in the basement pounding away on the treadmill bare-chested, a sopping headband over his eyebrows, sweat spraying everything.

My father may not have been especially European, but the fact that he could still breathe and walk on his own after his accident was something. At least the Neckless Wonder still had that. And fortunately, those were the only skills I required in a protégé. I would teach Dad to love bonbons and Gérard Depardieu movies. If he had a knack for this stuff (and why wouldn't he? we were related) it wouldn't be long before we were swinging around lampposts to the tune of my favorite Jacques Brel song, "Ne Me Quitte Pas."

Don't quitte me, I would sing to Dad.

Don't quitte me, Dad would sing back.

It could be I was born a bad traveler, but it wasn't until that summer I knew for sure. The day we left for France, Dad woke me at three to catch the first leg of our flight. As soon as we got to the gate, Monsieur Arnaud reached up and put his hand on my dad's shoulder. A petite ex-pat with a well-groomed beard and Halloween teeth, Arnaud was always smacking his lips and clearing saliva from his throat. His goal was maximum articulation, but when he spoke it sounded like he was snacking on a banana. "We will all follow *Boob* because he is the tallest," he said. "*Plus haut.*"

When we landed on the other side of the Atlantic, I found that Charles de Gaulle wasn't teeming with bakers and Pierrot-style mimes as I thought it might be. The French didn't amble around with baguettes stuffed under their armpits but hurried past each other, as they would have in America. We didn't drive by many cobblestone streets on our bus ride to the outskirts of Paris. Nor was there a single sidewalk chanteuse trying to earn money to treat her consumption. The motel we checked into was not charming but grungy, and that was fine. Maybe I would join a street gang. Nothing was definite yet, but it didn't hurt to make note of tattoo parlors and places I might get my ears pierced. We weren't exactly in the shadow of the Eiffel Tower, but every crepe stand might still serve the world's best Nutella. Every Tabac might be the one I ducked into to buy my first pack of cigarettes, my first naked postcards.

Paris turned nasty fast. On our virgin ride on the metro, a rising tenth grader named Verity got her camera pickpocketed. The girl emerged into the traffic of Place de la Concorde in tears, her bright fanny pack flapping open. Verity's mom, the only other parent chaperone, petted her daughter's stringy brown hair as cars no bigger than escargot swerved by. Motorists scraped their nails against their beards and shouted tongue twisters using every French swear word I knew and a lot I didn't. "Did that guy just call us Yankees?" I asked Robin.

"It's not about the camera," Verity sobbed. "It's that he just went and took it."

Ever the generous guy, my dad offered to buy Verity a disposable camera and when her mom shot down the idea, Dad started joking around to try to cheer her up. Snorting the exhaust-laden air, he said, "Ah, the smell of Par-ee in the morning."

It wasn't long before Verity's tears turned to laughter and Arnaud carried on with the tour, talking about the obelisk donated by Egypt and the gilded fountain in the square.

There was no note of condescension in his clipped English, and rather than blame my French teacher for leading us into danger, I blamed France. It would have been bad enough to have my own camera stolen, but it was worse imagining it being stolen, knowing that someone out there wanted to take what was mine. Maybe my favorite country in the world wasn't full of acerbic turtleneck wearers but of anti-American hoodlums, thieves.

When we arrived at the Eiffel Tower, it was raining. We still had more than two hundred days to go until Y2K, but the famous iron latticework was dressed for an epic party, a millennium countdown clock sparkling from its midsection. I had wanted to pose with my back to the monument, arms crossed, the way I might appear in the credit sequence of my own travel show. Now, with the rain popping around us, making the stone escarpment bubble, I just wanted to go back to the motel and empty out my leaky shoes. My hip was hurting, my big toe burning along the outer rim where it came in contact with the pavement. Turning my face to the miserable sky, I thought, *So, France, this is how it's going to be.*

One of those effortless travelers who packed nothing and yet always seemed to be prepared for the weather, Dad produced two black rain ponchos from his drawstring backpack. Once I'd gotten this monstrosity over my head, Dad gave Robin our camera and roped an arm around me. "On the count of trois say fromage."

For me, the day had turned into an exercise in endurance while for Dad it was clearly still a vacation. I couldn't help feeling annoyed at his unwavering enthusiasm, even though I knew he was right. Dad was the kind of guy who could don a trash bag in a rainstorm without ever worrying about the cruel or pitying remarks Parisians might be leveling at us. He could break his neck and bounce right back. "What sort of terrible accident were they maimed in?" I imagined a businessman remarking as he hastened by holding a wet newspaper over his head. "To get the neck of one and the leg of the other, *c'est terrible.*"

Dad and Arnaud shared a room that night. Their garret had two twin beds on opposite sides of the room. Looking back, this seems like an unremarkable arrangement. At the time, I remember being jealous in a way I couldn't articulate: two grown men were getting to have a sleepover. "I can't believe he's spending the night with Arnaud," I told Robin. "It's completely disgusting." When Dad came to say goodnight, I took a this-is-way-more-awkward-for-me-than-it-is-for-you approach.

"If you boys are all squared away, I'm going to hit the hay," Dad said.

"Aren't you coming in?" I asked.

"I need some shut-eye," Dad said. "I'm pretty sore from the plane."

I watched him disappear down the hall and up the stairs, each step cracking like a bad back, and told myself he was just being brave. I hoped Arnaud wouldn't give him a neck rub.

I'd heard there was nudity on French TV, but our room didn't have so much as a Bible. Robin fell asleep almost instantly and I was left staring at the ceiling, listening to drunken pacts being issued from the sidewalk below. Kids my age rode mopeds, probably speeding off to cafés in Montmartre, where they would smoke cigarettes down to the butt and then go home to their artist colonies and fuck each other's brains out. I wanted to be out there with them, not in a motel room next to my boring, bigheaded friend.

Dad knocked on our door the next morning. More than a year into wearing contacts, I still struggled to get them in without his help. Still, the fact that Dad was carrying a copy of *Le Monde* gave me pause. Few men enjoyed their morning constitutional as much as my dad; he usually did his business while catching up on stock prices. "Bonjour!" Dad said. "Pierre's getting ready. Can I use your *toilette*?"

"Pierre?" I asked. Was Dad already on a first-name basis with my French teacher?

Singing a ditty on the other side of the bathroom door, Dad told me about the café he'd visited down the street and I thanked God we didn't have a bidet. "Flush, Dad," I reminded. "And no little black hairs around the sink."

"They had two prices, one for standing and one for sitting. Can you believe that?"

Dad didn't fuss in front of the mirror, but he had brought along a brown pocket comb. After he'd flushed and sprung open the door to "air things out," he wet his hair and combed it into strips over his forehead, wicking it back to give his thinning part the texture of a Frisbee. "You know, you could run a comb through that hair," he told me. "It's looking a little crazy this morning."

I told Dad to put in my contacts for me and get out.

When I came squinting downstairs, my vision still swimming, Arnaud was making smooching noises at my dad, guiding him through a language lesson. Sleeping together one night had made them best buds. Dad had not buttoned the top three buttons of his shirt and his chest hair came spilling out. Among the dark mass, a pair of sunglasses floated from slender black chums. His tennis shoes were gone too, replaced by comfy brown lace-ups. Was he attempting to look . . . continental? "Pierre is really helping me with my *français*," Dad told me once Arnaud got up to refill his coffee. "He's a cool guy, isn't he?"

I pulled out my chair. "We'll work on your accent," I said. "Don't get discouraged. Just remember, Robin and I have been at this a lot longer than you have."

"Your eyes are looking a little red there, Greggo," Dad said. "If your contacts are bugging you, maybe you should just wear glasses today." His advice was logical enough, but I was offended. I hadn't come to Paris to be seen in *glasses*.

"I'll bring them just in case," he said, producing the case that held my glasses with a magician's flair. "Get it? Bring your case in case?"

Verity's mom smeared jam onto her English muffin, chuckling from the other side of the table. "Oh, Bob, you're a riot. I bet you two just laugh all the time."

I should have felt lucky having *Bob* with me in France. Besides putting in my contacts, Dad bought me metro cards, made dumb jokes on the bus, and, as per my mom's instructions, kept me alive. But Dad's proficiency, his Boy Scout readiness, had a way of making me feel like an urchin. "Bob's son? *You're* Bob's son?" kids on the trip wanted to know. They seemed genuinely astonished. Sometimes I felt not like Bob's son but like his genetic waste.

My dad, Robin, and I split from the group for lunch that afternoon, eating at a café near the opera house. A hostess greeted us and asked how many would be in our party. "How many in our *par-tee*?" Dad said, absentmindedly parroting her accent. "Three." He pointed to Robin and me and then to himself. "Uh. Duh. Twa." He wasn't being malicious or mocking. Something about hearing those flocked French vowels from a pretty girl apparently short-circuited his brain.

"Dad, don't talk like that," I said.

"What do you mean, Greggo?" Dad croaked. "Dis ees how I talk."

Dad thanked the hostess and, when we sat, told Robin and me to order whatever we wanted. "We are on vacation, no?" he said. "Let us kick back and eat some good grub."

I smoothed the tablecloth. "Dad. Seriously."

Our server was one of those guys I dreamed about, a beanstalk with a large Adam's apple and one pierced ear, not a waiter but a *garçon*. When I tried to show off, Dad stopped me. "What did you say his name was? Garson?"

"*Garçon*," I said.

"Right, Garson," Dad said, kissing the word off his lips the way Arnaud must have taught him.

If the hostess made my dad blush, this waiter guy, whatever you called him, was doing the same to me. Dad ordered a glass of *rrrrrr*ed wine, and I thought I might go into the bathroom, smash the mirror with my fists, and stab a shard of glass into my neck.

Instead of showing us the door, "Garson" smiled and tucked his spiral-bound notebook into his apron pocket. "You are American," he said, amused.

"Wee," Dad said.

Our chance to practice French became the waiter's chance to practice English. Dad explained that we were from Utah and the waiter said, "Mormon. Ski."

"Not Mormon," Dad said. "But ski, yes."

Apparently, the waiter had real opinions about the sport. He'd visited some resorts in the States. In America, my dad might have replied, "Isn't that interesting," but because this was France he rolled out the exclamation he'd practiced on the street, saying *sacre bleu* as three distinct words. "Well, Suck Ray Blue, mon frère. I hear the Poconos are great. But you need to come out to Utah. Snowbird."

"Snowbird," the waiter repeated.

"Our license plates say GREATEST SNOW ON EARTH for a reason," Dad said.

Tired of this flirting, I whipped shut my menu, prepared to flaunt what little French I knew. "Je voudrais un grilled cheese."

I wasn't about to say *fromage* and get Dad going again.

After some debate, the waiter came up with the phrase *croque monsieur.*

"Crrrrroque monsieur," Dad repeated.

"And a Coke," I said.

"Cooookee monsieur," Dad said.

Garson scowled. He probably just hadn't heard me. Coke was the same in every language, wasn't it? If I would have just said "Coca-Cola" he would have gotten it, but I was exasperated with France and this gorgeous waiter with his one earring. I told him again I wanted a Coke, but this time I said it with a French accent à la Dad: *Cock.*

Garson gave us a funny look. "Cock?" he asked.

"*Cock,*" Dad repeated. Attempting to be helpful, he held his fingers several inches apart. "Comes in a can, no? About zis big."

Embarrassed, Robin retreated to his pocket dictionary. Garson couldn't really have thought I was asking for his penis, and it took him mere seconds to come up with the word "Coca." "He wants you to penetrate him," my dad may as well have said. "You know, he is ze flower and you are ze bee."

I ate what turned out to be a grilled cheese with ham, chilled by the back sweat of defeat.

We headed to central France the next day. Dad sat with Arnaud at the front of the bus, head tilted puppyishly toward him, while Robin and I played cards. Our bus driver was girthy, with a mustache so buxom it could have been used to brush a horse and a gut that avalanched over his genitals. His name was *Jean,* the French equivalent of John, but Dad called him Gene. At the lamest of Dad's jokes, Gene would wheeze and lose control of the wheel, steering only with his cellulite.

"*Nekles*," he'd bellow, making a hand motion like he was chopping off his head. "*La Merveille Sans Cou!*"

I hoped they were talking about jewelry, a necklace, but no. A quick check of Robin's pocket dictionary confirmed it. The Neckless Wonder was in on the joke even when the joke was on him.

I bore my eyes into the back of Dad's neck, that familiar pinkish scar running down the middle of it. "That's what I tell people about *you*," I wanted to say. "It's my line."

It didn't seem fair that I couldn't be asked about my leg without running out of the room in tears but Dad could spin his spinal injury into an icebreaker.

We'd also picked up our official tour guide. His name was Hugh in English, but everyone on the trip called him Ewg. Ewg was a little too friendly and seemed like the type who would distract us with one hand and rob us with the other.

By this time, our group, not nearly large enough to fill an EF tour bus, had merged with a bunch of college guys from Wisconsin who were interested not in flying buttresses and rose windows, but in getting blacked out and picking up girls who knew better. The tension between our two groups was understandable. These guys didn't want to be with inbred Utah middle schoolers any more than we wanted to be with them. Sightseeing wasn't so bad because we could all spread out. On the bus, though, there was no escaping the chin chucks and joshing. Here I was, on another continent, stuck with philistines. I'd crossed an ocean and still couldn't escape them.

"Wisconsin is *très gauche*," I whispered to Robin.

From behind his big glasses, Robin pretended to squint out at the countryside.

"*Beaucoup de vaches*," he said.

Really, the Wisconsin guys didn't bug me as much as the camaraderie I was forced to witness a few rows up, where things had turned serious. Ewg, Gene, and Arnaud were having a deep conversation with my dad over the rumble of the bus. Occasionally, he looked back and shot me a thumbs-up.

Touring a castle later that day, Arnaud was like a maître d' motor-mouthing through the specials. It would have been nearly impossible to keep track of which Louis commissioned which massive estate, and how many weeks of the year he stayed there, and how many thousands of horses it took to transport the royal entourage, if not for my dad reinforcing the information at every turn. "Did you say twelve thousand horses? Jiminy Christmas! Can you imagine traveling with twelve thousand horses? You should really write that down, Greg."

"It sounds like a lot of *merde*," I said.

Verity, the girl who'd had her camera stolen, shot me a dirty look, and I wished they'd taken her fanny pack, too.

"You bet," Dad said, eyebrows steepling over his shades. "Old World fertilizer."

Verity snorted in delight. It didn't seem fair. My jokes flatlined but Dad's got *snorts*.

The town we spent the night in was not quite a village but not a city either. After a lasagna dinner, we were free to wander. Dad decided to go for a jog, and I lathered myself in Old Spice that crinkled under my armpits anytime I moved and tried to at least flatten my cowlicks before Robin and I took to the streets.

Calling Wisconsin boys *cows* was one thing, but Robin and I found it more daunting to speak French to anyone who could speak French back to us. Wander into a café and we would surely be forced to interact with nosy owners who would charge us more to sit than stand, so we just walked the city square, admiring shops that were older than our home state.

The place where we were staying didn't have much of a lobby. It was just a sofa, really, with a few uncomfortable chairs on either side of a coffee table. I almost didn't see my dad in the crush of men off the entrance, sipping cognac. It wasn't just Arnaud, Ewg, and Gene with whom he was carousing but also two men he'd met on his run. They were teaching Dad "La Marseillaise."

It turned out that after Dad left for his jog, he realized he didn't know the name of the motel. When he got turned around, it was this veterinarian and pharmaceutical salesman who had returned him.

I could understand the French loving Dad's crooked bottom teeth and the fact that he didn't wear deodorant, even the fact that he had no neck, but how had Bob turned not speaking the language into an endearing quality? Why hadn't these perverts abducted *me*?

We bussed it to so many castles in the Loire Valley over the next few days they started to feel like rest stops—places to stretch our legs and relieve ourselves before continuing on. After a château-laden day, during which Dad did not stop practicing the French national anthem, his new favorite song, we toured the wine caves of Azay-le-Rideau.

Despite the charming prehistoric setting, by the time of the tasting all the talk of yeast had turned my stomach. Still, I wanted a sip. "All right, Greggo. Now you're getting into the spirit." Dad signaled the girl behind the counter. "Generous pour here, s'il vous plaît." It felt good to clink plastic cups, but the wine tasted bitter and I worried it would stain my teeth.

"It won't stain them," Dad said. "It'll just turn them purple for a couple days."

Arnaud's mustache twitched. "Very funny, Boob."

Robin and I stuck our noses in our cups and sniffed, talking about the *notes* we detected in this particular vintage. All was going to pretentious plan until I swirled the cup, trying to give the wine one last breath, and a centrifugal dribble splashed onto my shirt. For the next few seconds, I watched the spill expand as Dad toasted with Arnaud.

"Viva la France!"

While I resisted being a tourist, Bob embraced it, stuffing his suitcase full of souvenirs and four-dollar bottles of wine. With no one to win over or impress, no inferior limb to hide, Dad was free to enjoy himself. At the beaches of Normandy, he helped Verity and her mom gather vials of sand. When I ducked into a foxhole to snap an artsy picture, Dad popped into the shot and pretended to be snagged on barbed wire.

It was on the coast of Brittany that I began to suspect my happy-go-lucky Dad was a shrewder observer of human nature than I'd given him credit for being. We grabbed lunch in the walled city of Saint-Malo, and then he asked if I wanted to check out a stretch of windswept beach before we had to get back on the bus.

The fact that the beach was populated with topless women shouldn't have been a surprise. Even *Max et Julie*, the French primer Monsieur Arnaud taught out of back home, pictured yellow-haired Julie on summer break in all her flat-chested glory. What alarmed me was that Dad and I found ourselves alone. Finally free of Gene, Ewg, and Arnaud, all I wanted was to have them back. The most basic blocking and tackling of male bonding was beyond me.

Being the middle of five kids, I could count on one hand the number of times it had just been Dad and me. That would change as I got older: road trips, Jazz games, hikes, tennis matches. The summer I was fourteen, though, I'd mostly been with my dad in a crowd of siblings, cousins, pets, or friends, impatiently raising my skis on the chairlift as he rambled on about Hobbits and Middle-earth. Now it all made sense: Dad gossiping with Monsieur Arnaud, his attempts to get me drunk on wine. He was gearing up for a talk, preparing to ask the question I'd been asking myself a lot lately. He couldn't possibly think a topless beach was something I'd enjoy. I was an honors student!

"This seems like a fun place." Dad smiled and his face shot back into his chest, creating multiple chins. "I wish we had more time to visit."

My arms remained frozen at my midsection as I shuffled in the sand like C-3PO navigating the pesky dunes of Tatooine. It was too late to feign gastric distress, make a run for the ocean. Carrying my shoes and socks in my right hand, I was the one who felt naked. "I think the bus is going to leave soon."

It wasn't a warm day and the gray fortress and crenellated walls that we'd just explored as tourists looked foreboding from the beach. Even the French flag was trying to wave us off, the wind picking up and dropping Dad's Frisbee of hair. When we made it back to the stone path, I dropped my shoes and put my hand on Dad's shoulder for support. "Women are more beautiful with some clothes on," Dad said as he surveyed the scene a final time from behind his aviators, a note of apology in his voice.

I hated myself on the walk back to the bus. A different son would have been able to enjoy that moment with his dad, might have bumped chests or exchanged knowing glances. I felt bad he was stuck with me. Angry, too. At having to pretend to be something I wasn't. At being who I was. And yet the alternative was outlandish, too, the possibility that I might confess. That I might want to. The whole premise of our adventure in France had just gone up in flames. Dad must have known all along. Straight kids didn't take French. They took Spanish.

Primed for Dad to ask if I was gay, not sure what I'd say if he did, I retreated into misplaced snobbery. Because we were a busload of Americans, paying next to nothing for an all-inclusive week abroad, I had plenty to work with. The cuisine was not France's finest. Busboys overturned bread plates on our laps; the menu promised beefsteak and they brought out hamburgers instead.

"I guess we're still waiting for that genuine French meal, aren't we?" Dad said.

I didn't dare ask what beefsteak was in the first place. Like beef sticks?

Driving back to Paris on our last day, Ewg got on the bus's loud-speaker and roared that we would at last be dining on the Champs-Élysées. It seemed like the authentic French meal that had so far eluded us was finally going to happen. A bistro that served raw horsemeat or sow heads drizzled in hollandaise sauce would go a long way in helping me recover from the culinary slights of the last week. Even a niçoise salad or strawberries dipped in balsamic vinegar would be fine. All the better if a waiter draped a cloth napkin over my lap and a deaf beggar handed me a rose.

What to make of the fact that we pulled up to a Planet Hollywood? If we had been in Las Vegas or Orlando, I would have enjoyed the movie props and costumes, the cardboard collages of Demi Moore, Patrick Swayze, and Christian Slater. I didn't mind a chain restaurant whose world-famous pizza tasted suspiciously like Tombstone. What I minded was that we were in France and here I was, a sloppy American forced to order a vanilla milkshake.

A late-night tour on the Seine couldn't save me from an aching sense of disappointment. Before the trip, I would have belted a trench coat and scrambled onto this *bateau mouche*, hoping to be mistaken for a jilted lover. Things were different now. This wasn't the City of Lights, as I had once romantically thought of it, but the City Where Your Dad Has More Fun Than You. Dad was ignorant and unstylish and yet he was comfortable with himself in a way I never would be. He was great at being French and he didn't even speak French.

Being best friends with my dad must have tuckered Arnaud out because he got us lost on the death march back to the motel. It was past midnight. Bands of Parisian teenagers languished in alleys, cigarettes dangling from their mouths.

"What's the French word for camel?" I asked Robin. "Do you think it's a cognate?"

Among these blustering derelicts I felt self-conscious about my clothes and my limp. My cargo shorts drooped below my knees and made my legs look like hairy sticks. My wine-stained shirt was yellow with a band of blue around the middle and I could have sworn one of the Parisian kids snickered, "Charlié Brown."

During the day, I had admired the public toilets that sanitized themselves and the street washers with their neon-green coveralls and neon brooms. That night, though, the word *ghetto* kept tripping through my mind. *We are lost in a French ghetto.* We passed a bus stop that had a swastika scratched into one of its posts, an ordinary enough sight in any big city, but one that sapped my longing for nightlife. "Get me away from these Nazis," I whispered to Dad. "They think I'm Charlie Brown."

"Hang tight there, Greggo," Dad said.

The indignity didn't end in France. While Dad brought back tricolored flags and international phone numbers, I brought back giardia. "I told you not to drink the water over there," Mom said, taking a swig of Crystal Geyser. Already home when I started pooping twenty times a day, I conceded that she had a point, but I also couldn't help but wonder how, of the twelve kids from my junior high who went to France,

I was the only one who got sick. It was the same with bacterial con-
junctivitis. Lots of kids wear contacts and their eyes occasionally get
pink and irritated, but the infection that started in Paris lasted through
the summer and for my entire freshman year. That week left me with
memories of châteaus and abbeys, but also with a lasting appreciation
for how difficult it was to find a grilled cheese sandwich without ham.

Expressing any sense of disillusionment was impossible once I
returned home. Even in my transatlantic grogginess, I understood that
the only thing more low-class than the French were the Americans who
scoffed at them, so I told anyone who asked what a great time I'd had.
"It's just so cultured over there."

My first week back in Salt Lake, Mom took me to the drive-thru Moto
Photo near our house and a few hours later I was filling two albums,
labeling each picture and postcard in my best impression of French. The
Eiffel Tower was *La Tour Eiffel*. It was *La Louvre, L'arc de triomphe, la
toilette*. We didn't eat at Planet Hollywood but at *Planète du Hollywood*.

"Why are you acting like you can speak French?" my brother asked.

"Because I can," I haughtily replied.

The other night at a dinner party, I learned the expression *petit moutard*
and was delighted at what I took to be its translation: "little mustard."
Familiar with the French saying about mustard climbing up the nose,
meaning a person getting angry or seriously annoyed, I assumed this
mustard referred to an ill-mannered child. A little brat. However,
when I asked my French-speaking friends about the phrase's origin
and meaning, each came back with a different answer. A few had never
heard it at all. As is often the case with these things, the most convincing
explanation turned out to be the one I liked the least: *moutard* without
an *e* is slang for "little kid" or "rug rat" and has nothing to do with the
condiment. "It's one of those f-o-r, f-o-r-e situations," my friend told
me. "Nevertheless, you'll always be my mustard en anglais."

Not one to be deterred by facts, I still greedily snatched up this
funny idiom and retroactively applied it to myself all those years ago
in France: I was quite the little mustard.

I had Monsieur Arnaud for another year after we returned. He and Dad would hang out at parent–teacher conferences and pass along well-wishes, always threatening to grab a baguette together at Normandy Café. "Tell Pierre *bonjour*!" Dad would say.

I didn't mind the idea of them being friends, particularly if it meant I'd keep passing French, except that the more time they spent together, the greater the odds their conversation might turn to me. Petit moutard might not have come up, but who is to say they wouldn't call me what I was: a little faggot?

Ninth grade was the year I finally metabolized my gayness. It was the year I came out in my *Wizard of Oz* journal. "This journal is for me only," I wrote inside the front cover beside a Technicolor image of Emerald City. "If you choose to open it, do so at your own risk." It was the year I practiced my broadcaster voice around the house and experimented with tinted acne cream and bronzer. I went on Accutane to clear up my skin and had my front four incisors shaved down to horrifying nubs and replaced with a set of Bugs Bunny teeth. I dreamed of becoming the next Ricki Lake, but blond.

The bathroom I shared with Danny was piled not just with scrubs, pills, pads, and peels but also with purple shampoos and Sun In. I got high-lights and wore out-of-season knitwear and experimented with plucking my eyebrows, imagining myself getting nailed at a boarding school on the East Coast as "Oops! . . . I Did It Again" played in the background.

It was also the year I started hanging out more with girls than guys. Tiffany and our best blond friend, Gretchen, and I would cruise around the valley dancing to Madonna's *Immaculate Collection* and make pilgrimages to the state's only Abercrombie & Fitch all the way in Provo. We'd come home with shopping bags covered in naked men, raving about crepes slathered in Nutella from a place called European Connection.

Given that his other son spent his days spraying Binaca into our cats' foaming mouths and smearing poop on payphones at the mall, Dad may have found my behavior peculiar, or, more likely, gay. If it bothered him, he never let on, chuckling to my news reports around the gazebo about male pattern baldness and red wine consumption that featured him as the main subject. The closest he ever came to calling me out was to gently float the idea that I should collect *Star Wars* action figures and stamps in addition to Princess Diana dolls.

Dad had tried to discourage me from going on Accutane—pointing out it caused erectile dysfunction and depression—but how could I trust a man who had grown up washing his face with bar soap? Anyway, he'd neglected to mention the worst side effect: dry lips. If I forgot ChapStick, Dad would drive the few blocks from his office to my junior high and park in the fire lane to hand off a tube in the hall outside Arnaud's class like he was my drug dealer.

"This ChapStick thing is really becoming an annoying habit," he would say as my mummified lips crackled and hissed under the balm. "Maybe you should try cigarettes instead. It'd be more French."

I wouldn't have smiled even if I found him funny. It hurt too much. And, in my current state, just the thought of cigarettes made the mustard climb up my nose.

THE JOHN

Having fixed everything else about myself in the lead-up to high school, I had just one body part that still needed work: my legs. I had surgery on my hamstrings the day after Christmas sophomore year and though they weren't the calf and ass implants I'd hoped for, I was excited at the prospect of waking up a new sixteen-year-old.

I was still probably a little stoned from Lortab as Gretchen pushed me to class like an obscene parade float, me smiling and waving all the way as I grumbled about the difficulty of pooping. Surgery had stuffed up my bowels and opened up my nostrils. Since coming home from Primary Children's everything smelled like Purell, even at school. I told Gretchen I was probably still sweating out anesthesia.

Still, I tried to treat it like a victory lap, the culmination of all that transformation. In terms of optics, my wheelchair was a major win. My lower extremities were half-piked in front of me in stirrups and dressed in Steri-Strips, gauze, and Ace bandages and packed into Velcro splints. My sweatpants were streaked with baby powder and my chafed butt was rigged onto an inflatable hemorrhoid donut. I couldn't have looked more pathetic. We hadn't even peeled the tape off my back from the epidural.

For weeks after my surgeries, success had been measured in less than baby steps: sitting up in bed without feeling nauseous, scooting up the stairs on my butt. My parents had hauled a TV on a card table into my room and hooked up a TiVo so I could watch reruns of *The Simpsons*, and when that got old they took me to see *Cast Away* at Century 16.

The theater had been crowded and a large man collided with my wheelchair in the lobby and spilled Coke and fat yellow kernels of buttered popcorn onto my lap. The worst part wasn't the collision. It was the group of teenagers who glanced sideways at me and then looked away. You would have thought I'd asked one of them to wipe my ass. "This isn't permanent!" I wanted to tell them. "I'm not really in a wheelchair."

"Don't worry," my mom told me. "You'll need stupid people to serve you coffee once you're a famous newscaster."

Getting back to school was a relief, even if I was in an enormous black wheelchair with a full rectum.

It helped that I had one of the most popular girls in school pushing me. I liked Gretchen, adored her, in fact, because she looked totally normal but wasn't. She had rosy cheeks and a round, kind face, but also a pacemaker and a bone spur hanging off one foot like a sixth toe. You'd think that extra little toe would give her traction, but she'd had to retire from cheerleading after flying off the top of a human pyramid and cracking her head.

Gretchen and I had been in school together since kindergarten. Our families belonged to the same country club. Our dads were both affable men named Bob who scraped our windshields after winter storms and made killer post-tennis pancakes. The summer after seventh grade, at an outdoor concert, Tiffany talked Gretchen and me into sharing our first kiss with each other as Jerry Jeff Walker played "Mr. Bojangles" in the background. I ended up kissing Gretchen on the hand and the cheek. Saved by a technicality.

It was for the best that our early passion had ripened into friendship. Now that we were in high school Gretchen and I had bigger, more political fish to fry. We were going to make a historic run for student body president and VP at the end of junior year—historic because in forty years no pair of non-Mormons had ever won.

The highlight of most days was when Gretchen wheeled me into Journalism and put on my parking brake. That's when the Greek guy I was secretly in love with, John, would trot up to me for a fist bump.

In a fateful twist, my old buddy Chip was now best friends with John. Chip and I were still on good terms, but we'd grown apart as I'd become more awkward around guys. The days of the massager and bareback were behind us. Now Chip was putting firecrackers in mailboxes and experimenting with partying while I was downloading pictures of Ben Affleck on the family computer.

"Face it. You've been dumped," Danny said.

Danny was right but what he didn't see was the upside: Chip's new social circle meant I had an in with John. The two had delivered some Algebra II assignments to the house while I was still recovering from surgery in what I came to think of as our first hangout session. Now John and I were a couple of fist-bumping pals, not to mention what passed as intellectuals in our high school: we used big words and our parents had HBO subscriptions.

Girls at school called John a smelly rock geek, but I'd lusted after him since before losing my kissing virginity to Gretchen. Nearly every day, he'd worn the same Grateful Dead tie-dye shirt to seventh-grade Utah Studies, a class about Lake Bonneville, Ute Indians, fur trappers, and Mormon crickets taught by a benevolent and bewhiskered old man in a back support belt named Mr. Fagg. Normally, tie-dye didn't do it for me, but this particular shirt was a send-up of *The Wizard of Oz*. Dorothy was a skipping, psychedelic skeleton with red roses for hair. Bannered in the swirling emerald sky above her were the words FOLLOW THE GOLDEN ROAD.

I'd sworn then I would.

John's arm veins were art. He had hot hands, fingers strong and calloused from playing guitar and writing with nubby No. 2 pencils. I even found his stutter sexy. "W-w-what the hizz, G?" John greeted. "Are you feeling s-s-superb this morning?"

Superb. What a stud.

"I'm pretty out of it," I'd tell John, trying to sound like a druggy rather than a teenager whose mom had been giving him suppositories.

Like all boys that age put under for anything more serious than a cavity, I considered it my sworn duty to squirt stage blood onto the dry facts of my case. My hamstring releases became, right there in front of John, a torrid story, a combination of what I'd picked up from checkups with Dr. Stevens and my own imagination.

Unlike certain sanctimonious others, John didn't squat on his haunches to make himself eye level with me in my chair but let me gaze up at him fidgeting joyfully under his squeaky black leather jacket. He'd clutch the backs of his thighs in sympathy as I went off about how Dr. Stevens had butterflied my tight tendons like chicken breasts. I'd conclude, into the fraying crotch of John's Carhartts, with some variation of the joke that the limb-lengthening would be totally worth it because it meant I'd get a new pair of jeans: my old ones would be too short.

John would raise his fists, stretching, and emit a tigery laugh-yawn. "T-tight," he'd say. The tardy bell would finally ring and, as Mrs. Jacobs tried to start class, I'd think about how I wanted to unzip John's fly with my coordinated left hand and go after him with what his friend Byron Bower once called, not in a nice way, my blowjob lips.

If we're talking blowjob lips, Byron's twin sister, Carlotta, is a good place to start. Carlotta was the other kid in our grade who walked with a limp and let's just say she sucked up to me like no other. She approached a few days into my comeback tour to inform me she'd be helping me get better. She'd been through surgeries herself and knew I'd need a friend.

I can't remember ever giving Carlotta the go-ahead to carry my books, open doors for me, or clear gawkers out of the way like an offensive tackle. She just went ahead and did these things. She was broad-nosed, with slender stemmed eyebrows that scattered well before meeting and enough hair on her head for two people. One of her arms was longer than the other, one hand allergically swollen. Sometimes she'd just stare at my Accutane-chapped lips and flaking chin and tell me I had a gorgeous smile. The consensus at school was that, unlike her popular brother, Carlotta was a little bit off.

It wasn't long before I was out of knee immobilizers and back to shuffling around on my own two feet, pushing a walker. John was downright chivalric during this brief and embarrassing interlude, carrying that walker up the icy steps in the courtyard at school with a single sexy-strong hand. Part of me worried he was only being nice to me because he'd seen me with his good friend's weird sister. Paranoia and plain old self-consciousness about my limp resumed as soon as the walker went away, wedging a real stick up my ass. Yes, my tight tendons were less tight, my limp less pronounced, but I still dragged my right foot and always would.

No longer a parade float, I went back to organizing my days around how I'd get from point A to point B without anyone noticing my funny walk. I didn't like to bend or move in front of anyone and had Dr. Stevens write me a note permanently exempting me from PE. Dashing into class, I took off my backpack and carried it in front of me to hide my skinny legs, hating myself when my right toe caught and sent me stumbling, as it still often does.

My beloved Doc Martens were only worn at home where there was carpet because the acoustics were terrible in the halls at school and I hated people looking over their shoulders to see me coming. My closet wasn't a closet. It was a shoebox.

I don't know if Carlotta's limp bugged her less than mine did, only that she didn't let it stop her from clomping down the halls and signing up for clubs. Operation Smile was one thing, but you had to hand it to her for galumphing through dance company recitals in the back row, her ribbon tosses two beats behind everyone else's, her butt sticking out, like mine did.

Her brother Byron was usually twisted around in his auditorium seat loudly hitting on a pretty girl during these *tour de thump* performances, a loose gold watch rattling on his wrist. It killed me that this supposedly cool dude barely acknowledged his sister when eye contact and some small talk made her light up, shake her head, and smile down at her pigeon-toed feet, too moved to speak. I figured I could at least return the favor—I'd look out for her if her own brother wouldn't.

By the spring, thatches of leg hair had grown around my red incision scars. The tennis bubble at the club came down for the summer and, as soon as it was warm enough, Dad and I started driving over there to get in a set or two after dinner. Grand old cottonwoods discharged bugs, seeds, and pulp onto the courts and the smell of duck poop permeated the grounds, but our games grew larger and more exuberant as we played through sunset and into the violet of dusk, fist-pumping like we were on a show court dazzling a small but devoted posse of spectators.

Every sports story is the same when fathers and sons are involved. The father teaches the son to play and the son eventually surpasses him, or doesn't. The twist in my rivalry with Dad, if you could call it that, was our joint lack of twisting ability, our physical limitations. It took Dad breaking his neck to make our matches competitive.

As I'd started to take my lessons and league matches more seriously, as I challenged kids on the ladder, Dad became more than my hitting partner. If anything, it bugged me that he handed me calls. Balls that landed six inches wide miraculously hit the line in my dad's estimation. If I missed a second serve, he'd dig a ball from his overstuffed pocket and have it bouncing my way before I could move to the other side of the center mark.

"Redo," Dad would say. "Take another."

"I know what you're doing," I'd holler to him.

"What's that, Greggo?" he'd say lamely, like he couldn't hear me.

Tennis was a good sport for a kid with tight tendons. Even on our cracked and weed-riddled court at home there was little to trip over besides my own feet. The worst I'd do was scuff up the baseline and burn a hole in the right toe of my tennis shoe. My New Balance sneakers were arch-supporting and orthopedic, one of my first online purchases, and there was something freeing about being in them, chasing down balls just to call them out, daring myself to net. Once I got there it was clear I didn't know what to do and I usually took a big swing and missed by several feet.

Since I already had a one-handed backhand (modeled after Pete Sampras's, not my dad's), I didn't have to wait for my clumsy right side to let me down. Believe it or not, I was more coordinated with a racket than a lot of kids my age. Some of this was the natural advantage of having a court in our backyard, but some of it was a bit of modest talent. It made me wonder what my life would have been if I hadn't crushed my umbilical cord on the way out of Mom's uterus. Could I have been an athlete?

"If you ask me, Greggo, you already are one," Dad would say.

There was another advantage to getting back on the court. With Dad's unwitting help, I sped up my return to John and Chip's tennis class at the Cottonwood Club and was in shape to try out for the junior varsity team at school. I made a point of wearing a sleeve on my good left knee. My excuse for playing with it was that the incision site had been mildly swollen since surgery, but my real reason was that I hoped it would spare me having to explain why I was limping. "It still looks like you're favoring your right leg," observed Coach Snarr, the seminary teacher.

Surprising both of us, I beat John in a scrimmage match at tryouts. He won the rematch, erasing my fluke victory, and went on to make the team. I was cut. I figured it was a win/win, but on the drive home, as "The Rain Song" purred from his car speakers, John broke the tense silence and told me he wasn't upset. "I j-just hate losing to people I know I'm b-b-better than."

I should have had him pull over so I could limp home, angrily bobbing and jerking on the side of the road, but John looked so cute in his red bandanna and this was the good part of the song. Robert Plant was cursing the gloom, letting us know that he loved us so. *Oh, oh.* John may have partied with Chip and Byron, but I was his measuring stick, the person he called when he needed to feel better about a lousy match or his unbelievably shitty performance on the ACT that was four points better than mine. "You're still going to get into an Ivy, John," I said. "Think about how great your personal statement is. What other kid is going to write about Keith Richards?"

One day in Journalism, cheerleaders came around distributing candy. John didn't take any, just turned it down. His gesture, small though it was, helped fuel a growing vigilance about what I was putting into my body. Gretchen and I started to trade diet books that issued edicts like "Orange juice is a meal" and "Muffin is just another word for cake." I would have had an eating disorder if I'd known what to call it. I'd exercise in the basement and then close myself in the pantry and consume an entire box of Honey Nut Cheerios or a whole loaf of French bread from the grocery store. For some reason, I thought bread was super healthy. I figured as long as I didn't put dressing on my salad I'd lose weight, though I had none to lose. I squeezed the grease out of fries, patted my pizza down with a napkin.

From being obsessed with John, it was a hop, skip, and a limp to shaping my whole world around his whims. I was already on the newspaper staff with him junior year, but I transferred into Art History, Honors Precalc with Trig, and the literary magazine so our schedules would sync up. John's Xcel membership motivated me to not eat the baby carrots Dad packed in my lunch (too much glycemic sugar) and pound away on the treadmill in the basement. Eventually, I could go more than five miles in forty minutes. "It's like you're punishing the motherfucker," Tiffany observed from the stairs.

I lived my life in a state of preparedness. The person I was preparing for was John. I blasted *Aida* in the car but kept a Weezer album in the CD changer just in case. I'd make Mom idle in the library parking lot as I tried to snap along to *Dixie Chicken* (totally different from Dixie Chicks, I'd discovered upon first reporting back to John). Mom would give me some serious side-eye as we pulled into traffic, like I was an imposter. "Who are you and what have you done with my Greg?"

"*Aida's* scratched," I'd tell her.

It wasn't all in my head, either. John skipped Monster Mash that October to take me to *Jackass: The Movie*. He started sneaking away from house parties at eleven or twelve at night to play ping-pong with me in the basement. I had to work hard to keep up in my AP classes, so I was usually just making art history flashcards in my room when my Nokia lit up with one of John's texts: *Shit's pandemonium. Utter madness. The debauchery has reached new heights.*

Knowing John would soon be inviting himself over, I'd run downstairs and dig out the paddles hotheaded Danny, now away at Berkeley, hadn't bitten or splintered in frustration. When I heard John come

through the side gate and dance down the outside stairs to the basement, his lively shag bouncing with him, I'd fix my wild eyebrows,
double check for boogers, and make sure my hands weren't shaking.

Just being around John caused a chemical, color-changing reaction
in me. I was ruddy and breathless for the first five minutes of every
rendezvous, running my hands through my hair, laughing too hard,
bracing myself against the pinball machine behind the ping-pong table,
and muttering "Oh God!" should his rugby shirt lift to reveal a swatch
of hairy belly as he tested sore muscles. "Shit, the gym was intense,"
he'd say. "I just went home *an*-and passed out."

That stutter, it was so dear to me. It reminded me of my leg, how it
would be its most debilitating when I most wanted it to go away. John
might not stutter once for an entire night when it was the two of us, but
the second he got in front of the Gretchens of the world, it was game
over. It intrigued me that John was almost opinionless about my leg,
not sympathetic or condescending, like he didn't see it at all.

Didn't he get how perfect we were for each other, how much we
had in common? I could literally complete his sentences.

When the serious conversation had run its course, John would
climb onto the orange Physioball I was supposed to use to stretch
my still-tender hamstrings and, balancing on all fours, regale me
with drunken yarns about how one buddy had peed in a hotel elevator and another had worn his boxers on his head as a hat. The fact
that Chip was on the scene for these bacchanals, that he could have
gotten into a peanut butter fight or gone streaking with John at any
time, left me envious. If John had asked me to run away with him, I
would have done it.

Early every morning there would come a time when he would peace
out, leaving me to record my thoughts in my trusty *Wizard of Oz* journal. It makes me cringe reading those entries now: the fake statistics,
the cloying use of the word *homosexual*, the certainty I'd die alone. I'd
joke with Gretchen and my girlfriends on the literary magazine about
butt fucking or gay porn, and publish a poem from the perspective of
one of Hitler's male lovers and title it "Mein Kampf," but that was all

just putting a good face on things. I was still very much in the closet. It was my destiny to fall in love with a "hetero" who found me amusing but nothing more. "The gay pop. is 3% of the world," I scribbled. "May as well stick my dick in a socket."

I consoled myself with the idea that I wasn't even homosexual. I was *John*sexual.

My hot weekend life with John made me take pity on Byron's dud of a twin sister, Carlotta, the way she treated me like a confidant and tried to make me feel good about myself. Didn't she see what a peripheral role she played in my life, not C- or D-team, not remotely in the same social circle? It's not like any of the drinkers were ditching parties to hang out with *her*. Carlotta didn't call me Greg. She called me Great, like that was my name, and she was as boy crazy as I was. She had a jerk of an ex named Bradley who had smashed her heart to mush. "I'm just sick of people thinking we're dumb because we limp," Carlotta would say, her eyes lowered, taking in my short, crooked leg, my bent knee, the heel that floated off the ground and the foot that stuck out no matter how many times I told them not to. "It's like, hello? They're the dumb ones."

Are they, though? I wanted to ask.

In my estimation, the biggest difference between Carlotta and me was not intelligence or looks. What it came down to was effort: she was lazy about hiding her limp, a regular clodhopper. It made me cringe to see her stomp down the hall, heedless of who might see her. I wanted to collar her into a janitor's closet. "Where is your self-respect? Don't you have any PRIDE? You can't just be walking in front of people willy-nilly. What will they *think*?"

Maybe our high school was tamer than most, full of Mormon kids who never tired of trying to convert us gentiles, humbly referring to themselves as members of "the Church of Jesus Christ of Latter-Day Saints," like we'd never heard of it. Meanwhile, we non-Mormons called anywhere beyond Colorado "back east" and talked up our parents sneaking kegs across the Wyoming border like they were drug traffickers.

All the same, I hated being asked about my walk, and though I tried to breeze through these encounters they were by far the most traumatic parts of my life, day-destroyers that left me breathless and humiliated.

Looking back, I can see that this was the shady side of my parents not coming clean about me having cerebral palsy. My clumsiness, like my sexuality, was shrouded in secret. The unintended implication being that it was shameful, that it deserved to be hidden: no Doc Martens, no shorts, no walking in front of other people.

In hindsight, Carlotta was right to not give a shit if kids in our class saw her limp. Trying to obscure mine was silly, but this being high school I had to try. I knew pitying Carlotta was the cruelest thing I could do to her, but I couldn't help but think of myself as a role model, an evolved being chosen to guide this village idiot through the struggles of being seventeen. Carlotta wasn't a staff writer for *Horizon*, she wasn't applying out of state for college. She wouldn't be reading Faulkner in Honors English and wouldn't have a clue about Keith Richards, but she could still be a valued part of our community.

The problem with seeing Carlotta as a charity case was that it blinded me to her wants and needs as a horny teenager. She was on the rebound.

We didn't have any classes together that winter, but Carlotta and her bestie, a big gal with wet, wandering eyes and a bald spot at the part in her hair, started eating lunch in the empty hallway across from my locker, a kind of picnic with their backs to the blue paneling. The Student Activity Board had to work around them to hang mistletoes and gossamer for Christmas dance. I should have known Carlotta was up to something. The dance was girls' choice.

After the five-minute bell rang, as I dug around my locker for a missing trig assignment or a tube of ChapStick, Carlotta would trundle up to me, a look of terrible concentration on her face, and ask if I was dating Gretchen. Once or twice would have been fine, but she asked every day for a week, and every day I turned red and started shaking, like she was John.

What a bizarre thought, dating Gretchen. In place of sexual tension we shared sushi dinners, Christmas sing-alongs, and powdered sugar fights. I tickled the underside of her arm to relax her. We carpooled. Gretchen didn't mind the bowls of half-eaten oatmeal I left to petrify in her Trooper, and I didn't mind grabbing the steering wheel so she could curl her eyelashes. We seemed almost subconsciously to color-coordinate our outfits, like we had gotten ready one changing room apart, tossing clothes over the walls. Trading all that for sex just seemed stupid.

Because they didn't drink anything stiffer than caffeine-free Diet Coke, the Mormons at Skyline (and, let's face it, the closeted gays) channeled their repressed sexual energy into arts and crafts, putting a premium on creative ways to ask potential dates to dances: scavenger hunts, puns, and minor acts of vandalism were usually involved. Why call up a guy when you could lather shaving cream onto his car?

I'd always thought John was too cool for dances. He had a fake ID and a case of Bud Light covered by a serape in the back of his mom's SUV, but even he got into the spirit. The bespectacled news editor of *Horizon* asked him to the dance by sneaking a "Keef" reference into one of her articles, something about that dollar past sunset burning a hole through her pants. Instead of blowing her off for this obviously desperate stunt, John responded with a stunt of his own, showing up on her doorstep wearing nothing but boxers and the word YES taped to his butt, like a real Jackass.

I was not so lucky.

One dark morning in late November, I walked into a side entrance at school, still stomping the snow off my scuffed tennis shoes, to find a glittery slab of poster board taped to my locker. I didn't have to read a single misspelled rhyme to know that Carlotta was the culprit. She'd addressed it to Great.

Carlotta staked out my locker for a week, looking like she was about to cry. Every morning, I dragged myself through the snowy lawn to school, the tracks of my wayward right foot illustrating my internal struggle. Being bound up with Carlotta for an entire night would be like hauling around the leg lamp from *A Christmas Story*. "It all goes back to my leg," I scratched in my journal. "I feel like I'm lugging it around, like a secret. When it comes to being homosexual, I call the shots. I can choose when people know, which people know. My leg is just there, staring you in the face."

"It doesn't have to be a big deal," Dad said at dinner. "Just tell her one way or another."

"One way or another, Bob, really?" Mom countered. "The world already treats this girl like shit. Does our son have to? It's one night, for Pete's sake, not the rest of your lives."

"This is what you get for not just asking Gretchen," Tiffany volunteered, chomping on an apple.

At the last minute the next morning, I abducted the little Christmas tree I'd been growing on my desk, belted it in the backseat of Sweet Potato, the Taurus I'd inherited from Danny via Grandma Rosie, and went to pick up Gretchen, thinking that with the clever RSVP I'd dashed onto a neon index card and staked into the soil the gift might make sense. The clue I came up with sounded like something the Jolly Green Giant might leave: *A green thumb makes for a great night.*

Gretchen unbuckled the shrub from the backseat and lifted it into her lap. "Oh my God, no!" she protested a moment later when she read my clue. "It sounds like you're going to finger her with a green thumb. You're going to *thumb* her."

Gretchen produced a felt tip marker from her bag and bit off the cap, writing out a less ambiguous message underneath my own: YES CARLOTTA I WILL GO TO THE DANCE WITH YOU.

"What about the handwriting?" I asked, examining Gretchen's rounded, bubbly script. The marker's fumes were making me light-headed. "She's going to think I write like a girl."

"You have better things to worry about," Gretchen said, pulling out her eyelash curler.

I had Gretchen drop the shrub off in the middle of Carlotta's World Civ class. Avoiding my locker for the rest of the day, I nevertheless heard that she carried the plant to her next period that morning, telling everyone it was her Greg tree.

After my plant-based degradation, just being around Carlotta made me queasy. I tried not to cringe as she backed me against my locker, talking excitedly about her dress, but I couldn't resist making fun of her behind her back, claiming to my tennis class at the club that I was going to the dance with a mentally challenged girl I'd christened Carlotta *Boner*. She had a crazy libido and would probably try to rape me. "Dude, you know that's not her name," John chuckled, shaking his head as he grabbed a ball from the basket to fire off a practice serve. "You're worse than Byron."

His rebuke left me shaken. I wasn't about to tell him I had feelings for someone else. "She's a cool person," I said. "We just have nothing in common."

"You're just nervous," Dad told me as we did the dishes that night. "You should have seen me around girls at your age. I was a mess. All these elaborate dances and ways of asking each other out, it doesn't have to be such a big deal. What's wrong with just picking up the phone and talking? If you like a girl, give her a buzz. Say, hey, Juanita, how's it hanging?"

Whenever Dad talked to my brother or me about the hypothetical girl of our dreams, she was named Juanita. I'm not sure why he picked that name, let alone why he assumed this imaginary knockout would want to talk to his teenage sons. It was just one of the things he did. "Is that Juanita on the phone?" he'd tease. "*Juan-i-ta!*"

"Her name is Carlotta," I said, scraping soggy Hamburger Helper down the disposal. "And I don't like her. That's the whole point."

"Think of it as practice then," Dad said, "like working on that second serve."

I gave him what I hoped was a withering look. He knew I had an excellent second serve.

The night of the formal I met Carlotta and her parents at the Olive Garden. Carlotta's dad, Albert, liked the fact that I was English-brained.

He gave me his thoughts on *Moby-Dick* while tonging salad from the communal bowl onto Carlotta's mom's plate as she tried to signal that she didn't want any.

Carlotta was uncharacteristically quiet for most of dinner, picking the toppings off her pizza. At one point, trying to strike up a discussion, Albert gloated about the eighty-eight Carlotta had scored on a recent quiz in World Civ. "That doesn't mean anything to him, Dad," Carlotta blushed, popping a mushroom into her mouth. "He gets all A's."

Albert picked up the check and made sure Carlotta had the tickets to the dance in her little handbag. Her mom helped pin a boutonnière of red roses and baby's breath to my lapel and eased Carlotta's pea coat over her corsage so she didn't crush it. Seeing how loved Carlotta was made me feel awful. This wasn't going to be a Winter's Night to Remember, as the tickets promised. It would be one we'd both rather forget.

It should have been a fifteen-minute drive to the student union at the U, where the dance was being held, but I got us lost for an hour. I was driving Tiffany's Ford Explorer that night and the headlights kept cutting out. It was well into the snowboarding season and the car was ripe with the tang of sweaty boots and gloves. Goggles and old hand warmers and Taco Bell wrappers shifted around every time I stopped too fast. As I tried to not get us killed, Carlotta jabbered in the passenger seat, worrying the tiny ruby on her crucifix. Had I ever had a crush? Did I like to go out? Did I like to spend time with people and just be their friends and then go out? Did I believe in kissing girls? What about on the first date? The second? The seventeenth? Would I kiss a girl on the seventeenth date?

"Carlotta, I've never kissed anyone," I admitted, my cheeks flushed. The thing with Gretchen didn't count.

When we finally parked and straggled into the student union, Carlotta waited for me to tie my shoe before pulling me onto the dance floor, hugging me like a trophy. She sprang around during fun songs and cupped my lopsided butt with her lopsided hands when a slow song came on. I only waddled to the music. Gretchen was in bed with strep throat, but there was still the risk that John might spot us and think we made a cute couple.

In line for pictures, Carlotta told me she liked that I didn't play sports. She was trying to say I wasn't a dumb jock, but I refused to give an inch. I wanted the night to go badly. "I do play sports," I told her. "I almost made the tennis team."

The backdrop for the picture was a cut-rate interpretation of a winter's night: a jagged white mountain range, the frosty silhouette of a tree line, stenciled snowflakes. Unseasonably green AstroTurf unfurled in front of this snowy scene, ruining the effect. I imagined being lost in that confused wilderness. The photographer didn't ask us why we were limping, but she moved and talked slower once it was our turn. With a wrist on her hip, she cooed, like she didn't think I could do it, "Can you get on one knee, mister?"

As nimbly as I could, I lowered myself between a lamppost and an unflocked Christmas tree, grimacing when Carlotta climbed onto my trembling knee, arched her back and, at the photographer's instruction, gently fell into my waiting hand.

Carlotta and I both screamed when the Explorer's headlights died for good on the way home. Nerves shooting up my leg, I pulled off the freeway and inched down 45th South to my house. With Mom in for the night, eating sunflower seeds on her heating pad and watching the news, I had to wake up Dad to give us a ride to Carlotta's. I was too rattled to drive her myself, yet I knew that with Dad behind the wheel of Big Dog I'd have to sit in back with Carlotta, holding her lobster claw as my dad dispensed dating advice.

"It's important for you guys to have fun," Dad said, taking in a handful of Chex Mix he'd brought along in the car. Carlotta squeezed my hand in the backseat. "It doesn't have to be hot and heavy right off the bat. These are the good times, you know? They'll be lots of time to get serious later on." Dad wiped his hand on his khaki shorts, catching my disgust in the rearview mirror. At least he wasn't just in boxers. "Sorry there, Greggo," he said, clearing his throat. "I'm being romantic."

Carlotta clung to me on the shoveled walkway to her door, our sensible shoes crunching over blue salt. I made a joke about the

lame leading the lame and Carlotta said, "What do you mean?" We
made it up the porch steps and I asked if she wanted her boutonnière back. I went to unpin it and she put her hand over my lapel,
over the three red rosebuds and baby's breath. "Dads can be really
embarrassing," she said, not needing to point out hers was obsessed
with *Moby-Dick*.

This was the moment we were supposed to be borne away with
passion, our breath mingling in the cold, our chapped lips sticking
together, but I couldn't make myself do it. I thought Carlotta might
reach for me with that large, sweaty hand of hers, which would depress
both of us. She was a nice girl. She deserved to be with a guy who could
get boners over her. "Thanks for the great night, Great," she said.

I went down one step, good foot first, and then another and walked
around to the passenger side of Big Dog. Climbing in, I closed the door
so softly behind me it barely latched. My friendship with Carlotta had
been one steady march backward, from awkward to unbearable. We'd
started out talking about big ideas, about our legs and the nature of
love, and ended a year later unable to offer each other so much as a
kiss after a school dance.

Dad turned down the sports talk radio and put a consoling hand on
my shoulder. "It wasn't your night, Greggo," he said, laughing quietly.
"That girl is your Gina Jones."

"Don't you mean Juanita?" I wasn't sure I was ready for another
femme fatale from Dad's fatherly arsenal.

Gina Jones, he explained, was the lady Dad had been dating the
summer he met Mom. Well, dating is a loose term. "I was writing her
community college papers and watering her plants while she was off
sleeping with the town drug dealer, Billy Nasser," Dad said as we pulled
up to a stop sign at the end of Carlotta's block.

"You had a town drug dealer?" I asked, slumping in my seat. I liked
talking in the car because you didn't have to look right at each other.
It made us more honest.

"It was mostly just pot, I think," Dad said, "but yeah, Billy Nasser
was the drug dealer in Twin Falls and Gina Jones had been a beauty

queen in high school, Twin Falls Junior Miss, and I was this dopey guy from out of town."

Dad had worked at a bunch of different newspapers after college and moved around a lot. He was always in a different apartment, a new dumpy small town in Wyoming, Illinois, or Idaho. "You wouldn't believe how many nights I sat at the bar by the freeway, not talking to anyone," Dad said. "I thought, *I could sit here for the rest of my life and not have a single conversation.*"

"Dad, that sucks," I said.

"It did suck," he said. "But then I met Mom."

Dad told me about how he'd been walking to his car after work at the paper one afternoon, too depressed to watch where he was going, when he'd bumped into a young, tan reporter with long brown hair and a Basque last name. "I took her out in my gold Firebird and . . ."

"Dot, dot, dot," I interrupted. We were on the freeway now, cruising along.

This was the part of the story I'd heard before, the part Mom was always bragging about. I remember wondering, even as the words came out, why I always had to be so sarcastic. Dad's gold Firebird was the best car he'd ever owned. The engine had melted twenty years ago but he still brought it up any chance he got.

"And dot, dot, dot," Dad said, playing along, "a month later we were engaged."

"You and Mom jumped each other's bones in your gold Firebird," I said. "On your first date. Thanks for the info."

Did I turn bright red after saying this? I did.

Did dad? I think so.

He tapped the steering wheel with his thumbs, tilted his head to check his mirrors. "My point is that I never gave Gina Jones another thought."

"Except for right now," I said, trying not to laugh.

I didn't glance over but I could tell Dad was smiling, too.

Gretchen and I kicked off our presidential campaign in style that spring. In the era before social media, we gleefully turned our life into a photo shoot. We snapped silly pictures of ourselves as we raised virgin margaritas to firefighters at an arts festival, drink umbrellas in our platinum hair, and booty-danced near trash cans swarming with flies in case we wanted pictures to go with the slogan NO BUTTS ABOUT IT. Our strategy was simple, and that was to make fun of ourselves. It proved to be as sure a course as any. The G's vanquished the bible study kids and the theater kids, the star baseball player being recruited by Annapolis and his outrageous girlfriend who wore jeans over pink tutus and peed on the kitchen floor at John's house parties. The election came down to a runoff between Gretchen and me on one ticket and a pair of adorable Mormons on the other. One was a corn-fed male cheerleader and the other was the yearbook editor. These were the upstanding young people Gretchen and I would have been if nothing had ever been wrong with us, if we didn't have to salt our happy childhoods with irony.

I knew we'd beat them.

The homestretch of the campaign was a blur. I hardly remember delivering our closing speech or bubbling in our Scantron ballots. What I remember is sitting together at a schoolwide assembly, our shaking hands locked together, and hearing our names called. Gretchen and I walked down the center aisle of the auditorium and onto the stage as blue and gold confetti rained down on us and Kool and the Gang's "Celebration" came over the speakers. We'd won.

Our families rushed the stage. Tiffany tried to act like she hadn't been crying. Moe danced around. Mitch played on her phone. My dad gave me a high five that turned into one of those shoulder-level victory handshakes that politicians do, fingers intertwined, palms flat against each other. "All right, my man. Leader of the free world."

Mom wrestled me into a hug, her diamond earring digging into my cheek like usual, her sun hat almost flying off. Sometimes she piled on extra lipstick just to leave her mark. "You weren't even supposed to *walk*, you little shit," she said. "You were just this little tiny guy, this peanut, and you had these *giant testicles*. It was like, 'Oh my God, those are the biggest things I've *ever seen*.'"

What can I say? Mom had her talking points and she stuck to them.

Despite the party going on around us, I could tell something was wrong. We normally only hugged gingerly as not to disturb Mom's port. Hugging me hard, it was like she was past caring. Sure enough, the next thing I knew she was pulling down her camisole to show me what looked like an unripe pomegranate growing on her chest. Her port was infected and needed to be taken out. Immediately. "I'm supposed to be in surgery now. I've ignored about a bazillion calls from Saundra. I'm septic."

"Is that serious?" I tried to sound worried but I was already looking past her for my friends.

"Most people die from it," Mom bragged. "Don't worry. I probably won't."

"Mr. President's got hands to shake, Deb," Dad said. "Let's put away your third breast and get you to the hospital."

"Hold your horses, Bobby Boy," Mom said, trying for merriment as she roped me into another disconcertingly firm hug. Into my ear, she whispered something but started to cry and had to begin again. "I just had to be here in case you lost."

Being the president of my high school was a complicated experience. The office gave me the permanent hall pass and padded résumé I wouldn't have had otherwise but also made me susceptible to bullying on a far larger scale than I could have anticipated. It was like real politics in that way, all my insecurities under the spotlight. At club sign-ups before the first day of school, a band of self-described Mormon hippies (no shoes, no showers) politely asked for my car keys and threw them in the dumpster.

In spite of being religious rejects, Gretchen and I did the little good we could in office. We funneled some of our Christmas fundraising money into Head Start, where Gretchen's mom worked, and knocked on doors for a Jewish woman, and proud Democrat, running to represent Skyline's neighborhood in the state senate. I even spoke out against the Iraq War on the senate floor of the state capitol.

But the best part of being president and VP was getting to hang out with Gretchen. We starred in assemblies, got free pictures at dances, skipped class whenever we wanted, and prowled the sidelines at football games wearing our Student Body Officer sweaters. "Have a good time," the Bobs warned us, "because it's going to be over before you know it." And we did. And it was.

Our final summer before college, John and I both got jobs as camp counselors at the Cottonwood Club. I had already decided to go to the University of Southern California when, after a day of filling bottles with colored sand and letting kids launch off my shoulders in the pool, I got talking to John in the parking lot about my other option, Northwestern.

John had gotten into an Ivy after all. He was headed to UPenn and was rooting for me to end up in Chicago because it was closer to the East Coast, just one time zone away. Mom had gone to a journalism grad program at Northwestern back in the seventies and hated it, passing on to me a dread of the freezing midwestern weather and depressed student body, though I told John, piously, I wasn't going there because I wouldn't be able to hack it academically.

"Fuck, you got in," John said. "If you don't want to be in Chicago then don't go, b-but you're plenty smart. You taught me how to say e-e-*erudite*."

Something else had happened to turn me off Northwestern that I didn't mention to John. Back in the fall of senior year, I'd done an alumni interview with a guy in an electric wheelchair. His wife had taken my coat when they had answered the door and I'd walked stiffly to the couch in their cozy living room, unsure whether I should mention my tight tendons, hoping this guy, an engineer in town, didn't think I was making fun of him with my shambling gait. I hadn't mentioned anything about my leg in my application.

Our conversation covered the usual ground, stories I'd written for *Horizon* and what I'd learned so far from being student body president. As we talked, one of the engineer's house slippers fell off. I kept wanting to bend down and help him put it back on, but I just sat there on the couch, hands on my thighs, biting my bottom lip and thinking about how I was blowing it. How many times had a slipper fallen off my partially paralyzed foot? My brother said watching me try to put on a pair of shoes made him feel like he was having a stroke.

That slipper brought back the sense of revulsion I'd felt for Carlotta. When I saw other disabled people—openly disabled people—I wanted to limp away as fast as I could.

Maybe this was part of my attraction to John, my polar opposite, a Greek god who could spell things right on his first try, ace the ACT, and make the tennis team. And there he was in the parking lot of the Cottonwood Club, feeling up his chest muscles and begging me to follow him eastward. I had Dad call USC and back out that night. My destiny was in Chicago with John.

The crazy part of my ploy to be closer to John is that it worked. Both homesick freshmen, John and I spent hours every week messaging each other on AIM. John would send me music files and I would put on my janky headphones to block out the sound of my roommate slathering peanut butter on mousetraps or streaming basketball games on his laptop to compose enthusiastic mini-essays on Bruce Springsteen and Bob Dylan. *Who are these guys? They're amazing!*

My all-male wing of the dorm was nicknamed the Mole Hole as it sat opposite the all-female Virgin Vault. I detested every second there. Not for the first time in my life, my queerness and my leg formed a perfect storm of insecurity. It's hard to make friends when you're scared to walk in front of people, when you're secretive and ashamed about something as obvious as your own body. *Thucydides says the strong do what they will and the weak do what they must,* I chatted. *I feel like I'm must-ing right now.*

A few seconds later, LovingCup5954 popped up. *Good reference!*

I trudged to the showers in the blue terrycloth robe I'd stolen from my brother, so shy I shaved and brushed my teeth in the shower stall rather than at the sinks. In a matter of months, I'd gone from being the student body president of my high school to being the gross, weird kid in the Mole Hole. How anyone could stand living with me I'll never know. I ran myself to the bone at the campus gym—trying to keep my legs stretched while punishing them for screwing up my life—and then hung sopping workout clothes from every corner of the room. I ate boxes of 365 Brand Cheerios in front of my laptop until the roof of my mouth was cut up, and then I washed it all down with gallons of pulpy orange juice. The mice were my fault.

Heading home for Thanksgiving break, John texted from the runway in Philadelphia, then again from the tarmac in Salt Lake after he'd touched down. All those hours over AIM would be worth it when we reunited in person for the scintillating talks we were sure to have about our new cities, our new lives, Thucydides. And who knows? Maybe the right moment would finally come along and I'd have the courage to put down my ping-pong paddle and tell him how I felt. Maybe we'd end up making wobbly love atop the table. I did some thigh stretches just in case.

I waited for him to text but John was always out with Byron and his drinking buddies. I had to swallow back a dribble of stomach acid when I thought of him pounding beers, no longer worried about brain cells and calories, no longer saving himself for his future with me. Did Chip realize how lucky he was?

I hadn't gotten drunk once since the start of college, but I made up for lost time over the break with Gretchen, barely making it to the toilet to be sick on more than one occasion. Rinsing at the sink one morning, I made my way back to bed, Mom trailing after me. "I just don't get why you're so upset. I mean, who's John? He's just some kid you knew in high school."

If he'd meant less to me, it would have been easier to express my disappointment. To call him a high school crush would have negated the hours we'd spent together, suggesting I'd only gawped at him from across the hall. At the same time, John wasn't my first love; he was my only love. The possibility that he could just be some guy I knew in high school felt like more of an indictment of me than him. If that were the case, what had I been doing with my life?

Being stood up for a week solid should have been enough to break John's hold on me, but once we were back at college, it was like we'd never left our dorm chairs, like Thanksgiving had never happened. John went back to being the smelly rock geek, repulsive to everyone but me, the guy who sent me love songs over AIM. Perhaps feeling guilty about Thanksgiving, or wanting to hang out with me away from his high school drinking buddies, John invited me to visit him for a campus-wide party at the end of the year. It was called Spring Fling.

Seriously, John wrote. *It's not for a while but book your ticket.*

I booked my ticket to Philadelphia and then woke up in a cold sweat every night for months. Three weeks out from the trip, I took a shot of my roommate's soju and sent John an email telling him I was gay because I couldn't quite bring myself to tell him the truth: that I loved him. I remember addressing the email like a letter. It began "Dear John" and was signed "Sincerely." If John didn't want me sleeping on the floor of his dorm, I understood completely. "Sorry if this puts you in an awkward position," I wrote. "I shouldn't have accepted your invitation to visit without telling you first."

I hadn't even come out to my parents yet and I was hoping one coy confession would lead to another. John's considerate, supportive, totally platonic reply dinged in my inbox a few minutes later. John told me how much our friendship meant to him and that he was still looking forward to my visit. And then came the dire final line: "This changes nothing between us."

I played it off like I was relieved but I couldn't help but be devastated. John didn't want to do me. Duh. We were just friends. Coming out didn't change that.

I took a long, weepy walk around the Lakefill that night.

Given the emotions roiling in me, the serves I uncorked on the hard-courts of a Palm Desert Marriott over spring break with my family were eminently more returnable than the veritable branches of lightning I could imagine emanating from my racket. Nineteen and still a virgin, I had things other than tennis on my mind. It was time to make like the macaw in the lobby and announce to my family I was *GAY*. Now that John knew I had nothing to lose.

In terms of set pieces, I could have gone for the dramatic, the clay courts, say, or the flamingo pond. When it came down to it, I chose the quiet of our villa, starting with my mom.

She had a range of reactions over the course of the day, from saying she liked gay men way more than straight men to telling me, as we treaded water at the main pool, that it felt like she had been hit in the stomach with a shovel. "I just don't want your life to be harder than it already is," she said. "I don't want to see you get hurt."

My dad's response that evening, when I told Tiff and him I was a "pickle smoker," was characteristically low-key. Eating Triscuits and sipping wine on the back patio, he said, "I see this as a non-issue, Greggo."

"Wait, what's a pickle smoker?" Tiff asked.

"Now hug," Mom instructed, and Dad pulled me in, like we'd just finished a tennis match. The next day we picked up a set right where we'd left off. "It makes sense if you think about it," Dad said, piecing things together. "Most of your friends are girls."

It's easy to deride the coming-out experience as trite. Part of the *over it* feeling I've settled into now that I'm older stems from a sense of annoyance. Once you start coming out, you never really stop. As a gay man and a person with a disability, I come out every day. "Are you limping? Did you twist your ankle?" Let me tell you: it gets old. It helps to remember the sun-drenched joy of that day in Southern California. And for what it's worth, while the rest of my family dined at P.F. Chang's that night, I was on the phone with John, screening calls from my mom, who had it in her head I'd left the table to grab a quick STD or off myself, not talk with a friend. Part of me knew she was right to be skeptical. Clearly, it should have been Gretchen on the other end of the line.

I still went to Spring Fling, but my heart wasn't in it. I slept on a blow-up mattress on the floor of John's dorm. His coke-snorting roommate was usually out, so we talked late into the night, me worried the entire time that I'd fart or go into cardiac arrest. Nothing happened.

We walked around campus not holding hands and ate Chinese food not feeding each other bites. Wyclef Jean had been hired to play a concert at the football stadium. That night, John and I didn't breathe in the scent of each other's neck sweat or bump hips no matter how extreme my hip-thrusting contrapposto. A kiss was out of the question. There may as well have been a ping-pong table between us.

Every morning, he came back from the shower in nothing but a towel, drops of water coursing down his happy trail. All I could do was crawl at his feet, deflating the air mattress as he modestly pulled on boxers under his towel, like he was getting dressed at the beach. A girl from his hall kept coming around. John said her name in Sanskrit translated to "poetry in motion."

Whatever you call the opposite of poetry in motion, that was me as I limped to my cab at the end of my stay, a hand on my aching liver, my roller bag repurposed as a cane. The proximity of John's garlicky beauty could still scorch me even if proximity was all I told myself I deserved.

On the plane back to Chicago, I draped myself in one of those thin airline blankets, scrolled to Joni Mitchell on my MP3 player, and emoted like a ghost, hoping my seatmates would assume I'd just gone through a breakup or been food poisoned. I didn't know if I'd get over John. And yet, I also knew I was ready to find a guy who wanted more than conversation and ping-pong. I had to put myself out there, even if all that meant for now was standing in the back of a Rainbow Alliance party at the student union, nervously crinkling a bottle of water as a Cher impersonator shook her fishnetted booty.

I didn't go on AIM for fifteen days.

MELK

My first summer out of the closet turned out to be a low point in the battle for gay marriage. It was 2004 and President Bush was running for reelection. Compared to the blunders of George W. Bush's first administration—fake weapons of mass destruction, the Iraq War—it'd be easy to see the homophobia of his reelection campaign as a historical footnote. To gay kids like me, it wasn't. Same-sex marriage bans were on the ballot in eleven states, including Utah, and in them we couldn't help but imagine the divergent paths our lives might take. Orchestrated by Karl Rove, Bush's chief strategist, these measures were designed to drive evangelicals and, yes, Latter-Day Saints, to the polls, to get them to vote for Bush and against gay people. Against *me*.

My gig as a camp counselor at the Cottonwood Club was only a few mornings a week and rather than fill the rest of my time with an internship at a newspaper or, God forbid, a second job that paid in money rather than vague promises of college credit or experience, I landed a volunteer position with an LGBTQ political campaign called the Don't Amend Alliance.

What we didn't want amended was the Utah constitution. Same-sex marriage was already illegal under the federal Defense of Marriage Act, passed under Bill "cum on her dress" Clinton. Utah's Prop 3 would only make it more so. The law was a double whammy. The first part of the amendment defined marriage as between one man and one woman. (This being polygamous country, there was a sanctimonious emphasis on the *one*.) The second part outlawed not only same-sex marriage but also anything like it—domestic partnerships, civil unions—insisting there would be no legal equivalent to the real thing.

My parents' wildly different approaches to having a gay son played out around the house that summer. More than a political cause, Dad saw

Don't Amend as a great way for me to find dates in what amounted to my summer of love. "Let's get you off that computer and around some other gay and lesbian gals," he said, knowing enough about my romantic life to be suspicious of AOL Instant Messenger. Mom remained more skeptical of human nature, the Mary Todd to Dad's Yankee Doodle, insisting that I try sleeping with boys *and* girls before I went around making any big announcements.

So, while Dad helped me stake a VOTE NO ON 3 sign in our front yard, Mom backed out of the driveway, trying to lure me away with a trip to the Estée Lauder counter at Nords. She was sick of me stealing her Night Repair. "Don't think for one second these people will ever accept you," she shouted from Big Dog, loud enough that our neighbors could hear. "You could talk to them till the cows come home. They think they can cure you, Greg, plain and simple."

Now that I was attending an out-of-state school—and subjected to the whims and prejudice of the Church only during breaks and major holidays—Mormons had become a joke to me, or so I claimed. It was easy to feign culture shock at their false cheer and self-righteousness, the fact that they believed they could cheat life's sorrows by going on missions and tithing, by cutting out swearing and caffeine. By keeping me from getting married.

The truth is I was hurt. I had gone to high school dances with more than my share of bright, interesting Mormon girls. In stretch limos we'd talk gun control, abortion, whether or not we believed in God. (They always did; I wasn't sure.) On the dance floor, while kids from John's drinking crew got wasted, these girls gave me salsa lessons, pitched me feature stories for the school newspaper, and didn't mind when I stepped on their feet. We never kissed, never so much as smelled each other's hair, and I think we all preferred it that way. It was now clear, however, that if they couldn't have all of me, these girls, they didn't want any of me.

When it came to the soul, there was no such thing as leftovers.

"You guys are a good family," I overheard Michelle's soccer coach tell my dad one morning when he dropped her off after practice. "What happened to Greg?"

It's the smallness of our ask that gets me now. It could have been called the *Don't Please, We'll Behave We Swear!* Alliance, the *Status Quo Is OK by Us* Alliance. We weren't asking for the right to marry, or even to be treated equally under the law. This wasn't Massachusetts where two hairdressers could get hitched at City Hall. Our senators didn't wear Livestrong bracelets or go windsurfing or climb into bed with Big Ketchup, aka Teresa Heinz Kerry. All we were asking was that our fellow Utahns not cross the street to kick us in the nuts, legislatively speaking. By passing a constitutional amendment for a law that already existed, they weren't just beating a dead horse, they were fucking one.

Trying to broaden our appeal to hipsters and ski bums—likely candidates for domestic partnerships—we talked more about wills, power of attorney, medical visitation, taxes, inheritance, and child support that summer than we did gay marriage. Don't Amend's carefully chosen slogan was IT GOES TOO FAR.

This also became my slogan for my boss at Don't Amend. Gail had initially rejected my application because I was on the quarter system and not getting home until mid-June. I'd assumed that was that until she called during finals week. I'd find out later her first intern had walked out on her during Pride.

Gail's Utah accent was so thick she sounded like a drunk Scandinavian. I recalled telling her in my first phone interview that my family had a Jeep that could fit lawn signs in the back. Her question reminding me of such came out sounding something like, "Do I remember *correcklee* your *famlee* has a *Jip* that can *fet* lawn signs?"

I eagerly took the job, "hired" being a word even Gail couldn't slaughter.

I wish I could say I spent those first months out of the closet going on dates or sneaking into bars. Even wearing white shorts would have been an adventure. What I did was turn being gay into homework: gay movies, gay anthologies, female impersonation.

I've always done voices at home. I spoke in a British accent for most of junior high, calling my parents *mutha* and *fatha* or *mum* and *pup*. Asked to do a chore as straightforward as carry my plate to the sink, I'd lurch around the kitchen counter and start in on the monologue from

A Little Princess, with my name substituted in. "Every girl's a princess. You don't have to be smart or pretty as *Greg.*"

The thing about a voice is that it takes you over. Once you start talking like that you can't stop, even when you really want to.

That first summer of college, when I was nineteen, I found myself doing Gail.

"*Theenk* you, sweetie," I'd tell my dad when he piled my plate with stir-fry from the grill. "*Awesome, awesome, awesome!* This looks so yummy, babe! Yahoo!"

"You are ever so welcome, son," Dad said, snapping his tongs and trying not to sound too disturbed.

It was like Gail was reading from a broken teleprompter, the way her eyes searched for the words. She had the eloquence of one of the pamphlets we handed out. Mormons were *LDS.* Cars were *vehicles.* People were *particular individuals.* The bland talk of committees and subcommittees, of volunteer participation rates, took on the lilt of a nursery rhyme when Gail intoned them. She'd dropped the "the" before Don't Amend and the "Alliance" after it, answering the phone with a "Don't *Ameend*!" She once tried to say the word *orange* in a meeting and it was like watching a baby try not to sneeze. She finally settled for "The thing *pumpkeens* are."

Gail was like a boss from a blooper reel: bizarre, tragic, easy to play for laughs. There was a staggering and rarified air of complete self-unawareness about her. I was jealous of it. I didn't know words like *appropriation.* Within the first few minutes of meeting her, though, I was struck by the sense that she had joined the fight for marriage equality to, I don't know, make her parents mad? She reminded me of the Mormon girls in high school who slummed it with skaters but only so they could talk about it at ministry on Sunday. Was she G, L, B, T? Q? Nah. Gail only referred to herself as an ally.

Whose ally, I wasn't sure. She looked like she should have been fighting for the other side. Dressed like Divine on laundry day, Gail rolled her jeans at her waist and pulled her hair into a greasy pony-tail. Her favorite hobby was collecting twisty straws that looped and corkscrewed Diet Coke to her small, puckering lips. "You know what they say. Three *mills* a day and a glass of *melk*!" She could finish off a rack of Oreos in her small front office after her *perfeect, wonderful, amazeen* boyfriend Randy had already brought Arby's.

Though Randy was nothing to look at I was dumbfounded. Gail had a boyfriend and I didn't.

Don't Amend was headquartered a few blocks from Temple Square. I'd drive there in the afternoon still in my green Cottonwood Club staff polo. Our office sat above a dress shop called Latter-Day Bride and looked, I'd think in later years, like a small-town gay bar with the lights turned on. Desks were piled with banners, pins, envelopes, rolls of stickers. The place always felt empty—there were more offices than full-time staffers—though we had our share of semi-unemployable volunteers milling about, too, including me: a teenager in high cotton socks with chlorine-damaged hair. Out but above it all, I was as sexual as the clipboard I hid behind. It was easier to make being gay about politics and progress rather than about my body.

A sense of humor about it all would come later: the boy band–loving returned missionary who told me I looked like Lance Bass; the only other kid my age being obsessed with horses and so bitchy he managed to look mean while licking envelopes; the bearded hippie in rainbow suspenders who always needed a ride; the tubby massage therapist who was in a sham marriage with his best friend. "She lives in Arizona, but it works out because she has a job at Southwest and I have a season's pass to Disneyland." It was good I'd come out before having a boyfriend, he said, looking me up and down. I tried to hyperextend my knee before his eyes passed over my leg but it was too late. "Otherwise, when you break up, it's back in the closet, honey. I've seen it a million times."

Honey? I thought. *Really?* Talking like that around the house was one thing but doing it in an office building, among staplers and a copy machine, just felt wrong. Yes, this was Don't Amend HQ but you could practically see the Temple from our window.

Meet people? Dad had no idea what I was dealing with.

"Those guys are just too weird for me," I told Mom when I got home, and then I made her take me to the Estée Lauder counter like she'd promised, and if we happened to stop by the naughty card store on 900 South to try on pink boas or buy shot glasses that read "YBU" and "I heart SL,UT" then so be it.

"Why did the Estée Lauder lady ask if I wear makeup?" I fumed on the drive home. "I guess it's gay now to put lotion on your face?"

"It is when the lotion costs a hundred bucks," Mom told me.

That summer was as bipolar as a pair of conjoined theater masks. My mornings were spent in my old life at the country club with John teaching Pee Wee tennis and my afternoons were filled with being gay, but only professionally: sign-ups and scheduling, data entry, asking for donations. I played ping-pong with John and drank gin and tonics in Gretchen's backyard. Thursday nights and Saturday mornings consisted of knocking on doors and talking blithely about my sexuality to strangers, like a confused missionary. In small towns outside Salt Lake, I didn't so much knock on doors as tap on truck windows and the dented siding of trailers.

No one we talked to fled in terror. We weren't beaten or shot or stabbed, but in my mind there was no pretense of heterosexuality on these outings. Two teenagers in matching shirts walking on the side of the road? Come on. The townies who drove by must be picturing us holding hands atop a wedding cake and then giving their sons and daughters faux-hawks and expensive lotion. For their faces.

Whatever my reservations, part of me was just plain excited. These were my first tentative steps into the rest of my life. They were supposed to be a little scary. I couldn't say it enough. I was gay! I didn't feel like an intern with a clipboard, gathering emails and petition signatures. I was the Johnny Appleseed of queers, spreading my spunk all over the valley. Limping around neighborhoods I'd driven through a thousand times, I got to come out to a hundred disgusted stay-at-home moms. They'd tell me bravely through their screen doors that denying me the right to marry was a wonderful idea and I'd answer their follow-up questions, bravely, I hoped. I never cried until I was back in the car.

Gretchen went with me to canvass the Pioneer Day Parade that July. We non-Mormons call it Pie and Beer Day to make ourselves feel better about being outnumbered. It's also a state holiday so everyone has off work. True believers, and local news stations, refer to it as the Days of '47 Parade, as in July 24, 1847, the day the first Mormon settlers descended Emigration Canyon and Brigham Young declared, "This is the place."

I can only speak to July 24, 2004.

Gretchen and I donned our yellow Don't Amend shirts, got out our clipboards and pamphlets, and worked that crowd of Mormons like we had in high school, this time sans wheelchair and with more handcarts, marching bands, covered wagons, and women in bonnets waving from the back of pickup trucks. We called each other Prez and VP, smiling and high-fiving like we were holding our own parade on the sidelines.

We'd always known the odds of our mission were long. The quickest stroll through downtown Salt Lake put it in terms of real estate. Don't Amend's office space resembled, as I've noted, a small-town gay bar flickering under fluorescent lights. The pro–Prop 3 side had museums, monuments, libraries, the Temple. The Church Office Building looked like it belonged to the FBI and boasted an egg-shaped map of the world engraved on its gray flank. The other night, I'd overheard my brother griping to his Mormon friend Tigg about Utah. Tigg had replied, "If you don't like it here then leave." Looking up at that stone map from the street, I thought, *And go where?* Utah was the only home I'd ever known.

The Mormon architecture may have been intimidating, but it was the church's human counterparts who were filled with vitriol on Pioneer Day. A ruddy guy in a trucker hat came up and asked me if my parents knew what I was up to, like shame alone might get me to leave. In his prune-like eyes I wasn't a kid in a yellow shirt asking, with heartbreaking earnestness, if he had a moment for equality. I was a pervert. If I wanted to marry a man, he'd go ahead and propose to goats and sacks of flour.

No being mistaken for a pioneer now.

Before I could stutter out a response or feel my leg betray me, those prune-like eyes went wide with fear. What this shame-slinger hadn't counted on was the one among us for whom shame was wholly ineffective.

"How's it goeen, sir?"

Bestride the double yellow lines of a street closed to morning traffic, Gail looked as colossal as a boiling tea kettle with all its zippy rage. She'd curled her hair, improvised new shades of yellow into her home highlights. "Puteen on war paint" was how she'd described it. Adding to the air of Mormon mom respectability, Gail's nails were a most Republican pink, her ring finger adorned with a small brick of cubic zirconia. "Are you haveen a super awesome, *amazeen*, wonderful Pioneer Day?"

The ruddy man blinked twice, stepped back with a shallow swallow I could hear from two feet away. "Isn't it nice the sun is *shine-een*?" Gail's mouth was a mean little horseshoe and though we both knew she wouldn't be able to get the guy to take a pamphlet or sign anything, her presence created enough of a diversion to let me haul my lopsided ass to safety.

It was strange putting myself out there like that before I'd so much as kissed a guy and I wondered why I was doing it, this awful work of telling people I was gay again and again. Who was I fighting for? The urbane, slutty boys back at college who couldn't bother to friend me on The Facebook? It wasn't as though I had a gorgeous hunk with whom I could speed down the aisle. Who would want to spend an eternity with my imperfect self?

Later that day, I found myself resting in a patch of shade with Wynona, the lesbian older sister of a high school friend, telling her how over it I was as I tore at clumps of tidy municipal grass: over being gay, over trying to fit in, over wearing rainbows and bright yellow shirts for other people's target practice. I wasn't any better match for Don't Amend than I'd been for the Mormons.

"We're target practice whether we wear matching shirts or not," Wynona said. "It's more about figuring out who's on our team than who's on theirs."

From our spot on the grass, we watched Gail sweat it out on a stretch of scalding pavement nearby, trying for every signature she could get. Her curls had gone flat but her eyebrows hadn't, lending her the irksome imperturbability of Tweedledum. She looked like a cupcake that had sat too long in the sun.

"Why is she even out here?" I asked. "What's her deal?"

"You know her boyfriend is trans, right?" Wynona asked.

"Randy? The fat, bald guy with the goatee?"

I had to admit the fake wedding ring on Gail's finger took on a different sparkle in this gayer light. I'd never met a person who had transitioned. I'd mostly only wandered into the lands of the L and the G of my new acronym. I suppose in my first trans guy I expected a cliché of masculinity: a dude in a biker jacket or a pool shark. In my unindoctrinated state, it was odd to me that Gail's boyfriend had gone to all that trouble only to embrace the ugly parts of being male: the sweating, the giant pores, the hair loss. Didn't he care about looking good?

"Oh Gregory," Wynona sighed. "You gay boys are funny. He doesn't have to look good. He just has to look like himself."

"But it's weird Gail doesn't talk about it at all though, right?" I asked. "Even with us she acts like they're a straight couple."

I'd only recently surrendered the throne of presumptive heterosexuality and I wasn't sure how I felt about Randy so easily filling my seat, passing without a hitch.

"They *are* a straight couple," Wynona said. "Randy is a guy and Gail is . . . Gail."

"But they're in the closet," I said. "How can you tell people to be proud when you're not?"

"Are you proud of your leg?" Wynona asked.

I can still feel the peculiarity of that question as a tightness on my entire right side. On the grass that day, I felt the lift and drop of every step working itself into a spasm, the kind that splayed my toes for painful minutes. Too tired for fight or flight, my measly muscles and tendons skipped straight to fainting goat. If I weren't lying on my stomach I'd have tipped over for sure. Stunned, I tried to play it cool with a little gay humor, like Jack on *Will & Grace.* "My leg? What did she do?"

"Are you proud of her?"

"Proud of my leg? Is that even a thing?"

"Say it is. Would you want to talk to all these people about her?"

I must have looked appropriately pained because Wynona didn't wait for my reply. She got up from the lawn and wiped the damp spot on her butt. "We tell people stuff when we're ready," she said bluntly.

Once I was back at the house, post-pancakes, I peeled off my yellow shirt, showered, and returned to my bedroom, letting my bath towel fall off my knobby hips. I slipped on my student body president sweater from high school like an old wedding dress, flopped onto my bed, and flipped morosely through my senior yearbook. Miss Havisham at nineteen, with a hairy ass.

I couldn't get Wynona's question about my leg out of my head. *Was* I proud? I'd sculpted my body in the name of becoming myself: the leg surgeries, the constant exercising. For all the attention I lavished on my appendage, though, I was only proud of it when I could successfully conceal it, when I sidled into my seat at a basketball game or carried a chair across a lumpy lawn without detection.

Gail would never acknowledge being anything more than an ally in the fight for gay marriage because doing so would mean outing her boyfriend in a state that was so conservative it hadn't allowed Pride banners downtown because they featured the words *gender, sexuality,* and *justice.* But having spent most of my life with at least one foot in a closet, I was beginning to distrust a world that demanded secrecy for safety, one where passing was a requirement, not a choice.

Our golden retriever puppy, Berkeley, had taken a bite out of the cover of the yearbook, but my presidential headshot survived the attack. It didn't matter that my friends had hugged me and told me they loved me after I came out. They were my friends. That was their job. I dwelled on the rejection of acquaintances and strangers. I was the same person I'd been before announcing I was gay a few months ago, my smile broad and white, my cheeks covered in bronzer, but a lot of the kids who had voted for me and Gretchen would now be voting against me. And to think I'd done the salsa with them.

"You want to know why they hate you?" Mom told me at dinner, jabbing a fork in my direction. We were under the gazebo watching wasps carry away chunks of leftover flank steak. My parents had that awful Norah Jones album going on the CD player. "Because they're total *cocalos.*"

That is Mom's made-up word for crazy. Sometimes she claims it's Basque but it's not.

Dad knew I was having a tough time. I didn't like Northwestern and now Utah didn't like me. Playing tennis that night at the club, as the crickets tuned up for an orgy on the fairway of the ninth hole, he tried to comfort me in the only way he knew how: by bringing up Gina Jones. "I was dating a gal who didn't give me the time of day and I thought I'd never find anyone." He took a sip of water from a paper cone as I hugged my racket to me.

"I know, I know," I interrupted. "The parking lot, the gold Firebird."

"It feels weird now because it's all new," Dad said, shifting his tone to something more serious. "No really, Greg. Listen. It's new for all of us and we're all figuring it out. But you're a great guy and you're going to find another great guy and you two are going to fall head over heels for each other, just like your mom and I."

"Your mom and me," I corrected.

"And you know what, Greggo?"

"What?" I scooped up a stray ball using my racket and my shoe, refusing to look at him.

"You guys are going to get married."

I wanted to say something snarky but when I went to speak I found that I couldn't. I didn't even have the energy to mock Dad with an *amazeen.*

In the fall, a few months after I returned to Chicago for my sophomore year, Prop 3 passed by a wide margin and President Bush coasted to a resounding electoral victory. I watched John Kerry's concession speech in the basement of the student union, eating a soggy tuna sub. According to conventional wisdom, the success of marriage bans like the one I had fought against had cost Kerry the White House. They had gone eleven-for-eleven across the country. Utahns favored Prop 3 by thirty-two points.

"Thirty-two isn't that bad," Dad said over the phone as I staggered from the student union in the wind. "That means a lot of those girls from high school voted your way. You probably helped change their minds. Anyway, I don't think you'll need long johns tomorrow, but don't forget an umbrella."

Dad had the annoying habit of checking the weather in Chicago every day from beautiful Utah while I had to actually suffer through it. The phone shivered in my hand. "*Dad!*" I barked. "You know I don't own an umbrella."

"How about a clean shirt then?" he asked. "You never know who you might run into in the parking lot."

I was taking a lecture course called Gay and Lesbian History in America that quarter. I'd turned from doing figurative homework on being gay to doing actual homework in the form of term papers about George Chauncey's *Gay New York*, the myth of isolation, and the social construction of the closet. Most of the material was jubilantly affirming: bathhouses, cruising, imaginative uses of Crisco. Plato liked guys, some Indigenous Americans revered androgynous or intersexed tribe members as two-spirited shamans, and Abraham Lincoln shared a bed with another man for most of his twenties. For Halloween, our professor, Lane, a tall, slim man who did yoga, came to class in a Lycra wizard costume. His TA, Deb, showed up as Smee.

The post-election lecture was more somber. Lane slid red and blue transparencies on the overhead projector and pointed out that Bush's victory map had the same contours as the Confederacy. He turned out the lights and told us that we were going to watch a documentary about San Francisco's first out city council member, a man with the funny name of Harvey Milk.

Lane warned us that the movie was a little dated but he couldn't have known how precisely dated for me. Harvey Fierstein's gravelly voice came on over a porny dirge of synthesizers, flutes, and keyboard, and I was sucked through a wormhole and found myself sitting in Mrs. Palmer's Life Science class. I realize now that the *Afterschool Special* took its inspiration from the documentary, not the other way around, that one is schlock and one is a classic, but with the lights out in that lecture hall on north campus I felt the sugary breath of serendipity tickling the back of my neck, making my shoulders shudder. That voice.

Sitting there, my stupid summer of clipboards and pamphlets and having doors shut in my face took on new significance. Harvey Milk talked about the necessity of coming out and I had. I'd come out to my high school friends and the lady who worked at the naughty card store and to the one at the Estée Lauder counter. I'd come out to strangers at free concerts, rodeos, arts festivals, parades. I'd come out because I knew people like Gail—people who didn't know me, people who annoyed me, people I made fun of, people who weren't even my friends—would have my yellow-shirted back.

Walking to my single-cell dorm after class, a Counting Crows album on my MP3 player, I imagined my own misadventures being whispered into a microphone. If the voice in my head began as the crackle of Harvey Fierstein, it soon morphed into someone else's, mine but not exactly. We weren't part of any one campaign or candidate but about a candidacy, a movement, like Milk. I may not have had muscle tees with piping around the neck and sleeves, may not have waved from the back of a convertible in a Castro parade, but I'd found a sense of purpose, of we-ness, even if it wasn't the kind I was looking for. Some days that had meant phone banking and knocking on doors and other days it meant sitting in a quiet office above a bridal shop, sharing a rack of Oreos and waiting for other volunteers to trickle in after a long, hot parade.

SEKSI

Some combination of Delta, Lufthansa, Air France, and Croatia Airlines lost my luggage on the forty-five-hour flight from Salt Lake City to Dubrovnik, but neither lost luggage nor prudishness can account for wearing my jeans into the Adriatic. Stripping down to my reindeer boxers wouldn't have raised a balkanized eyebrow, not in this coastal nation of Mediterranean climes and attitudes where, if my Frommer's travel guide was to be believed, topless women ate oysters and rode Jet Skis from islands to shady bays.

Nor was it a lack of alternatives. A freckled tuba player named Nick had offered me his spare trunks. I was too shy to take them, picturing my genitals tangled in the netting like some pink urchin. When I cheerfully turned him down, rolling up my jeans and saying I was going for the Tom Sawyer look, the disturbed expression he shot his girlfriend, Christina, a poli-sci major also on our study abroad trip, was all too familiar. "O-kay," he said, pulling Christina closer.

As we strolled through city streets to the beach, I intentionally hung two paces back and feigned utter absorption in my surroundings. Was that a palm tree? A convenience store where they sold water and stuff, just like back home? I'd learned that stealing even a glance at my feet was a dead giveaway. It worked until it didn't. Nick asked if I was hurt. Was that why I didn't want his extra swimsuit? "Were you worried you'd get blood all over it?"

My leg went stiff.

"Nick, stop," Christina said.

"Sorry, no, I walk with a limp," I said, apologizing for him.

"Permanently?"

"It's no big deal. It's just tight ten—"

"Wait, is your leg fake?" Nick hiked his hip and began swinging it in a wooden half-circle under him, pirate-style. That was not at all how I walked. Was it?

Christina broke away from Nick's big dumb grip and whacked him on the back of the head.

"Ouch?" Nick said, all that boyish full-of-beans joviality going out of him. It was up to me to save the vibe, so I gave my thigh a playful punch. "Not fake!" I could feel my leg wanting to come up short, like I'd stubbed my toe. I guessed we still had a good twenty-minute walk to the beach and I had no clue where I was going. "I was born with it. I'm not in pain or anything."

"Shit, my bad," Nick said, chastened at last. "I wouldn't have asked if I thought, you know . . . I just wondered if something happened on the plane or whatever. I dunno, how they lost your luggage and everything."

"I get stiff, is all." I felt like I was about to cry. The trip had just started and I was already off on the wrong leg. Didn't matter. What did I care about some fire crotch's opinion of me? When we made it to the beach, I dropped my backpack, took off my shoes, and trundled into the surf before anyone could stop me.

Alas, I swam in my jeans because I didn't want Tyler Townsend to see my leg. Tyler Townsend, past whose lifeguard stand I had limped countless times back on campus, always on my way to grind it out on a treadmill that looked out onto the ice floes of Lake Michigan. Tyler Townsend, whose lips knew how to accommodate a whistle, whose Popeye arms knew how to pull in a lane line, who was this very second stripping off an Axe-scented pink polo shirt (at least I thought I caught a downwind note of Dark Temptation) and unfurling a beach towel. On the shorter side, he had the stocky stride of a circus strongman. His aquiline nose and unmoving coif could have been swiped from a Roman bust and though only a white boy from the Northeast, his skin already radiated the golden hues of buttered toast. If I had a type, I was looking at him.

Hell, maybe I swam in my jeans because I wanted Tyler Townsend to save me.

What was it that made someone capable of obliterating shyness, of laying out like his limbs were counterfeit Coach bags he was determined to illegally hawk?

Not having tight tendons, for one.

By age twenty, I occasionally trotted out the terms "hemiplegia" and "hemiparesis," but "tight tendons" was still my go-to in casual conversation. I liked how it sounded tossed off, like nothing. And in a funny way, it fit me best. Spending my childhood and teens in physical therapy had introduced me to gyms—treadmills, thigh presses, stationary bikes—and turned me by degrees into the most dogged kind of athlete, one in competition with himself.

Like gay guys who hit the weights to develop beefcake bods and dispel notions of sissyhood and illness, I worked assiduously to make tight tendons the truth. My tendons were skinny and tough from working out, that was all! I'd never play intramural sports but if my legs were going to be sore, it'd be because I'd just run my regular five miles on the tread, not because I had a disability. If I was tired and needed both hands to hoist myself up from a chair, if I had to lean my hip against the sink to brush my teeth or keep at least a knuckle on the wall as I walked up stairs, so be it. I earned the "pulled" muscles the term "spastic" implied.

This internal tug-of-war—between fitness and physical limitation—may sound high-minded, but it played out in the form of run-of-the-mill social anxiety. No matter how in-shape I got it was never enough to make my limp disappear, or even improve. For as much as I could transform my body, one appendage I just had to accept. But I would not. I approached every interaction with my face contorted in concentration, like I was holding in a fart. If I merely came across as serious, I counted it as a success. While every toe drag brought renewed worry that my friendly cohort of Northwestern Wildcats would call me *handicapped* or some variation therein, Tyler filled his social calendar, racking up more besties in one afternoon at the beach than I had made in two years at our alma mater.

Like me, Tyler was a journalism major, but unlike me he was not on the gray newspaper side of things but in Broadcast, and he had the clean-cut look and highlights to prove it.

In the one broadcast unit I'd taken so far, the professor had pulled me aside to tell me I had talent but that I needed to stop tilting my head to the left on camera. We'd used old-school video editing machines that were too confusing for me, and I'd heard that the broadcast kids were responsible for every facet of production, lugging what were then heavy over-the-shoulder cameras to wherever a story was taking place and setting up their own shots. I didn't think I could manage it, technically or physically.

My failings left me humbly smitten with the Tylers of the world. He may have pledged Pi Kappa Alpha and been anything but out of the closet, but he made no apologies for the fact that he had a weakness for entertainment news. His minor was *voice*.

It was that lilting alto I caught wind of as I crawled to shore after my swim. My body went rigid, as if I'd been struck by an oar. Was that "hey" for *me*? The waves smacked my back side. Slimy rocks sucked at hands and knees. Denim rubbed in weird places. It took probably ten separate steps, squats, and little kicks to exit the ocean and drag myself to my feet, like a Russian dance in reverse. Trying to save face, I treated each move like a contemplative yoga pose. It didn't help that the pebble beach hurt my overly sensitive feet. When I made it to the little pile of rocks Tyler was lazily building at the lip of the tide, he wedged himself up on an elbow, narrowed his pretty brown eyes, and asked if he could ask me a random question: Was I limping?

Jesus, this again. With a sinking feeling, I realized I'd inadvertently signed myself up for a six-week crash course in my least favorite conversation.

It was a compliment, being asked, I reminded myself. It meant Tyler thought I might have twisted an ankle or tweaked my back or been attacked by a stray dog. Something might have happened on the plane ride over, like Nick had imagined.

"I walk with a limp," I said, trying to sound breezy.

"That's what Nick said. I was just checking."

I could try for over-jazzed, explain about surgeries, roll up my soaking jeans even more to show off my Achilles tendon scar, or I could just say what I felt for once. "Nick can go fuck himself."

The words escaped me before I had time to consider their repercussions. Tyler rendered his verdict with a loud *ha*. "That's what *I* said." Next thing I knew he was shouting down the beach. "Did you hear that Nick? Go fuck yourself!" Other kids in our program picked up the call. Christina jumped on her boyfriend's broad, pasty shoulders in the sparkling surf and repeated the phrase for his benefit. Playing the comic, Nick slapped himself with salt water, scrubbed his face, and flopped back onto a baby wave. "Fuck me!"

Tyler and I couldn't help but smile at each other. He dropped down to his towel with a moan that sounded genuinely exhausted. It was the lifeguard in him, always making sure everyone was OK.

I'd come to Croatia to try to salvage my college experience. After an initial dash of exuberance at telling the world I was gay, I'd found no one cared. It was like the emergence of Chicagoland's cicadas every seventeen years: anticipation and then mild disgust and indifference.

My first full year out of the closet was so lonely it was almost funny. I'd somehow managed to become a rising junior without making a single friend. This is a real achievement considering that I lived among thousands of nice-enough kids on campus in Evanston. It didn't matter what courses I took or how many classmates I friended online. I never had anything to do but go to the gym on Saturday night.

It was no mystery why I was floundering. Coming out had made me more self-conscious about my leg. Studious to a fault and always solo, I was too formal for my peers, too paranoid about preserving my dignity to let my guard down. Good manners felt like the only thing I could trust. With girls out of the way, it was time to get physical and I couldn't so much as walk beside someone. My footfalls made potential mates turn in terror at me, the campus Igor. My ass was writing checks my leg couldn't cash, or maybe it was the reverse. My early years in the closet could be characterized by an obsession with AIDS; coming out brought a different horseman of the apocalypse, this one riding in wearing distressed cargo shorts and flip-flops. To call him "body image" would be too banal. Instead, let's refer to him as Abercrombie &/or Fitch.

My diet of gay books and movies, my classes on Shakespeare's comedies, Greek mythology, human sexuality—they only reinforced the idea that gay boys were preppy fuck machines, cruising the world for D. Sometimes these guys were the embodiment of physical perfection à la Brad Pitt in *Troy* (I was fresh off an English Department award for a poem about Patroclus, Achilles' lover), and sometimes they were just regular human-gorgeous like the guys jumping on the bed to George Michael's "Faith" in *The Rules of Attraction*. Gays may get sad, may even hurt themselves, but never because there was anything wrong with their smoking bodies.

Making matters more humiliating, my hair had started falling out in the shower, ropy strands that covered my bottle of Tea Tree shampoo.

When you consider the amount of Sun In I'd used, I should have been grateful it had hung in there as long as it did, but Dad maintained that I wasn't going bald. I just needed to relax and have some fun. "It's the stress, Greggo," he said. "Get out of your head. Go to Europe. Get a rail pass and have an adventure."

Because I'd dropped out of my one quarter of college French, and NU had a foreign language requirement to study in Western Europe, a return to Paris was out of the question, but Eastern Europe was still a possibility. The Prague trip was full but a six-week summer course in Croatia wasn't and no one could be expected to learn whatever language they spoke. I'd heard that Tom Cruise vacationed on the Adriatic. Another bonus, at least in my eyes, was that I'd travel with Northwestern kids rather than doing homestays. The friends I'd make overseas could stay my friends on campus. A pre-trip orientation sealed the deal for me. Among the dozen music majors and pre-med geeks sat square-shouldered Tyler Townsend, doing bicep curls with invisible weights. I had no shot stateside but get that guy on a beach halfway across the world with a bunch of people who didn't know me and I just might have a chance.

There wasn't any wild sex those first days, what with the jeans-related chafing, though I did hobble along the ancient fortress walls that encircled Old Town and hop as best I could from one ATM to another, feeling like a Disney prince, freshly exfoliated. At least my tight tendons were out there now.

When your primary point of reference is Sleeping Beauty's castle, it's hard to fathom a medieval wonderland like Dubrovnik. Altars, arcades, cloisters, monasteries, and palaces pile atop each other in architectural Darwinism, like the Cheesecake Factory at the base of the Hancock Building. Sixteenth-century cannons take aim at docking ships, and ornamental green men hammer away in the bell tower in the center square. You can fill your water bottle from a pissing cherub and then skate down the shiny marble boulevard to check out one of Europe's first pharmacies or a Balkan War museum with a bullet hole behind plate glass.

We stayed in a nunnery, by which I mean a dormitory run by nuns. It was called Učenički Dom, which sounds exotic but translates disappointingly to "student dorm." As soon as my late-arriving roommate Frank deposited his backpack on the bottom bunk, he took the crucifix off the wall and stuck it in a desk drawer. "What?" he said. "I'm Jewish."

Učenički Dom sat behind a barred green door at the end of a stone alley. It was so close to the main gate of Old Town you needed only poke your head around the corner to see costumed guards standing sentry on a drawbridge, conspicuously not posing for pictures, and thus giving cruise ship tourists, those lowest of the low, exactly what they wanted. A nightclub called Fuego rocked out next door, and a five-star riverboat of a Hilton loomed not far down the road.

In addition to taking in wayward girls and college students, the nuns had a side hustle doing laundry. For seven kuna a load, the Sisters of the Sacred Heart washed, dried, and folded anything we handed over, giving us the stand-up collars of vampires and making us itch from the starch. A tabletop Athena statue with what appeared to be an extended middle finger greeted curfew breakers in the foyer. Thanks to Cece, a homesick economics major, *Roseanne* episodes dubbed in Serbo-Croatian played loudly in the homey living room. A black-and-white portrait of the Dom's founder, the gently double-chinned Marije Krucifikse, presided over doilies and lampshades. In a crooked frame a few inches lower hung a portrait of the Pope.

Mornings were rosemary and bougainvillea. If you pushed open our shutters, you could see a cluster of terra-cotta roofs in the distance. In the backyard below, my jeans and reindeer boxers desalinated on the line. (Thankfully, my luggage eventually arrived.)

The view that concerned me most, though, was the one you could only get from sticking your head clear out the window and twisting due east: the little sliver of Tyler's window five or so down from ours. While Tyler and his new gang partied and puked into the lilac bushes in front of stone villas, I became a clumsy spy, stumbling over my shoelaces to keep track of how much sugar he put in his morning espresso and the dance moves he'd picked up at Fuego the night before. "It's called the hula hoop," he'd tell the wayward girls. Everything he said sounded like it was part of a morning news segment. I was obsessed.

Northwestern provided us with live-in tour guides for the trip, scholarship students who hailed from the quarrelsome remains of the former Yugoslavia: Croatia, Bosnia, Serbia, and Albania. During our long lunch breaks, the student guide from Zagreb, a young art-critic-in-training named Barbara, would take me to a swimming hole about a quarter mile down the road from the palazzo where we attended lectures. Barbara was serious yet romantic, the kind of oddball whose modest swimwear, Snow White hairdo, and love of Literature destined us to seek each other out. She was always pushing her cat's-eye sunglasses up her tiny nose and calling me her "Dear American."

Obscured by a kayak stand, the cove was a local hangout with little more than a concrete sundeck and a swim ladder fastened to the rocks, but it was closer than the beach and, unlike the beach, required descending no winding steps cut into the face of a cliff. A stone wall doubled as a water polo goal. A lap lane slapped between two cliffs. Croatians may have invented the necktie, but the official outfit of the Dalmatian Coast was a Speedo, a tank top tie-dyed in sweat rings, and what my mom would call a Gilligan hat. I'd float in the ocean and feel so far from home. Weird how it felt good for once.

One afternoon, Barbara and I came back from swimming laps to find Tyler and his harem colonizing our usual spot on the sundeck with inner tubes and umbrellas and bottles of *pivo*. (The only local color any of us had picked up was the word for beer.) Usually when laying out, Tyler struck starfish pose to maximize his tan and yelled up at the sun, "End me! End me!" Today he had my journal open and was tossing a page from hand to hand, inspecting a poem I was working on about a fisherman's wife. Thank God I had accounted for this contingency and written about him only in the context of gutting fish. "Hey stalker," he said.

Stalker? By rights, he was being the stalker, unless he'd noticed me following him around these past few days. Unless I'd been more obvious than I thought.

Dad was always telling me to put myself out there. My shoes half on, my journal broken into, my furry chest bracketed by a *Beauty and the Beast* towel I'd brought from America, how much more out could I be? Too insecure to ask Barbara to apply my SPF 70, I had gone the DIY route for a day or five and missed a few spots, turning myself into the Coppertone girl. Handprints on my back and stomach suggested assault, like someone had tried to paw me to death. White patches under my arms only underscored my paleness.

"A diary is a private matter!" Barbara protested. She'd swum in those cat's-eye sunglasses and now she pushed them up her pale forehead and into her dripping bangs so we could see the outrage in her bloodshot hazel eyes. Chastened, Tyler handed my journal up to me. "I like the line about sliding out the fish spines," he said, and then, embarrassed, he wiggled his toes and did that framing-a-shot thing people do with their hands. The shot was of his small, tan feet and his fun-colored Havaianas. "A bunch of us are going to check out the sunset tonight," Tyler said, like The Sunset was a private back room in Fuego. "It's going to be stunning! You two are coming."

Our handsome Bosnian student guide, Mehmed, led us to an outcropping of rocks on the other side of Old Town that evening. Before us, the ancient peninsula crumbled into the sea, the horizon stripes of red and violet not unlike my peeling nose. "*Seksi*, huh," Mehmed said.

I would have taken a picture but my digital camera was dead and would remain that way for the rest of the trip: I hadn't thought to pack a charger. Trust me. The scene was as perfect as a postcard.

From a beach bag tumbled a sweating bottle of white wine that was wrapped in a sweatshirt for good measure. It made its way around the circle until the last shaving of sun simmered in the ocean and the city was torchlit and clanging with church bells, those little green men at it again. Yachts weighed anchor outside the battlement, cicadas hummed, and I forced one butt cheek onto a piece of driftwood beside Tyler. Properly petrified.

After a few rounds of spin the bottle, Tyler, Barbara, and I were the only ones not necking. Tyler felt his way down the driftwood and I scooted after him. "So, what do you want to be for Halloween?" came his phony attempt at small talk. It wasn't even July Fourth.

The old me might have lobbed back a pleasant answer. *A Chipotle burrito?* But this was Croatia, land of Greco-Roman forefathers, seedbed of homosexuality. My heroes from Gay History, that life-changing elective back in Evanston, spurred me on. Abraham Lincoln was delivering the Gettysburg Undress in yonder tide. Walt Whitman was humping the sand. Eleanor Roosevelt was uncapping a can of Crisco. Lane was casting a spell in his Lycra wizard cat suit, *Fantasia*-style. Crouched on a neighboring log, chin resting against her knuckles like a major Rodin, Barbara kept egging me on with that timeless Queen/David Bowie duet sung just under her breath. Tyler was *under pressure*.

"I'm going to be a lifeguard," I said. "Lifeguards are sexy."

Brave or shameless, you be the judge.

"People think it's all about looking good but it's a serious job," Tyler said gravely. "Lives are on the line."

I didn't dare look down but I thought I heard his foot slide an inch closer to mine.

Excelling at queerness academically but still struggling in practice, in my short time out of the closet I'd given all of two, no *three* hand jobs. Sure, I'd had a boring threesome on Dillo Day, NU's end-of-year music festival, but generally speaking it was tough to get physical when I worried the whole time if I could stay hard. If my twentieth year were a bumper sticker, it would read: POLITICALLY AROUSED, SEXUALLY SLUMBERING.

Every body is different, of course. When it comes to mine and sex, you can play the fortune cookie game. Take all the symptoms of a nonprogressive motor disorder and add *in bed*. Less flexibility . . . in bed. Trembling, clumsy hands, charley horses, stiff joints, misfiring muscles . . . in bed. Or maybe you can take those symptoms and add "erectile dysfunction."

I'd been around enough other dicks by then to know I had a plumbing problem. Mine didn't work right, not in the throbbing, full throttle, instantly-at-attention mode of movies and, let's be honest, most other twenty-year-olds I'd encountered. Having a broken dick so perfectly aligned with the story I'd always told myself about my body's damage, I didn't question it all that much. Never whole, neutered was my natural state.

A urologist could have talked to me about poor blood circulation, nerve damage, cock rings, and Viagra, but that would have required learning a language I was even worse at than French. Diagnostically orphaned, I figured seeking treatment would only make me feel more powerless. Any discussion of my penis would circle back to my leg, and there was no springing myself out of that bear trap anyway. All that was left to go off were the physical manifestations of my tight tendons that remain to this day. The surgical scars on my hamstrings and heel are easy to irritate and my sphincter can be restrictively tight. Slow to rise, even robust erections turn to putty if left unattended. Vigorous fondling is usually the ticket, as if God took a look at all the masturbating I've done over the years and said, "Why stop now?"

Limp in more ways than one, milestones hadn't come easily for me. A game of quarters at a house party the previous summer had come to a head when one of John's best friends and I absconded to the bathroom to pee—I'd gone in the sink, like a Croatian cherub, he the toilet. It had been a Tilt-A-Whirl of drunkenness in there. My balance was donzo. Our follow-up hookup that Christmas break soured when he stated bluntly, "You're not hard."

This time I didn't have booze or balance issues to blame.

The first sexual encounter I had at college during that dull winter of sophomore year began when a strapping Pole who played Willie the Wildcat at home basketball games IMed to see if I wanted to walk around Barnes & Noble. Within a few hours, I had left behind my sad single room in the Foster Walker (Prison) Complex and was on an unmade bed in a funky college dorm, the kind with chili pepper lights, taking hits off a bong decorated with an ironic Macaulay Culkin sticker, watching the greatest gay date movie of all time, *Shakespeare in Love*. It was like I'd boarded the campus shuttle in Sadsville and alighted in the village of REGULAR COLLEGE. I should have known to be wary. When it was time to choke each other's chickens, flaccidity wasn't the problem. He got me off in seconds as I bucked and writhed and squirmed in for a kiss, my hairy nostrils in his face. The dexterity to reciprocate eluded me. "Stop," he yelped. "You're hurting me."

The guy who eventually popped my anal cherry spring quarter only went through with it after I lied and told him I had *accidentally* jerked off before he'd come over, hence my lack of erection. "Oh, that's the problem!" he'd said, relieved.

It's little wonder my first year as a fruit had turned out to be so unfruitful. Keenly aware of my physical limitations, I spent my weekends rereading my favorite Supreme Court decision, *Lawrence v. Texas*, the one that declared sodomy a basic human right. Forget my tight tendons. Even my foreskin was as tight as the knot on a party balloon.

I'd like to say I was horny that night in Croatia but the truth is something thornier: I was determined. I didn't want to be the guy who swam in jeans his whole life. Impotence emboldened me, like the hemi-, demi- eunuch I was. I had nothing to lose. Compared to a life alone, being a slut felt almost aspirational. My knees bumped with Tyler's, our leg hair stuck together. You couldn't have called it smooth, more like pushy. My heart was thumping so fast I had to fake yawn to catch my breath. My toes mashed together in my tennis shoe as I leaned toward my terrified target. There in the dark, Tyler looked panicked, his tan like a bad photocopy. At the second I thought I might make contact, Mehmed's kissing partner, a Theta from Seattle, came up greedily for air.

"*Seksi seks*," Mehmed growled. "Radical. Awesome."

Everyone but me laughed.

Tyler jumped me in the communal bathroom at the nunnery that night. I figured since he was "straight" it would take more than one game of spin the bottle to get him to do it. Maybe all that baiting Apollo to *end him* had fried his brain. It could have simply been being on vacation, hundreds of miles from the brothers of Pi Kappa Alpha. One minute I was sipping a little tap water, quieting a tickle in my throat, and the next Tyler had spun me around and was coming at me with eyes squeezed shut and lips bunched, like he was about to blow his lifeguard whistle.

Seconds later we were rolling around the soggy floor outside the shower.

Our proverbial tumble in the hay had a nativity feel. Even the bathroom had a crucifix on the wall, one my roommate Frank hadn't gotten to yet. This was our manger, the showerhead our twinkling North Star, the always-running toilet our lamb. Tyler assumed the role of Virgin. I guess that made me baby Jesus since, like I said, I was only fifteen months in gay years, still learning to walk and talk and see more than fuzzy objects.

Completing this Christmas scene, a wise man bowed at the door. Wait, what?

Frank's doughy silhouette required a double take. If he was coming to check on me, he racked up some serious friend points. If he just had to pee, he would have to hold it. All I could do for now was flap my hands in the universal gesture for *am-scray* as Tyler sat me down on the toilet and bounced on my lap. God bless this early test of my gross motor skills, this cosmic hand job redo. Willie would have been impressed. Tyler's pump barely needed priming. A few jerks produced a divine squirt of semen as Tyler threw his head back in Saint Teresa–like ecstasy. He had managed to wiggle out of his underpants when I hadn't been watching. *Look ma, no hands!*

After making sure I was not the victim of assault, Frank welcomed me back to our dorm room with a baffled high five that slid into a shoulder-bumping handshake of appreciation he wished he could take back once he felt the sticky spot on my shirt. I'd come out to Mom and Dad before even kissing a guy because I hadn't wanted to fib when it came to the family jewels or where I planned to put them. Now I was hooking up with a closet case, swearing Frank to secrecy using the crucifix he'd taken off the wall.

The next morning, we broke from our usual class schedule to go sailing.

When he wasn't trolling for sardines, Captain Josko claimed to be a folklore professor at the University of Split. His rambling pirate stories made us wonder if we'd been kidnapped. "Who is this guy again?" I asked Barbara. "This is part of the program, right?"

Captain Josko's first mate, Tonko, was a thin, potbellied man who stripped to his sagging underpants and flopped into the water at the slightest suggestion. Tacking and rigging around the narrow vessel, Tonko managed to fan our sails against the midmorning sun like a bit of laundry on the line at Učenički Dom. He had a way of getting only the girls wet.

Usually a pro around water, Tyler clung to the side of the boat all morning, ready to spew. Evidently, he was still coming to terms with what we'd done in the bathroom. He looked a little green when I spotted him some Dramamine, thanking me for the pill with a solemn *hvala*.

"Having a blast?" I pressed. "Isn't it magical?"

He smiled weakly. "You know it."

Given how NU's LGBTQ crowd usually shunned me the morning after, even his modest gratitude, if that's what it was, felt like a victory. The white-capped horizon didn't captivate him out of acknowledging my existence. His head didn't snap away anytime I crept into his peripheral vision. For as hard as it was to believe, the kid was suffering not from motion sickness but with a condition long ago stricken from the DSM: desire. I couldn't believe it but Tyler Townsend was gay for me. Now playing with house money, the ocean breeze galloping through my suddenly voluminous, not-falling-out hair, I flirted back, "And was that a *hvala*? I didn't know you were a local."

Captain Josko parked our sailboat outside a grotto whose cerulean waters were so unnaturally tinged we joked the Blue Man Group must have been offed there. Even the anxious kids like Frank and me couldn't resist shrieking and saying *Geronimo* before cliff jumping. Not having a beach to play on was a bummer, but then again that meant no sand could cloud our sparkling blue and turquoise landing spots.

Drunk on salt water, starving, nostrils stinging, blisters forming with each squish of my holey right shoe, I was having the best day of my life. Tyler had swatted four horse flies off me and dug in my suit pocket for sunscreen.

When our two weeks in Dubrovnik came to an end, we boarded a bus to Serbia-Montenegro, a country so sketchy it doesn't exist anymore. Tyler and I were still in an "everything but" situation, and we were still only hooking up in the privacy of the communal bathroom at night. Figuring the Laundresses of the Sacred Heart were holding up our tryst from playing out in the godly light of day, I let a hoot escape me as we left The Dom shimmering in our bus exhaust. This was sexual liberation: Tyler and I could swap roommates and make this thing official.

I wasn't naïve enough to think that sex and love went hand in hand, but it'd sure be convenient to wake up next to a consenting adult. Fifteen months of hooking up in bathrooms, grody dorms, and parents' basements had made me long for the simple pleasure of a shared bed. It didn't seem outside the realm of possibility. "Afternoon Delight" was the group's unofficial anthem. Even our bus driver, Dragan, was doing kissy kisses in the rearview mirror, checking out his cheekbones. "Is he looking at me?" whispered Cece, fan of *Roseanne*, dodging around in her seat.

The one hitch in my internal Pride parade was Tyler Townsend himself. His ongoing boldness in the bathroom was rivaled only by his tentativeness outside it. Brushing our teeth could turn into minty make-out sessions, provided we were alone, but no nudging on my part could get him to own up to our tryst. Tyler didn't need to issue a proclamation about his sexuality, nor did we need to be a couple. But after so long wandering a college campus alone, filling my camera with pictures of squirrels rather than friends, I wanted a buddy. With benefits. Tyler sat next to me on the bus and, at my request, read aloud from our course pack in his announcer voice, looking up from the rattling page to make profound eye contact with a camera that wasn't there.

It was tricky admitting you liked a guy, saying the words, knowing you couldn't ever take them back, but this was getting ridiculous. I needed to get laid.

Tyler and I didn't share so much as a peck that night.

"If you were a girl, I'd say you were having PMS right now," Mom liked to chide whenever a foul mood overtook me. If that were the case, it was with PMS I climbed the infamous 461 stone steps to Lovćen's peak-top mausoleum. For Tyler, the trudge became 461 chances to credit card his friends, swiping hands through butt cracks. "Visa! MasterCard! Discover!" Protests bounced off limestone ridges and sinkholes as Theta and company scampered, holding their tailbones.

The bus ride to Ostrog Monastery served as my wake-up call: I didn't want to die boyfriendless. Even my increasingly tattered Frommer's described the road as "terrifying," to which it added "twisted" and "pot-holed," a match for Dragan's twenty-seven-point turns. Fear inspired an outpouring of PDA. The girls sweated through the long skirts and sleeves modesty required. Fingers entwined. The bickering picked up, as did the snuggling. Pet names were deployed. It was "babe" this and "babe" that. Cece asked to be let off. Nick climbed to the front of the bus to "check on things" as Tyler and I swayed in our seats, hands chastely clutching armrests, jeans in need of a laundering nun. The guidebook said to expect signs of the cross, the kissing of lintels, floating mosaics of the Holy Trinity. I hadn't thought it meant on the way there.

The dormitory in the lower monastery where we stayed the night was more homoerotic than the chant-filled shrine carved into the cliff half a mile above us. All the guys in our group were shut into a windowless sanctum and the urinal down the hall was a trough, just like in the clubs of Boystown back home. Too pee-shy to go in front of anyone else, I had to loiter until the bathroom was empty and then follow the one-liners and farting noises back to my bunk beneath Tyler's. As I sat there, eyes adjusting to the dark, a meaty toe from above poked my cheek.

Which sort of pissed me off: Tyler would only touch me on the sly. Here he was, sitting up in bed, swimmer's legs dangling well into my personal bubble, joking and laughing like he was one of the guys, all the while *poking* me.

Mixed signals much?

Light-headed from the alpine air, sore from a day of crawling through ecclesiastical caves, I was tired of playing footsie, dancing around the main event. Time for Bottom Bunk to take control. Surely the way to get Tyler to publicly embrace me was to publicly embrace *him*. An ankle grab would be too much, perhaps leading to recoil. The trick was to not stir his reflexes. I'd be lying if I said there wasn't an ultimatum in this S&M fantasy. If Tyler wanted it to stop all he had to do was say so, preferably by calling me "babe."

I began an unsolicited leg massage. The only protests from top bunk came from squeaking springs. Tyler shifted around, tightening up like he was the one with tendon issues. But he didn't pull away. His strong, almost hairless calf remained in the thrall of my half-circling thumb. If any of the other guys in our group could see what I was doing from their bunks, they had better night vision than I did. It was that dark. And if they did see, so what? In the morning, on the bus to Split, Tyler caved and asked to room with me. When I ran the idea by Frank, he bounced up from his seat and hugged me like a proud parent, offering in benediction the magic words that would at last shove Tyler out of the closet: "You gay bastards!"

We were all eager for a fresh start, and Hostel Spinut was the perfect place, a modern complex with bold color blocking that must have been modeled after sets in *Saved by the Bell*. Within walking distance of Diocletian's Palace, its backside led onto an inlet with majestic ocean views and a jogging trail called, delightfully, Trim Staza. More importantly, each room had its own shower and toilet and two single beds separated by a nightstand, leading to the kinky prospect of turning out the lights like a wholesome TV couple and then ruthlessly making panky. Tyler's first night as a homo would apparently end in domestic bliss. I was jealous.

Dropping his bags in the doorway of our dorm, Tyler's libido rebounded from our brief monk/bunk-induced hiatus. He started licking my face, clawing at his shirt like Wimbledon champ (and local hero) Goran Ivanišević. Good. He was ready for another lefty. Now what?

My plan from the outset of the trip pretty much began and ended with hitting on Tyler. To forecast a kiss would have been optimistic. It hadn't occurred to me to pack lubrication, let alone condoms. The best I could produce from my overnight kit was Cetaphil, a face cleanser from my days on Accutane with the texture and color of semen.

An A-student of Gay History, I failed this early practicum. What can I say? The chance to be penetrated for only the third time in my life was too good to pass up, condoms or not. Lube or not. Sex made me stupid. This was true for Tyler, too. It didn't seem to matter to him, as we stumbled toward bed, that the internal fluttering of my penis produced no discernible stiffening. I was as unaroused as anything to fall off Dalmatian antiquity.

Missionary gave me a front-row seat to my most hated part. Once I had my insides slathered with dermatologist-recommended goo, I cannonballed onto my back and lofted my hairy chicken leg over Tyler's sunburned shoulder. The gnarly nail of my big toe, folded behind my second toe over thanks to a bunion, was its usual black and blue from the impact of being dragged. My nether region's other imperfections, like my disproportionate calves and ankles, were harder to discern. Plus, you know, I was a grower.

Just when I thought I'd have to ply Tyler with a self-deprecating joke about being asymmetrical, my rump met the challenge. Blissful pain, broken sphincter seal, and then grateful acceptance. Lift off, ladies and gentlemen.

Two minutes later, I was on the toilet. Twenty minutes after that, Tyler and I were wandering the chambers of Diocletian's pleasure palace, craning our necks up at the Roman arches, columns, and friezes that recalled one of the more dated hotels in Vegas. It was funny how the real thing always reminded me of the fake thing.

So began our era of regular copulation.

My first times with Tyler Townsend were fumbling, passionate, painful, and awkward, modern and ancient smashed together, like Split itself. Starved for experience, we caressed and cuddled and Frenched. We drank espresso among bellowing cruise ships, rubbed the toe of an Ivan Meštrović statue for good luck, undressed, dozed in each other's arms, and took turns keeping an eye on each other's thick iPods on crowded city beaches. My boner usually joined the party just long enough to throw up its white flag of surrender.

The ancient ruins of Salona provided the backdrop for an epic credit carding battle. The highlight of a weekend excursion to Sarajevo, where there was still a US Travel Advisory in effect, was not a steaming pile of *cevapi* or Brutalist architecture bombed in the Bosnian War but under-the-sweater hand jobs on a night bus. The stain on my shorts wasn't much to look at but the smell was unmistakable. Perhaps onto us, the driver double checked my passport at the border and told me sternly to put back on my shoes.

We weren't a couple, really, but I liked looking out for Tyler. If I bought dried mangoes at the farmer's market in Fruit Square, I'd save him a handful; if he needed baby Q-tips to clean his tiny ears, I didn't mind going to more than one convenience store.

Day after day in went Tyler, out squirted Cetaphil.

Sodomy left me swampy but content. I'd done it with someone . . . more than once! My performance as a bottom improved with practice. Rigid muscles loosened. Flaccid muscles flexed. Mouths relaxed around erections, stifling gag reflexes. Pelvic angels taught me to tuck a pillow under my ass, when to hug my knees to my chest and how not to buck and pull away when I came, only the toes of my left foot pointing. "Someone wanted to make a baby tonight!" Tyler would tease, finger-painting with the splooge I'd deposited under my belly button. Calling home, I'd nauseate my mom and Tiffany with tall tales about how I'd spent my first weeks abroad hooking up among nuns.

The only news I remember being relayed from home was that Mom's former reconstructive plastic surgeon, Alice, had flown in for a visit. Alice had done her surgical fellowship in Salt Lake when I was in high school, helping repair a hole in Mom's head from a nasty bout of skin cancer. Shortly thereafter, Alice had moved back to her native Delaware. She and my mom had stayed in touch, however, and when Alice had written to say she was returning to Salt Lake for a conference, Mom insisted she stay in the guest room in the basement, where we used to hide the back massager. "I couldn't let her come to town without seeing her masterpiece," Mom said. "The top of my head."

"Just don't let her look under the bed," I wanted to say.

It was an ordinary trip—horseback riding, the Alpine Slide—except for one thing. Before leaving for the airport on her final morning, Alice came out to Mom and Dad.

"Honestly, I think you inspired her, Greg," Mom said. "We talked all about you being gay and how great you're doing in college.

It made her feel comfortable with us. She's got a girlfriend now and everything."

Tyler was going through a transformation of his own. Gay lib hit him like a bag of dicks. My shorts stiffened from sexual stains, his shrunk. Mirrored aviators appeared on his nose. On the rare occasion his "look" required sneakers, socks stayed balled in his duffel bag. From his time in television—a quarter-long internship at a station in Rhinelander, Wisconsin—Tyler had picked up the habit of shaving twice a day, and he taught me to do it, too. Treading water in the ocean, he suggested I'd get fewer boogers if I plucked my nose hairs. He took me to get a haircut and told me, post coitus, that I had a face for TV. He'd been insecure at Northwestern, too, until a journalism professor told him he'd be fine as long as he kept his smile bright and his skin clear. Somehow, this advice made me feel better.

The other part of Tyler getting in touch with his gay side meant becoming more adventurous . . . in bed. Over the course of a few weeks, we gradually switched roles. Tyler became the aggressor, the goader, the serial leg rubber, and I the meek Utah boy living in the closet, too embarrassed to go full disclosure about how my bad leg and faulty brain wiring might get in the way of anal pen. I had questions about sizzle reels, but it was hard to ask them with my nipple being chewed. More and more, he'd jiggle my fleeting manhood and ask if I was enjoying myself. "Just stick it in there. Seriously, babe. I want you to be the one. Just end me." He'd half-smile, aware of how goofy he was being. "End me!"

Now I knew how the sun felt.

Unable to maintain a boner firmer than tofu, I'd make excuses about drinking too much *pivo* or relay fears that his rectal orgasm would be so intense it would castrate me. And then I'd go to the bathroom to silently yell at myself in the shower. This boyfriend business sent me straight up onto my right toe with apprehension. Considering the most I'd talked to another guy, sexually, was when I was teaching Chip to use my mom's vibrator, my inability to communicate was hardly a surprise. It still hurt. We needed a socialist sex manual, stat. "Forget it," Tyler would reply from the other room. Only he didn't forget it. Coming home from jogs around Trim Staza, I'd find him reading pantsless, ankles crossed, a checkered shirt giving way to the ghost of a swimsuit. Fallen pencils made him drop it like it was hot. (It was. Sort of.) The urge to do jumping jacks hit him at irregular intervals, usually while I was level with his pale butt, struggling into my shoes.

It's not that I didn't want to stick it in Tyler. It's just that I knew I couldn't. Tyler's smuttiness made me feel soft-core, half-paralyzed. Disabled. Limp. Doubt has a belittling effect that sends all the blood to the face. Wrap yourself in rainbow flags all you want. Worship Whitman. Study bathhouses. At the end of the day, it's studs like Tyler Townsend who climb steamy human pyramids and cripples like me who ogle them at a safe distance through history's binoculars. I'd waited years to proclaim my sexuality, and another harrowing year-plus to find a boyfriend. Now here was a guy who hardly noticed my tight tendons and I couldn't deliver.

Naturally, tensions arose when my penis didn't.

Little things I'd liked at first were starting to annoy me. Tyler's failed *American Idol* audition, one of the most devastating moments of his life, was hard to find upsetting. His dream job of doing the voice for Aladdin if Disney should ever make a sequel was hard to take seriously. And those ears, they really were disgustingly small.

Every morning, Tyler woke me up by singing in the shower. First, it was a Clay Aiken–inspired rendition of "Bridge Over Troubled Water." Next came "Defying Gravity" from *Wicked*. When I countered with a crackly "Castle on a Cloud," he came dripping out of the bathroom to politely tell me I was in the wrong key. Tyler would disappear for hours and return to the hostel blacked out. He'd come inside me and then ditch me for lunch. After weeks of regular plowing, he asked, on the advice of one of the straight guys in the group, if I had AIDS. We still didn't bother with condoms.

Minus the sex, I preferred Frank.

Our final excursion of the trip was to Vis, an island of fishing towns, vineyards, and communist hideouts. Having been a military base for Yugoslavia until the late eighties, Vis was the Cuba of the Dalmatian

Islands, or at least how I imagined Cuba to be—isolationism rapidly transformed into off-the-beaten-path tourism. Rowboats littered shabby front yards, buoys dangled like wind chimes beside brightly painted front doors. Some road signs consisted of just an arrow spray-painted onto a stone wall. Even the construction trucks on the island were cute, compact, and bright orange, like they belonged in a Hot Wheels playset.

Post-closet Tyler never failed to point out the suggestive shape of a gourd or the muscled figures on ancient Greek vases that had been pulled out of shipwrecks. "There's a guy in jeans on this one," he'd joke, feeling up his toned thighs. He kept one earbud in during our tour of a maritime museum in Komiza, marking the choreography to a campy club song about soccer practice while I scribbled notes for one of my poems. Hiking to Tito's World War II cave bunker on Mount Hum, hazy bits of coastline in the distance, he snuck amorous squeezes of my crotch. "My dick is bigger soft, but you're bigger hard," he observed playfully.

I barely touched my Ketchup-drenched pizza at dinner and drank too much of a local vintage of white wine that dated back to the Greeks. A tropical thunderstorm rolled in as we finished eating and we had to book it back to our crummy motel, taking cover in doorways and under awnings. It would have been romantic if Tyler hadn't torn off his tank top and sprinted ahead of me.

When I waddled into the room, ready to wring out my cargo shorts, Tyler had pushed together our beds. Sopping boxers were draped over the reading lamp to set the mood. My left arm started tingling. All the Ketchup was catching up to me. I was having a heart attack. "It's OK, babe," Tyler said, plopping down. His fingers were cold when he petted my face. "Let's just take it easy. Do you want a lap dance? No? Here, why don't you pretend we're back with the nuns." We kissed softly for a while and then he pulled back and whispered, "You really do have a face for TV."

I tried. I really did. We attacked it from every angle, on our sides, on all fours, with him on top and vice versa. I just couldn't stay hard. It was like trying to squeeze a jellyfish into a Coke bottle. The only crack that widened was the one between our beds, threatening to swallow us, tangled sheets and all. For all the success I was having at nailing him, Tyler may as well have been John. He may as well have been wearing pantyhose. "Are you sure you're not?" I asked. My attempt at humor left him sulking. In this be-careful-what-you-wish-for twilight, Tyler wasn't Aladdin, he was a moody genie I'd released from a bottle of Cetaphil.

We rode the ferry back to Split without sharing so much as an earbud. Tyler didn't come to bed that night, one of our last at Hostel Spinut, though I could hear him drinking and carrying on down the hall. In the morning, he barged in reeking of wine in a toga bedsheet, dressed as Diocletian.

Over the next two days, as we half-assed final papers on lab computers and packed, a new vagueness about the future set in. I was doing a newspaper internship in Tucson in the fall and, nautical innuendo about ship knots aside, Tyler didn't want to be tied down his senior year. You couldn't say we were breaking up, just that we were balkanizing, dividing back into sovereign entities. Like Yugoslavia, we weren't built to last.

Rather than keep it as a souvenir, I chucked the last of the Cetaphil in our small, cylindrical wastebasket and spent the hours before my flight chugging apricot juice and listening to the *Garden State* soundtrack as I wandered Fruit Square and rubbed the toe of the Ivan Meštrović statue. My leg had to be the cause of my lackluster performance in bed, the reason I was always falling all over myself, making excuses when I should have been making love. It just couldn't leave the rest of me alone. It had to spoil every adventure.

It had only been a couple days and I already missed kissing him.

The lights were off in our room when I went to get my bag. To my surprise, Tyler was waiting for me in the lobby when I came downstairs. And were those tears in his eyes? He must have missed kissing me, too, because that's what he did, right there in front of everyone. Even Frank got a little misty as we nastily made out. After a good minute or so, I pulled back and put my hand on Tyler's puckering deltoid, where he had been talking about getting a tribal tattoo once we were back in the States. "You were the freshman experience I never had," I squeaked.

"It was a blast," he said. He told me to keep my smile bright and my skin clear and then I limped proudly out the door, tugging my bag behind me.

Why was I so bummed to say bye to Tyler? Probably because I figured six weeks of unsafe sex in a foreign country was as good as it was ever going to get for me. Compared to whatever awaited me in the coming months of my gay toddlerhood, what Tyler and I had didn't seem too shabby. The world was so big that summer and my boy trouble so comforting and normal. Then I boarded a plane and Croatia shrank to the size of a scale model, something I could accidentally wipe out with a single toe drag. I guess that's what people mean by "experience." You come, stay for a while, and leave with nothing but a poem about a fisherman's wife, a bag of dirty clothes, and a feeling.

OUR LEFT FOOT

While I was navigating the ups and downs of the college dating scene—poking around Manhunt.net, doing poppers with my roommate Katie, having a guy I'd been seeing cheat on me in a bathroom stall at O'Hare—Dad began an adventure of his own: long-distance running. Now in his fifties, the guy lived on swag-bag gel packs and in bright marathon shirts. Danny and Tiffany and I accompanied him in 5ks and 10ks. When it came to marathons, though, I was strictly spirit team.

The fall of my senior year, after qualifying for Boston, Dad decided to enter the Chicago Marathon. Honored he wanted to run in the city where I was living, I took the El into the Loop and waited for hours so I could high-five him as he jogged by. The weather was glacial and after taking pictures around Buckingham Fountain we all needed a post-race soak in the hotel pool to warm up. It was the indoor kind with a metal bottom, like swimming inside a tin can. Dad had lost a lot of bulk in his chest and arms and a muscle in his shoulder wouldn't stop twitching. His internist had said it was probably the result of a potassium deficiency but nevertheless referred him to a neurologist. My siblings and I took turns in the pool pressing our fingers into his chest. "Stop," we said, speaking directly to the trembling muscle. "Just stop!" It didn't listen.

In late October, I came home from class and flipped on the TV in the living room of the filthy apartment at Ridge and Davis where I was living with three roommates and a Boston terrier. I caught the end of a segment about the golfer Tom Watson and his caddy, Bruce, who had died of a rare neurological disorder, Lou Gehrig's disease, also known as ALS. This was years before the Ice Bucket Challenge and I'd never heard of it, not by any name.

My parents called a few minutes later. Mom was sobbing so hard I couldn't understand her but Dad was his usual mellow self, saying he was sorry for bugging me, asking about classes.

"Classes are fine. Why does your voice sound scratchy?" I asked. "And why is Mom losing her shit?"

"We had Stana's chicken soup last night and I choked on a bone," Dad said, referring to one of our Polish cleaning lady's specialties. In addition to bone-in chicken soup, Stana's other go-to dish was a potato salad whose main ingredients were mayonnaise and eggshells.

"Is that why you called?" I asked. "Because Stana tried to murder you?"

Dad managed a mirthless, gruff laugh. "It sure wouldn't be the first time. But unfortunately, no . . ."

"*Dad has Lou Gehrig's disease,*" Mom screamed, breaking into a fresh whimper.

"For real, Dad? I was just watching a segment on ESPN and . . ."

"Don't you get it, Greg?" Mom interrupted. "Dad is going to die."

After hanging up, I called Katie. She came back to the apartment and we looked up everything we could find about Lou Gehrig's, all of it sounding bad: *orphan disease; no known treatment, cause, or cure.* It was bizarre to hear Dad report his fate in a voice not his own and I clung to the idea that a mistake had been made, that Dad would be spared, that, as his strange voice implied, this was happening to someone else.

No such luck. The twitch in Dad's shoulder was a fasciculation. A common early symptom of ALS, it's the product of nerves and muscles that aren't communicating properly. Not every muscle in Dad's body would twitch like that, but they'd all waste away. Mom was right: Dad was toast.

Even after the worst Google search of my life, I didn't imagine Dad's arms would soon go limp and that, when he went to take a breath, his diaphragm would be about as useful as an airless whoopee cushion. Anyone who has had his childhood pulled out from under him is lucky enough to have had a childhood in the first place. Still, the prospect of being a caregiver left me drained. The man I'd always taken for granted would need me to turn the pages of his newspaper, answer his phone, type his emails, get him Hot Tamales from the candy dispenser after eating out. He wouldn't even be able to shoo away flies.

Dad and I played a set of tennis in the bubble that Thanksgiving. During one point, he flubbed a backhand, got jammed up, and tried to use two hands instead of one to carry the racket across his body. I'd never seen him struggle to do anything physical. "Dad," I called across the net, trying not to sound worried. "Are you doing OK?"

I beat him by an unprecedented margin, 6–2.

"The racket felt like it weighed a ton," Dad said with a baffled smile.

"Really?" I shook his limp hand. "I didn't notice a difference."

We thought Dad might live for years with ALS. A lot of people do.

ALS didn't follow the script we'd learned from cancer. Mom always said life went on after the Big C, but it didn't with ALS, not for long. Maybe that's why there weren't cool nicknames for it like the Big C. People who got it died, left you an orphan. Lou Gehrig didn't care about the Marshalls' wacky, dark sense of humor, self-absorption, or ability to whip up a poem or a silver lining. For once, we couldn't just roll our eyes, make the jerking-off motion with our hands, and tell ourselves Mom was probably making it all up anyway. In a matter of months, Dad went from being the guy who never got sick to one who had a date with death. Our grief wasn't just for Dad but for the sense of order and calm he brought to our lives. Once you stop believing everything will be OK, the world takes on a pallor, and then you do.

One of Dad's first acts as a dying man was to book us all on a Mediterranean cruise in July after I graduated from Northwestern. If Mom's slogan was NEVER, NEVER, NEVER GIVE UP, Dad's was ALWAYS BE TRAVELING. The cruise was both our final family vacation and Dad's last chance to drink wine before getting a G-tube put into his stomach. You'd think the G would stand for gastrointestinal since it is essentially a bong delivering Promote and water directly to the belly, but it turns out the G is short for gastronomy. It sounds sort of French, *un tube de gastronomie*.

My natural inclination is to recall the uncomfortable parts of our sea voyage: dancing with Tiffany and Danny to the Pussycat Dolls' "Don't Cha" in the ship's nightclub, trying to run on the treadmill during a sea squall, getting crabs. But there was all the good stuff, too. It's the exception in life when you know you're doing something for the last time and can really savor it but that's what cruises do best.

Our last family trip was so full of finality it became a running joke: Dad's last towel animal left on the bed after turndown service, the last dinner roll he'd see Moe throw at Mom at the banquet table, his last flaming Baked Alaska for dessert, his last mediocre magic show in the ship's theater. Even with the tacky pomp of a cruise liner gliding into Venice at sunset blasting Pavarotti's greatest hits, I'm not sure I appreciated how precious our time was, how much I'd miss it once it was gone. At twenty-two I was grown, but barely. We'd had such little time to know each other as men, Dad and I. It was a loss I felt more acutely for not having come out of the closet at fourteen in France. Why had I been such a little moutard?

The cruise ended in Barcelona and we spent an extra week at a hotel on the beach. Dad had always been an early riser, and on the last leg of our last trip together I'd get up with him and we'd walk the shoreline as the sun rose.

Once we were home, our days weren't filled with sightseeing and sand but with clinic appointments, an ALS support group, and a breathing machine called a BiPAP that had to be refilled like a humidifier. The mask was so ill-fitting it rubbed the bridge of Dad's nose raw, leaving behind an acne-bright scab. He slept on a firm wedge of a pillow with other pillows tucked under each arm and that new G-tube pinned to his shirt, his existence a blunt reminder of physical need.

"This isn't drama class," Mom told me after I made a face helping him blow his nose.

Out of a mix of frustration and exhaustion one day, I told Mom I couldn't spend my life wiping Dad's ass. I told her his body grossed me out, that it was disgusting. It wasn't true and Mom and I both knew it.

"Dad has a beautiful body," she said. "It just doesn't work anymore."

Since the start of college, Dad and I had gone on hikes together. It surprised us both, I think, the fact that I had inherited his love of the outdoors. Dad was too air hungry to hit the trails in the weeks after our family cruise, but one afternoon we took a scenic drive up the canyon near our house and brought along the BiPAP just in case. Parking on the side of the road, we walked a few feet to some wildflowers. I had forgotten to bring anything for us to sit on, so we lowered ourselves awkwardly onto some sharp rocks. I'd never seen Dad looking so gangly and long-limbed, so much like me. He must have been thinking along those same lines because he said, "I'm starting to get a sense of what it must be like for you with your leg. It just never goes away, does it?"

I hadn't assumed Dad would understand what it was like to be disabled. It's not a feat of empathy a lot of fiftysomething men would have been capable of back then, especially not with their gay sons. I'd always taken his good nature as a form of absentmindedness: Dad the space cadet, who could gently guide me down the ski slopes while I swore at him and then come home and singe his eyebrows lighting the grill. What I didn't see is how generous he could be, extending his failing body to me like a form of communion. *Don't you see it now?* he seemed to say on the rocks that day. *How alike we are?*

I'd watch in the years ahead as most of Dad's ski buddies hung on to fading notions of their former selves, keeping the shaggy hair and bushy beards as long as they could, wearing short shorts that showed off their wrinkled thighs and knee-replacement scars, treating even major health catastrophes as minor setbacks that would barely delay their backcountry treks. "Got in a hundred days on the slopes this year," they'd proclaim, fiddling with wristwatches that measured the distance they'd skied in vertical feet, like that wasn't the most moronic thing ever, and exactly what my dad would have done in retirement.

In acknowledging my leg that day on the mountain, Dad had found a way of guiding me onto a new path of inquiry when he should have been his most frustrated and angry. There was some of that, too, of course—sardonic jokes about his G-tube ("Filet mignon tonight, again?") or moments of pique when he'd get trapped in the bathroom while clearing out the small office he rented near our house—but Dad had a way of acting out of loyalty and love even in the worst of times. I'd wanted to distance myself from him all those years ago in France. Now, I only wanted to protect him. *Don't quitte me*, I'd imagined singing to Dad. Even at my crankiest and gayest he never had. I wouldn't *quitte* him either.

My siblings and mom might tell a different story—five different stories, in fact—but for the dog days of that summer it felt like Dad and me against the world.

Mom was embarking on another round of chemo and was overwhelmed with grief.

Tiffany had bought a house fifteen minutes away in Sugar House and moved out. Retired from competing in half-pipe snowboarding, she now worked at Fidelity and wore all-black except for a pair of gold-clasped pirate boots that jangled when she walked.

Danny was living in Los Angeles. He had a job in corporate communications, an apartment off Sunset Boulevard, and a college relationship to keep alive. No matter how much Mom or I guilted him, he wasn't coming home until he absolutely had to, which ended up being in the middle of September.

And the little girls were still just that, little, though in fact they were well into their teens.

That left me. A scary thought.

I worried I'd be too butterfingered to help Dad button his shirt or zip his fly. I worried I wouldn't be able to lift him in and out of bed or that I'd drop him. I worried I'd crash his car driving us around town. It wasn't just the physical part that worried me, either: pouring cans of Promote into his G-tube, helping him shave with an electric razor or brush his teeth or blow his nose or put on his shoes or wrestle on his complicated BiPAP mask. It was the figuring-stuff-out part that overwhelmed me. I've never been good at puzzles, assembly, or following directions.

"This would be a lot less embarrassing for both of us if you'd just go insane," I told him as I sorted through a bag of spare tubes for the

BiPAP. "If you just weren't in your right mind at all, I wouldn't have so much performance anxiety."

Before I moved home, my top concern was what it would be like to handle Dad's penis. It was an understandable anxiety when you consider I had been out of the closet for all of three years when Dad was diagnosed. What if I were *attracted* to my own father, some kind of incestuous reverse pedophile?

Out of respect to my younger self, I don't want to dismiss this worry out of hand, but it proved to be so at odds with the reality we faced that I unconsciously put it to rest. Bathroom stuff was mercifully unsexy. I'd pull down Dad's pants and ask a question about the Jazz or the stock market and he'd opine from the throne, shaking off with a wiggle. There was a certain screwball logic to caregiving. To put on his Maui Jims, Dad would have me angle the sunglasses on the bathmat so he could squat down, prop his elbows on his knees, and scoop them onto his face with what strength remained in his biceps.

"OK, maybe you *are* insane," I'd tell him, straightening the glasses on his face.

If my parents never questioned my ability to lend a hand, it wasn't because I never messed up. The first time I helped Dad shower, I turned off the water to hunt for a towel. When I came back, he was shivering. "What's wrong?" I asked. I didn't understand his response. "What? Can you say that again?" This time he spoke clearly enough for me to get it: "*I'm cold.*"

He could have so easily diminished me or chewed me out. He never did.

I broke down one night in the sunroom, saying I couldn't believe this was happening to him. When I went to hug him, I found that my leg was unwilling to let me to walk the few feet toward him. Dad made the journey for me and rested his chin on my shoulder, his arms Gumby-like at his sides. He felt so slight in my arms.

One of my responsibilities that summer was to chauffer Dad to the office or on errands in his Lexus. "Rex is yours now," he told me, using his car's nickname.

Like my driving skills, my car etiquette hadn't improved since high school. The luxury sedan I'd once been scared to drive to prom was now brimming with old bowls of oatmeal and glasses of dried smoothie. I'd swiped off the side-view mirror backing out of a narrow driveway. It hung by a single thick cable. "Is Greg driving you around or did he move into your car?" Tiffany asked when she peeked inside. Dad was in the passenger seat among the mess, arms braced helplessly at his sides.

Our ALS support group was held in the basement of a church. It's true we'll all be disabled eventually, but the support group made this point with economy and remarkably little optimism. People would go around the table saying where they were from and why they were there. The real reason for showing up wasn't solidarity but to scope out what was in store. The full spectrum of ALS affliction was usually present, and it was affliction. We came to see who could still use their hands or legs, who could speak or breathe independently, who had become a full-time wheelchair user since the last meeting. I wondered if, in some strange way, I was looking into not just Dad's future but also my own.

After every terrible update people concluded, "But we're hanging in there."

When it was Dad's turn, he'd introduce us. Head down, my toes would crinkle in my shoe, making me wince and sit up straighter. I'd press a fingernail into the leather of Dad's day planner so I didn't have to look at everyone nodding like they understood.

Talking at a whisper was the equivalent of shouting for him now and I quietly noted his talent, even in his current state, for putting people at ease. He was still handsome, maybe even more handsome than he had been before he'd begun losing weight, and he could still make people laugh. "Like a dad from TV," my friends called him. A dad from TV who'd never live to replace his AOL email or learn to pay bills online. I wanted to scream at all the families around the table just barely holding it together. This wasn't a basement. It was a crypt.

"The feeding tube's helping," I said brightly. "But he's having to spend a lot of time on the machine. I guess he's been pretty air hungry." It was funny sitting at a table in the refrigerated recesses of a church basement and summing up, in two words, how Dad would die: air hunger. He would suffocate slowly, breathe and breathe and still not get enough air. "But we're hanging in there."

At the end of the meeting, Dad would have me stay and fold chairs.

Getting ready for bed one night, he asked if I had any dates lined up and I got out my laptop and pulled up Cheetahboy's profile. Cheetahboy was a mechanic from Ogden who had stood me up the other night. One of his pictures showed him in a tucked-in American flag shirt and a cowboy hat. In another, he was straddling a chair in his underpants.

"It looks like that guy has other intentions," Dad said.

ALS had not stopped Dad from believing I'd end up with a great guy, not when I'd come into his room red-eyed and half-drowned from trying to join the gay swim team, not when the only guys who messaged me were forty-five-year-old Mormon dads on the DL.

Stretching Dad's atrophied legs a little too hard, I'd bitch about how I'd never meet anyone who wasn't a human AIDS germ or too stupid to *construe* a sentence. I was gay because I liked men, not because I liked bishops and little girls. (Internalized homophobia was as ingrained as my misuse of big words.)

Dad saw through my intensity and bitterness, saw that I was just a scared kid. He may have been on his deathbed, but he still considered it his job to call me on my baloney, to lift me up when it hurt too much to hope. I'd take off his BiPAP and he'd replace my moans with Gina Jones. "You're going to meet a lot of interesting people," Dad would say. "But the right guy is out there."

Besides support group, clinic was our big regular outing that fall. It managed to be both subdued and nerve-racking, especially as Dad got closer to needing a tracheotomy. The medical staff would try to make small talk by asking what I was doing now that I'd graduated and I'd tell them, well, *this*.

Dad's final visit before he went on a respirator is the one I remember best. In the waiting room, I thumbed through out-of-date magazines fanned out on the table until a nurse called us back to another, smaller waiting room that made me claustrophobic. I turned to the back of Dad's day planner and quizzed him on our social security numbers and frequent-flyer miles.

A nutritionist came in and asked him to step outside so she could weigh him. I stayed in the exam room, avoiding a woman in a wheelchair. The woman was staring at the wall beside our door, groaning. The blanket wrapped around her had partially fallen off. What came out of her mouth was a jumble of sounds, impossible to decode. She covered one eye and then the other. It took me a minute to get that she was reading from an eye chart. All these years after my alumni interview with the engineer whose slipper had fallen off and I was still skittish around other disabled people.

Later, a respiratory therapist knocked on our door and popped her head into the room, greeting Dad by name. She clipped his nose shut and had him blow into an electronic spirometer, essentially a stopwatch with a mouthpiece that measured the strength of his breath. I stood there thinking, "Blow! Blow!"

"OK," she said. "Good job." She looked discouraged and told us what we already knew: Dad wasn't getting enough air. It was nearly time for him to get a tracheotomy, a surgical opening in his windpipe, the kind I'd seen in anti-smoking ads.

Dad blew again.

I wanted to rip the spirometer from her and blow for Dad, the guy who had clipped my toenails until I was twelve and helped me put on socks. The guy who took me skiing and hiking and to play night tennis at the club. "Like this!" I wanted to say. "Do it like this!"

Another readout, another discouraging smile. She gave Dad a hug and hung his charts on the door.

I thumbed through the calendar in Dad's day planner.

"How's it looking?" he asked. Besides a birthday he'd filled in at the beginning of the year, when he could still write, the dates were blank.

"We can squeeze it in," I said. I penciled in *trach* for the middle of November.

Dad struggled to breathe so much that fall he looked perpetually panicked, his newly bony shoulders jumping up and down. He had to take a break to catch his breath if he walked more than ten feet, and he spent more and more time attached to the BiPAP. His body was working so hard for oxygen, and the disease was so aggressively attacking his muscles, he became rail thin. Old man thin. Massive amounts of dandruff fell from his scalp and eyebrows and his hair was turning gray and falling out. It looked like he'd aged twenty years in a couple months.

Two days before Dad was scheduled for surgery, almost a year since our final tennis match in the bubble at the club, I walked into my parents' room and found Dad panting on the edge of the bed. We tried taking deep breaths together. When that didn't work Dad told us to call an ambulance. "Are you sure?" I asked, thinking, idiotically, of how expensive it would be. "We could just drive."

The paramedics arrived a few minutes later. "Up here!" I shouted.

They tried to lay Dad down and I told them he couldn't breathe that way. Instead, they made a chair for him out of two transfer boards and took him down the stairs and out to the ambulance. Mom and Danny climbed in after him. The sirens started up and Berkeley and Mazie whined at the back fence, the way dogs do when they hear a siren, like they're calling out to a distant wolf relative.

I went upstairs and changed into a fresh shirt and jeans and drove Dad's Lexus to the ER. I didn't bother trying to keep the broken side-view mirror from thudding against the door.

When it was my turn to go back and see him, I pulled away the curtain and took in Dad's bloodshot eyes, the tube down his throat. I had no idea why no one had put a blanket over him, why he was as naked as a corpse. The attending physician explained that he had been sedated before he was intubated. The tracheotomy would be performed in a few days, the breathing tube moved from his mouth to a hole in his throat beneath his Adam's apple. I pondered that word, performed, like Dad were part of an act, the magician's assistant about to be sawed in half.

In rehab, Dad's roommate was even worse off. He wanted more and more morphine, already turning into a fiend. Either he'd skied into a tree or he'd hit a tree coming down the canyon after skiing. It was hard to piece together what was going on. His girlfriend didn't say much. She just came and sat by his bed and tried not to cry, probably wondering how long she'd have to wait before she could break up with him. His family drove down from Idaho when he turned twenty-one and filled the room with balloons. *Twenty-one*. He was younger than I was.

"Why do you keep looking at that paralyzed piece of ass over there?" Danny asked. "You gonna go blow him?"

Living in West Hollywood after college had exposed Danny to plenty of gay culture, and his jokes about my sexuality made me laugh even when they shouldn't. The truth is, we were all more relaxed with Danny around and glad to have him home. Together we turned caring for Dad into a buddy comedy, executing lifts and dips like gawky ballroom dancers and wiggling a tube down Dad's throat to whisk away green mucus plugs like Ghostbusters. It helped that Dad was doing better on the respirator. Now that breathing wasn't a struggle, the fear was gone. Christmas was just around the corner and his first words when he could speak were, "Ho, ho, ho."

"Pretty fucking corny, Dad," Danny said, trying not to cry.

Dad turned fifty-five that December. We didn't bring him any balloons of his own but some still drooped around his roommate. I went to take a load off in the chair next to his bed and woke up a while later to the sound of his favorite nurse singing "Happy Birthday" in a creepy whisper. Tiffany and Danny were behind her, blocking their smirks with Starbucks cups. Mom was at Dad's bedside too, bald and in her floor-length coat. She was singing along a little but when she saw me looking at her, she put two fingers to her temple and pretended to shoot herself in the head.

* * *

For Dad's homecoming on Christmas Eve, we wore Bob shirts: *I'm with Bob, Bob's Babe, Bob's Son, Bob Almighty*. We'd converted Tiffany's childhood bedroom into a kind of triage station for Dad. At some point over the years, Tiffany had ditched the grungy snowboarder vibe of her teens for Tommy Hilfiger, turning her room from a Petri dish into a patriotic demonstration. Even the pillows shone red, white, and blue. Stars and stripes cascaded down the wallpaper and behind the furniture, skipping among pillows and bedsheets.

Since Dad couldn't really go out at night, these were the only stars he would ever see again. I'd lower the railing of his bed and make him scoot over when I was on night duty so I could lie next to him, the anti-bedsore air mattress shifting under us, and pick out shapes in the plaster of the ceiling or connect the dots of a new set of constellations, not the Big Dipper and Canis Major but the darkened outlines of stuff around the room: La-Z-Boy, Oxygen Concentrator, Respirator, Flat-Screen TV.

Mona's martial arts teacher, Mr. Arishita, commissioned his classes to make hundreds of paper cranes for my dad that now dangled against one wall from fishing wire, swaying to the whoosh of the respirator. Marathon medals clanked from a row of nails behind his bed. Looming above the bed was a portrait one of my high school friends had drawn of Dad running the St. George Marathon two years earlier.

For as much as we worried about mucus plugging Dad's airway or his inner cannula popping out, it was comforting having him home again, within earshot of Moe banging on the piano in the living room and the dogs scrambling on the hardwood floor in the kitchen. The whoosh of a respirator replaced his snore, but Dad was still Dad, just hooked to a machine. I was still me, maybe more now than I'd ever been. After the lonely years of college, I was out of the closet and I had my family back, even if that family was falling apart.

For Dad to talk, you had to deflate his cuff—the bubble at his neck—so air could pass over his vocal cords. That's when I'd plop onto Dad's bed and set upon him with a cheap microphone plugged into the jack of my third-generation iPod. I wanted to record our conversations, apparently so I could know, years later, how vulnerable and clueless I sounded in my early twenties, how I misused big words and called everyone, even people my age, a "kid."

"What were you saying the other day about how you used to be able to go to the bathroom with just a cup of coffee?" I asked as he hunched on the commode, the mic an inch from his chapped lips. "You were saying on Christmas you'd rather have Lou Gehrig's than be hit by a truck or have a heart attack. Can you explain that?"

Danny interrupted these self-serious interviews by pulling out a digital video camera and shouting questions about first kisses and early sexual partners, all the stuff you'd really want to know. Meanwhile, I had a knack for poking at the wasp's nest of the ineffable. I smoked pot only occasionally, maybe two or three times a year, but to listen to these voice memos you'd think I was a hard-core stoner. "What does it feel like to be alive but not breathing . . . by yourself, I mean. Are you still alive right now?"

"I'm still alive," Dad would moan.

I wanted to know if Dad had Lou Gehrig's in his dreams, what it felt like *inside* his body, and if he thought of himself as innately disabled or if he saw Lou Gehrig's as an outside condition inflicted upon him, a leading question if ever there was one. "Has ALS changed your ability to focus at all?" I asked. "Like when you're moving your foot do you forget you moved your foot?"

"It's more how long I can keep a list of things in my head," Dad said.

"Does that mean you can't listen to me talk for the same amount of time?"

I might duck out of my line of questioning with a joke, but my inquiries were more than idle philosophy. They were a cross-examination of my own subconscious. Dad had a condition that couldn't be pushed aside or minimized and in asking about his struggles I was hoping he would tell me about mine. I don't mean that I expected him to wail, "We lied to you all these years, Greg. You don't just have tight tendons. You have cerebral palsy. Look it up! You're *disabled*." For one, I still had no idea I had cerebral palsy. For another, my dad wouldn't have seen me as disabled any more than he would have seen me as being gay before I came out. It just wasn't a nice thing to say about someone you loved. What I wanted was recognition, for the silent part to be said out loud, not dwelled on or pitied but explored.

Dad gave me backrubs with his feet and relayed wordless zingers with a raised eyebrow and a downturned lip. When I came home with a tattoo still bloody and Saran Wrapped on the underside of my left bicep—the Roman numeral seven for the seven people in my family—Dad told me he wanted one too: a butterfly on his butt. He didn't mention what I'd only realize after the fact, that I had essentially put a symbol meant to honor my family in my armpit.

To keep his legs strong, Dad would walk with Danny and me down the hall, one of us pushing air into his lungs with a tracheotomy bag, the other with a hand on his gait belt. We learned to synchronize our breathing, inhale and exhale together to keep the bag from popping off or from pumping too much oxygen into him. "And here's my room," I'd say. "You remember my room."

It was eerie at first to disconnect Dad from the respirator and leave the machine beeping, the readout of his vitals flatlining, his bed empty. The days of Dad hopping in the car or on a plane, going skiing or running or hiking were gone, as was the time for teasing him about having no neck. The wasting of his muscles made him a little pencil-necked, actually. What once seemed like a solidly fused slab of vertebrae was now frail and skinny.

Dad and I were doing his stretches one day, my fingers wrapped around his heel, the pads of his toes pressing into the underside of my arm, when it occurred to me that my handsome left foot was almost identical to his. It was even the same size: eleven or eleven-and-a-half depending on the shoe brand. The family resemblance didn't extend to my right foot, with its narrow heel and bunched toes, but one matching limb was enough. I'd been walking around on Dad's foot my entire life and not known it. I'd keep walking on it after he was gone.

I'd only known Kevin for a couple weeks when my mom walked in on us having sex. It must have been jarring for her to see a bald thirty-one-year-old Mormon dude thrusting into her physically disabled youngest son. Then again, only moments before, looking for someone to help get Dad out of bed, Mom had taken the new elevator to the basement and folded back the accordion door to see my brother having sex with a girl who had once been my dance partner at cotillion. If death is the opposite of desire, our house had plenty of both.

Privacy was nonexistent. The respirator was always going off down the hall, and if it wasn't the respirator it was the doorbell Velcroed to the base of Dad's Medicare bed. His ski buddies, running buddies, and former co-workers came and went without knocking. They hadn't seen me in the throes of intimacy, but they had seen me afterward, stranded in front of the fridge in my boxers.

That winter had been snowy and bleak. Mom was struggling to mend from a round of "big guns" chemo and Dad's legs were getting weaker by the day.

After a brief stint selling day planners at the mall, I'd gotten a job that March as a community newspaper editor thirty miles up the canyon in Park City at the *Park Record*, but in the larger scheme of things I'd fallen off what you might call the accomplishment horse—the accomplishment horse, the mechanical bull, the rainbow phalluses of Boystown, and anything else a young gay man with tight tendons might want to ride. Before Kevin, I'd been as celibate as celery.

I met him one soggy Saturday in April while judging packets at the Utah Future Problem Solving Bowl. FPS is one of those after-school activities for teenage nerds, a mix of a sci-fi convention and a debate tournament, with kids running around in crushed tinfoil costumes, dressed as genetically modified produce, developing nations, microchips, nanobots, and splices of DNA. I'd done FPS from the fourth grade until I was a sophomore in high school, coming back as a judge for most of college and now beyond. I was cool like that. Needless to say, Kevin was the first guy I'd ever picked up at an FPS conference. I liked the hole in his jeans.

Though Kevin was eight years older, we had a lot in common. We'd gone to the same junior high and high school. Not only had we both competed in FPS, we'd also had the same coach, a vegan with a Chihuahua named Atilla. Kevin was an FPS legend because his team had won first place at the international conference in 1990, when he was in the eighth grade. The closest I'd ever come to winning was top ten.

Now we were no longer imagining the future and its problems. We were in the thick of them.

Dad had a talking computer he could supposedly control with his eyes, but it more closely resembled the Speak & Spell we'd had as kids in the eighties than Siri and Alexa, who would debut a few years later. Danny had programmed the computer to say only dirty words and phrases. To move the cursor, Dad had to wear a reflective dot on his forehead, like a bindi, that fell off constantly. We mostly just depended on reading Dad's lips and deflating his cuff so he could moan out a few words. Even though breathing wasn't a problem with his respirator, the rest of Dad's symptoms progressed rapidly.

Communicating with Dad now could be like chatting with the Caterpillar in *Alice in Wonderland*, a mess of hard vowels that looped into short, cryptic sentences. You had to repeat after him, reduce complex ideas to one-word answers. Pillow? Pee? Suction?

To chat, your first move was to suction away any mucus that might clog his airway. We'd all piled into my parents' room to watch *ER* every Thursday night when I was a kid, and I liked to pretend I was a doctor, or at least a respiratory therapist. I'd call for "three cc's of saline." (They were actually milliliters.) "The little pink vial thingies," I'd tell Kevin, wagging a finger at Tiffany's old white dresser.

Once I'd twisted the top off the vial of saline and given a few good squirts down Dad's trachea, I'd tell Kevin to turn on the suction vacuum. "Ready for a suck!" Then I'd wiggle a tube through the joint at the hollow of Dad's neck and down his inner cannula, the tube in his windpipe that had popped out a couple of times. The machine would beep, coughs would rattle Dad's body, but with no air passing over his vocal cords they were silent coughs. We joked that we'd finally invented a mute button. "Don't worry," I'd tell Kevin. "He only looks like he's dying."

I didn't bring many friends around my dad. I suppose I felt protective of him, not just of his modesty but of the able-bodied guy they'd grown up admiring. Kevin was an exception: older, wiser, part of my new life as a gay man, not my old one as a child in the closet.

Kevin never handled any of my dad's bathroom needs but he was good for a hang. Kevin's dad was a retired physician who had counted among his patients the recently deceased president of the Mormon church. From a young age Kevin had grown used to being in medical situations. He absorbed my lessons like one of the little pink sponges we used to wet Dad's mouth. Striding into the bedroom, he'd shake my dad's emaciated shoulder and then pull up a chair. "Hey, Bob. How's it going?"

"Hey! Not too bad to-day," Dad would say, humming and coughing weakly between words after I had deflated his cuff. Hot Mary, his speech therapist, had taught him to articulate every syllable, like he was just learning to read. Even at his best, Dad sounded like he was talking through an electric fan. "I just got back from a run. Now I'm going to have a cup of coffee and read the paper."

ALS hadn't affected Dad's dorky sense of humor as much as his diaphragm, a fact some of his friends, understandably, found confusing. Bob was going for a run? Drinking coffee? They never said as much but you could tell they weren't sure at first if their buddy had lost his marbles. I liked that Kevin went along with our dumb jokes, rarely missing a beat. "He's just saying how much he loves me," I'd translate.

"Forget coffee, Bob," Kevin would say. "Next time, I'll bring beer."

Kevin saw my dad the way I did, not as a dying man gurgling out last wishes, spit bubbles popping over his teeth, but as a prankster who'd stick his tongue out the corner of his mouth and, with what smile he could manage, pretend to be dead.

The weirdest thing about Kevin was that he actually *enjoyed* the chaos of my family. He began calling as soon as I got off work; a few times, he was already at the house when I pulled up. I rang Kevin from work one afternoon to see what he was up to and he gayly reported, "I'm at lunch with your mom and sister. They're right here. Should I pass the phone?"

"Is this part of a twelve-step program?" I asked. "Are you a saint?"

Kevin had studied at Le Cordon Bleu in Paris and always brought over a basket of fresh ham-and-cheese croissants or a pan of double-chocolate brownies. Mom savored those brownies so much she hid them in a Tupperware container in the office so she didn't have to share. Kevin made dumplings from scratch at the kitchen counter and never failed to whip up a snack from whatever was in the fridge. He complimented me on my articles about reiki therapists, high-speed chairlifts, and frozen yogurt shops out at the junction. I liked having Kevin around to feed me and tell me I was doing a good job, that I was a good son.

It was no small blessing that, by May, the renovations to make the house wheelchair accessible were mostly complete. The problem was they'd come too late: Dad was deteriorating faster than anyone had expected. We'd planned for the long haul, spent too much money on amenities Dad couldn't use anymore. The elevator broke bimonthly. The squirt of the in-toilet bidet was as weak as a Camano clam. A ten-dollar commode and a baby wipe did just as well.

It could get stuffy and crowded in Tiffany's room with all those sputtering machines. As the spring thawed, Dad perspired freely, like he was running a marathon in bed. He was most comfortable in an adult brief, running shorts, and an old running shirt split down the back so his limp wrists and rigid arms could be steered through the sleeves one at a time. His feet were red and swollen and stayed white when you pressed them. On walks in Liberty Park he wore sandals, as one of the few joys remaining to him was feeling fresh air between his toes. My mom would tuck her nightgown into a pair of jeans and Danny would drive the silver Dodge Sprinter van in his bath slippers.

"That's the kind of family we are: clothing optional," I told Kevin.

Kevin came with us on walks so often he got sunburned. He was happy to be an extra set of hands. After we steered Dad off the van's ramp, Kevin would lug the suction device, spare tubes, pink vials of saline, and sundry medical equipment around the duck pond while I brandished the new Nikon I'd bought to take pictures for the paper. More and more, I was using the camera to document my own life. My chemo-shorn mom and be-tubed dad competed for backwards glances with dudes tossing devil sticks, tightrope walkers practicing a foot off the ground, and Mayan dancers rehearsing in ceremonial headdresses.

Every morning before driving up the canyon to the newspaper, I made Dad kiss my cheek and tell me I was his favorite. I had mixed feelings about being away from home so much in what was already looking like the final spring of his life. Still, I think it did Dad good to see me going off to work in the Lexus he could no longer drive. Dad had to sell his community newspaper business to pay his and Mom's medical bills and keep our family solvent, and I liked the idea that I was carrying on his legacy in some small way, albeit at a paper he had never owned. He said his biggest regret of dying in his fifties was that he wouldn't get to see how it all turned out. I wanted to show him it was going to turn out just fine.

As the business editor of the *Park Record*, I wrote every article in the small section, hammered out briefs, took photos, did basic layout, and plugged any holes with press releases. I'd roll in at ten A.M. on production days, my heels crushing the back of a pair of moccasins, and get to work accidentally cutting off my articles mid-sentence and introducing typos into my clever captions. Despite my shortcomings,

I was probably the best gay editor with tight tendons to ever work at the paper.

What I remember most about those early months at the *Record* was being exhausted. My dad's aide, Regina, worked full-time during the day, but we still had to contend with nights and weekends. We were the graveyard shift: Danny, Mom, and I. Even when I was off-duty, I stirred before sunrise to the polite but insistent single chime of my dad's doorbell and rolled over, praying for someone else to intervene, only to hear the machine go berserk. Coming to my senses, I'd charge down the hall in my boxers, hoping my negligence hadn't killed him.

Being that tired made me even more forgetful than usual, and "usual" for me includes a damaged cerebellum. I locked my keys in the Lexus about once a month and racked up speeding tickets. During my lunchbreak, not wanting to get caught dozing in the car, I'd sneak off to my family's rental condo near the *Park Record* building and come back to the newsroom with cowlicks and pillow creases on my face.

Kevin was a nice escape, the calm amid the chaos, sort of the way Dad had been in the old days. After work, he would take me out for root beer floats or to a lookout point behind the state capitol where we could watch the sunset, never daring to steal a kiss in public. We went deer spotting in Salt Lake Cemetery, tested the physics of Gravity Hill, and drove by the house in Federal Heights where, a few years earlier, Elizabeth Smart had been abducted and then miraculously returned.

I was a kid given to abstraction and flights of fancy. If I were running on the treadmill in the basement, I'd keep the TV on mute and Dad's room monitor near me. If Dad, Danny, and Regina were upstairs watching a movie—*Saving Private Ryan* was a favorite—it created an audio mix on my end that was part real world, part sound effects; part medical machinery, part movie magic. I liked to imagine that if I went upstairs I'd find my dad and Danny in the midst of a great adventure, battling Nazis from Dad's hospital bed.

It did sound stupid saying it aloud, but Kevin insisted I was in good company. "Like Snoopy and the Red Baron!"

Let's just say the man egged on my creative side.

Our dates took on a dreamy, giddy quality. We'd talk about the documentaries we'd make, the places we'd travel. I wanted to take Stana to Poland to research her origins. Stana's dad was Jewish and she had survived the Holocaust as an infant only because her parents had thought to hide her in blankets at the foot of their bed when the Gestapo had come to take them away in the night. Stana would tell her harrowing life story to anyone who would listen, usually when she should have been vacuuming, and had once given my mom a priceless crystal vase, a family heirloom, that still had the TJ Maxx sticker on the bottom.

Being around Kevin reminded me of my Future Problem Solving days; he thought way, way outside the box. He could talk for hours about sustainability, Zoroastrians, the Sadducees and the Pharisees, and the Angel Moroni. He also just liked being along for the ride, liked writing poems with me under the gazebo at night, or playing water basketball with my brother and his friends in the pool.

It felt right to bring him back to my childhood room, to the school awards and sportsmanship trophies gathering dust on my desk. When I moved home from college, Mom hired a painter to gloss over the sports wallpaper from my closeted teen years. My walls were now a sophisticated shade of burgundy and my room still smelled like paint. A stack of frames that included my *Wizard of Oz* poster and a caricature of myself at SeaWorld were piled against one sticky wall. With Dad sick, I didn't have anyone to hang them for me. My stuffed animals were in garbage bags in the freezer room. I was trying to be an adult.

Kevin was shy about sex at first, saying it took him a while to get going. The truth is, he was starved for it. He made vague allusions to a guy who'd pursued him back in Phoenix but I was his first boyfriend. After I showed him how to top me, I'd wake up to him pulling down my boxers, his stubble scratching my thighs. Following my Croatian fling with Tyler Townsend, I'd dated a couple guys back in Chicago, including the bathroom-stall bandit. A chlamydia scare senior year, and the prospect of having a Q-tip shoved up my urethra, transformed me from a casual condom user into a diehard, but I still felt self-conscious about my spazzy right leg and couldn't stop myself from making silly comments about how I wasn't bad in the sack if I stretched first. Blushing a little, Kevin would tell me about his famous pioneer great-great-grandpa who had hobbled to the Salt Lake Valley on a wooden leg, pulling a handcart. "At least you still have the original set," Kevin said.

He didn't talk much about his ex-wife, a concert cellist, though she was a professor and easy enough to find on the internet. They had traveled the world together in their twenties, shacking up in Paris, Moscow, and Manhattan. Mostly during those years Kevin managed his wife's career, securing grants and making meals, but during their stint in New York, he had enrolled at Yale and took the train up to New Haven several times a week.

The plan had been for him to major in urban planning, but somewhere along the way his marriage had fallen apart. This is where his story got hazy, a kind of smash cut that plopped him in Phoenix, a newly out divorcé with joint ownership in a catering company. The business had started hot but gone belly-up after nine months, or Kevin had simply abandoned it. Either way, he'd ditched his partners and moved home to meditate under a tree in his parents' backyard for a while, which is what he'd been up to when he'd gotten a call from his middle school FPS coach, the vegan with the Chihuahua named Atilla, asking him to be a judge at the state bowl.

In retrospect, Kevin's byzantine backstory should have been the first sign something was amiss.

For an unemployed guy living with his folks, his past was as adventurous and far-flung as a race around the world, with even more checkered flags. Understandably, the divorce was the part he was really hung up on. He called himself the prodigal husband. "I pushed her too hard to succeed," he would say. "She was tired of being a nomad."

"And being married to a gay guy," I'd add.

I teased Kevin but I was bowled over by him. He hadn't spent his twenties at his dad's deathbed, jerking off and sobbing in his childhood bedroom. He'd lived! A sham marriage, an aborted Ivy League education, the not-so-subtle hints of a nervous breakdown . . . and he could cook? Come on. Kevin was almost too good to be true.

* * *

We were in the hot tub in the backyard finishing root beer floats the first time Kevin brought up wanting to start a church. "A church!" I exclaimed. I wasn't sure whether to smile, if this was a joke. Kevin described himself as a seeker, not a fundamentalist, and too skeptical of the powers that be to *attend* church. Now he wanted to start one? Had someone implanted a chip in his brain, like in an FPS skit?

Kevin drifted over to me and wiped some dried ice cream from my chin with his thumb. The chlorine dispenser spun in his wake like a flying saucer. Not like the Mormon church, Kevin chuckled, but a church to save the planet. We'd get around using horse and buggy, build houses that faced west to soak up natural light, burn candles, brew beer. As part of this new religion, he wanted to move to London to start a microbrewery and artist commune where folks could come together and create, like the Carmelite nuns in town who made fudge.

"What's the free pot situation going to be?" I asked. I was trying to doodle a penis onto my empty Hires cup, the wax piling up under my fingernails. I only ever drew flaccid penises. I thought they were cute.

"A little pot would be fun," Kevin said, grinning wickedly. He tugged at my leg, pulling it onto his lap, and dug his thumbs into my small, hairy calf. It felt good. "Just don't touch my scars," I said, because that made me nauseous. I let my cup shoot off into the bubbles as Kevin's fingers crawled up my swim trunks.

The AC unit next to the hot tub chugged on and, as if it were attached to a fan large enough to cool the whole backyard, a corresponding breeze moved through the aspens and cottonwood trees, carrying away twists of chlorine-smelling steam. Dad's bedroom window was open on the second story. If his machines weren't too loud, he could probably hear us splashing around in the hot tub. It was surreal to be down there talking about wanting to smoke a joint as he lay above us, breathing through a hole in his throat.

The next I heard of the Church of Kevin was at his cousin Trisha's new apartment on 45th South. We were passing around a two-liter bottle of Diet Shasta and a bag of baked barbecue chips—Holladay's version of health food—when Kevin asked if we wanted to see the logo he'd had a graphic designer mock up. He pulled it up on Trisha's computer. It looked like a coat of arms.

"Now for the big surprise," Kevin said. He asked Trisha to turn off the lights as he scrolled through his inbox to find the link to a real estate listing. Trisha and I closed our eyes and when we opened them, an Edwardian mansion lit up Trisha's computer screen and most of her tiny living room and kitchen.

The estate was surrounded by oak trees and bluebells and had mullioned windows and a ballroom with a two-story ceiling. "I'm putting an offer on this place," Kevin said. The house was in Hampstead, "the heart of literary London," according to the listing, and cost millions of pounds. Kevin called it, accurately enough, *the abbey*. Its real name was something like Wenton House. It was the kind of house that had a name.

I'd just met Trisha but she reminded me of the Mormon girls I'd gone to high school with: she was big and athletic, with a short blonde ponytail and an irrepressible smile. It was comforting experiencing the abnormal with someone so down-to-earth. She seemed used to dealing with blowhard boys.

Trisha set down her Solo cup of Diet Shasta by the keyboard and pulled her ponytail tighter, wrinkling her nose. "I wouldn't want to live in such a big place, would you?" she asked, trying to give Kevin an out.

"The size worries me not at all," Kevin replied, clicking through photos of a cozy study, an entryway with a crystal chandelier, and a kitchen filled with gleaming modern appliances. That was one of Kevin's verbal tics: he'd say the opposite of what he meant and then add "not at all" to the end of it. It gave his every utterance a preliminary feel. "It's a fairly modest property for what I have in mind."

Unsettled, I begged off to meet some high school friends. After ordering a Coors Light at the bar, I realized I wasn't sure how to explain Kevin and his antics, what I felt about his spiritual side or my own. What did a brewery and a swanky English estate have to do with starting a church anyway? When I came home an hour later, my clothes perfumed with smoke, Dad was banging on the footboard of his bed and bucking his hips. Thankfully, the green and red numbers on his respirator weren't flashing. "Can you breathe?" I rushed to his side without thinking to turn on a light. "What's going on? Do you have to go to the bathroom?"

Dad nodded yes and clicked his tongue so I fished through the commode until I found his urinal. To think I'd been worried about the prospect of handling Dad's dick. I was now so comfortable I could do it in the dark, almost without thinking.

I started to unfasten his brief and heard Mom creak out of the bed we'd squashed against the window seat for whoever was on night duty. "Greg," Mom said. "Dad's masturbating. I've been up with him for forty-five minutes and he doesn't respond. He keeps making kissing noises. He's having a wet dream."

Dad shook his head the little he could in vigorous disagreement. *I have to pee*, he mouthed.

I stopped unfastening his brief. I'd come a long way as a caregiver but I wasn't in the mood to be jack-in-the-boxed by a Dad boner. I held out the urinal to my mom. "Here. You do it."

"Oh Bob, whatever," Mom retorted. "Then how come you didn't respond when I was asking if you had to go to the bathroom?"

She got out of bed and cinched her robe, ran a hand over the short hair that was growing in unevenly on the crown of her head. "I have this under control."

Did she though? Mom's caregiving had taken a turn for the worse since she'd gotten a prescription for fentanyl patches. There were a lot of painkillers and muscle relaxants floating around Dad's room, antidepressants and sleeping pills, too. I had never paid much attention to them. This was in the days before the word *opioid* started appearing with the word *crisis* in the news. Back then, I didn't know what an opioid was, but I remember bottles of Oxycontin, Klonopin, and Vicodin lined up on Tiffany's dresser. We'd grind them up in a pill crusher, mix them with water in a beaker, and feed them into Dad's G-tube.

Fentanyl was stronger than all those pills combined and proved fantastic at mitigating Mom's bone pain and calming her. I'd gotten used to her operating with a kind of whacked-in-the-head, out-of-it quality that made her appear like she wasn't in her body so much as hovering above it on a kite string. The downside was that she had become so scary behind the wheel that one motorist had tailed her home and told her she shouldn't be on the road.

It could be toxic to put a fentanyl patch in the same spot twice, and Mom often needed help sticking them on out-of-the-way places on her back. One morning before I left for work, she had me take a patch out of the wastebasket in her bathroom so she could lick it.

"You mean the one I just peeled off your shoulder and threw in the garbage?" I asked.

"It's not really the garbage, honey. Just grab it." Mom was naked from the waist up and staring me down in the mirror.

"Whatever you call it, it's full of dirty kitty litter," I said.

It wasn't but it could have been.

"Quit being such a sissy and give me the patch," Mom said.

I retrieved the used patch and handed it over. If Mom was going to be an asshole, I'd let her lick whatever she wanted. She uncrinkled the patch and spread it taut, pinching it between her thumbs and index fingers. After her first pass with her tongue, lapping at the patch like she would a lid of yogurt, she said, "I'm a fucking addict, OK?"

Home sometimes felt like an anxious dream, too staged and dramatic to be real. Kevin's deceptions were beginning to add to the feeling of uncertainty. A few days after he told Trisha and me he was buying an estate in London for his church, Kevin called me at work to tell me he'd just purchased a new Prius. He went on and on about fuel efficiency until I told him I had to go. Once I hung up I felt bad for being impatient. I hadn't even asked the color of his new car. I couldn't reconcile Kevin's practical new Prius with his larger-than-life real estate scheme. If he were fibbing, why settle for a Prius?

Nah, I was being too hard on the guy. He wasn't a liar. He was just a dreamer, like me—not a BSer but an FPSer, solving his problems with imagination. I was only a little taken aback when he pulled up to our house that evening in his mom's 4Runner, same as always. "I didn't want to take the dogs for a walk in the Prius," Kevin said. "It still has that new-car smell."

Driving home from work the next afternoon, I decided to get off the freeway one exit early and cruise by Kevin's house. His neighborhood was familiar, one street over from our old junior high. I wasn't out to catch him in a lie. I wanted to catch him in the truth, preferably a shiny blue one with temporary plates. I wanted there to be a Prius to celebrate. I'd leave a note on his car, like a high school girl, and he'd take me for rides.

There was no Prius anywhere on the block.

OK, but that didn't mean anything. The car could be in the garage. I parked on the street, hiked up Kevin's steep driveway, and rang the doorbell.

Kevin's mother cracked open the door. I'd visited once before, when no one but Kevin was home, and remembered the kitschy painting of Joseph Smith and the Angel Moroni hanging in the entryway. Kidding around, I'd said I resembled the Prophet and Kevin had agreed. We'd made out, Kevin smelling, like he always did, of a few too many squirts of cologne. Now his mother looked shell-shocked at the mention of her son's name. She treated me like I was a predator from behind a barely opened door. No, she said. Kevin wasn't home.

After the Prius, Kevin purchased a loft across from Pioneer Park, the Hampstead of the crystal meth scene in Salt Lake. It was a loft, not an apartment: high ceilings, exposed pipes, walls that only went up three-quarters of the way. Unlike the car, Kevin let me check out his new pad: I went with him to sign the contract of sale one warm May evening.

The loft was comfortingly modest, the kind of place Kevin could afford with a little help from his parents. It had a frosted-glass front door, like in old detective movies, concrete floors, and red railings.

Like my room at home, it still smelled of paint. It was small, sure, but Kevin had big plans for this bare-bones industrial space. He was going to deck out the walls in art and take advantage of the downtown view by putting a grand piano in the living room. It would have to be lifted in with a crane. This bothered him *not at all*. It bothered me slightly more.

If you asked me, business editor par excellence, Kevin had picked a bad time to buy a new loft. It was the spring of 2008 and the housing bubble was starting to burst. Because it was a ski town full of second homes, Park City was hit even harder than Salt Lake. Without hefty real estate inserts to fatten up the newspaper, the publisher of the *Park Record* cut the business section altogether. Rather than lay me off, my boss saved my job by moving me to the Scene section. I became the arts and entertainment editor, covering spelling bees, school plays, and Sundance.

My second week on the new beat, Kevin called to ask if I wanted to check out a couple of paintings by a local artist he was buying from a gallery on Main Street. He thought it might make a good story. "Anyway, I'm just downstairs in the parking lot."

The funny thing about Kevin's fibs was that they built on each other: if he could afford a Prius and a modest loft, he could afford a few abstract paintings of aspen trees to hang on the walls, and if those abstract paintings happened to be slated to spend the next six months at the de Young Museum in San Francisco as part of a special exhibit, well, Kevin would buy them anyway and wait to take them home to his flat in London. He had no problem loaning out his private collection to the public. He was buying fine art, after all, not a TV.

A flat in London? I thought. *Jesus.*

Kevin had one condition for the sale: he wanted the gallery owner, who was maybe six months pregnant and in a zebra-print maternity top, to take us to see the paintings that afternoon. They were at the artist's studio a few blocks away. Kevin signed some contracts and nonchalantly reminded the gallery owner that he did all his finances through the Bank of England. Money transfers could take eighteen hours. The gallery owner said that was fine and asked, very nicely, for one of my business cards, which she flexed between her swollen fingers. "They say I'm the business editor but I'm arts now," I attempted to clarify.

It was amazing: being around Kevin made *me* feel like the fraud.

It was only about five minutes from upper Main Street to the artist's mansion in Deer Valley. In a chichi resort town, even the artists were rich and lived in mansions. They traveled, too. Since it was that muddy time of year between the end of the ski season and the first days of summer, the artist was somewhere else drinking Campari in the sun, but a house manager every bit as fretful as Kevin's mom invited us in and asked us to take off our wet shoes.

The basement studio was set up to look like the artist had just stepped away and would be back any minute: easels and canvas tarps and buckets of brushes strewn about. The three paintings took up an entire den wall, each the size of a front door, each a study of the same stand of aspen trees with minor variations of color, like Monet's haystacks. Each cost thirty thousand dollars. I was sweating. Even my tailbone was sweating, Impressionistically. Kevin kissed my temple. "You should see your face right now," he said. "I told you they were worth the wait."

Acrylic on canvas, I copied down in my notebook. *Large. What is acrylic?*

On the ride back to the *Record*, I finally confronted Kevin about his mountain of dubious claims, trying to keep my leg from shaking. "It's OK if none of this is true," I said in a wobbly voice like Dad's. I put a thumb under the shoulder strap of my seatbelt to help me breathe. I was trying to project confidence but I'm sure I sounded like I was about to cry. "If you're just a dude living with his parents, meditating under a tree, trying to figure stuff out, that's fine. I just need to know how you're paying for all this stuff." I thought his pranks might get me fired. I was barely hanging on to the job as it was.

Kevin looked terrified and seemed to momentarily forget which pedal was the gas and which the brake. As he tried to regain composure, swerving a little, he stammered that he was a majordomo. "A major what?" I asked. I'd never heard that term before, though I hadn't heard of composting before I met Kevin, either. Maybe this was another thing only old people were into. Was a majordomo like a maître d' or a drum major?

"More like a personal shopper," Kevin said.

"You're a personal shopper?" I asked.

It was after five and the *Record* lot was nearly empty except for some cars in line at the drive-thru taco place next door. That's when Kevin put the car in park and finally told me the truth: he worked for a French millionaire.

I had to pinch my thigh through my jeans to squelch a scared laugh.

The gist of Kevin's story was this: The year he was enrolled at Le Cordon Bleu in Paris, a kind, elderly man in one of his pastry classes befriended him. This man turned out to be a monk from a secret religious order charged with serving a reclusive businessman named Monsieur Degeunet. Stinking rich though he may have been, and of noble blood, Monsieur Degeunet lacked taste. This is where Kevin came in.

The monk and his brothers had been watching Kevin from afar for a long time and they were impressed. Very impressed. Kevin was special, though he must have already known that. The monks couldn't save Kevin's crumbling marriage, but they could offer him salvation of another kind: the credit cards to the kingdom.

I forget the exact choreography of loyalty oaths, aliases, blindfolds, and heavy church doors in Kevin's story, only that it culminated in Kevin being hired as one of Monsieur Degeunet's personal chefs. Kevin quickly rose through the ranks of house staff and kept working for the grand pooh-bah even after he left Paris, officially becoming Monsieur Degeunet's majordomo just a few weeks before meeting me. This promotion meant Kevin could now buy top-of-the-line art, clothes, cars, and houses—for his boss. His job was not to spend money, but to spend it *well*. The only catch was that Monsieur Degeunet was notoriously discreet, even paranoid, with entanglements all over the globe. Kevin had to keep his work secret, even from his family. He used the word *clandestine* a lot, like he was living in a spy novel.

Kevin spoke so logically, so reluctantly, at first I was honored he was giving me the inside scoop. I remember staring out the dirty windshield, feeling a fleeting glimmer of hope as this intelligent, good-natured person who had been inside me, who regularly hung out with my family, baked up a fantasy every bit as flaky and delicious as a ham-and-cheese croissant. Then I just wanted to help him save face. *Degeunet* sounded a little like Huguenot. Did Kevin mean the Huguenots, like French Protestants, the ones from AP Euro? Was he talking metaphorically?

Kevin put a hand on the back of my clammy neck. "It's a lot to absorb, Greg. Take your time."

I unbuckled my seatbelt and told Kevin I had better get home to check on Mom and Dad. When I went to move my leg, it was quivering under me. "See you tonight," he said. Pulling me toward him, he planted a kiss on my lips.

I managed to get into Dad's Lexus and dump my things on the passenger seat before submitting to a panicked cry. I was already on the hook to take a road trip with Kevin over the upcoming Memorial Day weekend and I didn't feel like I could bail without a good excuse.

The plan was to fly to Minneapolis to pick up a handicap-accessible van (a silver Dodge Sprinter, like my dad's—what were the odds?) for a woman with MS in Kevin's parents' ward. The ward had raised thousands of dollars and shopped for the best deal. Now they were counting on us to drive the van back to Utah so they could surprise her with it.

I had an entire week to back out of going to Minneapolis, but that would have meant admitting I'd gotten myself into a sticky situation in the first place. Just as in life before he got sick, Dad was the person whose advice I most wanted. I told him about the Prius and the loft, the abbey, the alleged flat in London, and the paintings. Then I deflated his cuff and prepared myself to receive his fatherly wisdom, carefully decoding and repeating each word to make sure I was getting it right. "Sounds . . . like . . . Kevin . . . has been . . . fucking the dog."

"That's one of Dad's old expressions," Mom explained, snacking on Kevin's brownies.

Upon more considered inquiry, Dad was concerned but he also thought Kevin might just be trying to impress me. I tried to make myself think the same thing. Far-fetched as it was, the broad strokes of Kevin's story did match up with what he had told me about his nomadic twenties, reconciling the image of the brilliant burnout with that of the big-spending visionary and erstwhile caterer. He'd gotten divorced and hit a rough patch, lost a small business, moved home. That was all. His situation wasn't so different from mine. And Sprinter vans didn't have trunks, so I couldn't be locked in one.

"It's only an eighteen-hour drive back to Salt Lake," I rationalized, helping Dad strap on the blue arm splints he wore at night. "One of Kevin's bank transfers takes that long, right?"

Heading out the door to the airport at the start of the long weekend, I made Dad kiss my cheek and tell me I was his favorite, like usual. He mouthed the words *be careful* and I told him to call the cops if he didn't hear from me in a few hours.

"Don't wait for the trail to go cold," I said.

Kevin and I arrived in Minneapolis around midnight that Saturday morning. We took a cab to a gas station near the airport, where two guys as baby-faced and midwestern as I could hope for were waiting for us. I kept my phone out, tossing it from hand to hand, flipping it open and pushing buttons to keep the screen glowing green. The van looked and smelled as advertised, gently used, like a rental. This time there was no talk of the Bank of England. Kevin paid using a certified check the bishopric had issued through Zions Bank.

The hotel in the City Center sat across from a giant Chili's. All night, as we lounged in bathrobes, I could tell Kevin wanted to talk to me about something. I had the same feeling the next morning at the Institute of Art as Kevin inspected a famous Rembrandt of a woman brandishing the bloody knife she'd just pulled out of her gut. I knew how she felt. My stomach was in knots, too.

I kept waiting for him to bring up Monsieur Degeunet or the Church of Kevin as we hopped on the freeway and headed west, but he was only charming and fun as ever. We stopped at roadside museums, Mount Rushmore, and a Wal-Mart in South Dakota to buy the new Leona Lewis album and the greatest hits of Dolly Parton and Queen. "In high school, I was very uncool for listening to these guys," Kevin said. "It was a Guns N' Roses world."

I rubbed his shaved skull. "You're old," I said, a little awed.

I started to relax, like I was on vacation.

Kevin's weird was becoming normal again.

We passed road signs for Casper, Wyoming, and I told stories about my parents' happy, childless life there in the late seventies and early eighties, when they both worked for the local newspaper. Even now, Mom would sing the old Dick Jurgens song "Oh Why, Oh Why, Did I Ever Leave Wyoming?" It was her ode to a simpler time, something akin to "Oh Why, Oh Why, Did I Have These Brats and End up in Utah?"

We stayed the night near the Utah-Wyoming border in a motel off the interstate. The one painting on the wall was of a lonely cowboy on a ranch. I told Kevin about the time I'd tried on a pair of cowboy boots in a vintage store in downtown Salt Lake and gotten stuck in them. When I get tired, I can't stop talking.

I hoped we might just drift off, but Kevin rolled me onto my stomach and started giving me a leg massage, claiming I must be sore from the car ride. I remember feeling both relief and disappointment at being so close to Utah again, having to go back to that circus. I hadn't realized how much I needed a break until it was almost over.

Kevin returned to bed after throwing out the condom and brushing his teeth to gather me in his arms, his Hanes undershirt stretched, his bright eyes resting on blue-gray bags. Picking dandruff out of my bangs, he told me he'd had a dream shortly after we'd met of a golden army. He sounded so peaceful as he described it. "You were marching at my side, Greg," he said in a low, serious whisper. "And you know what? You weren't limping, not a bit. Your legs were just really healthy and strong."

It didn't take long for Kevin to start lightly snoring. Short of breath, my heart thumping wildly and my leg rigid with nerves, I struggled into my boxers and tried not to let my right foot come crashing down as I crept outside to the Coke machine.

Mom answered on the first ring. I told her everything was fine and that I loved her. "Why are you being nice to me?" she asked. "Now I'm really worried." I was surprised at how early it still was, only ten or eleven at night. It had been a long day.

Mom held the phone to Dad's ear so I could say goodnight and then up to the dogs so I could say goodnight to them, too. I didn't have the heart to mention what else Kevin had told me about his dream: my parents had been in the golden army, too, walking arm in arm. Thick brown hair cascaded down my mom's back and my dad was unencumbered by a respirator. Kevin could cure us. All we had to do was believe.

Kevin gently shook me awake at dawn so we could get back on the road: I had to put together my section of the newspaper even though it was a national holiday. We drove straight to Park City. I thought Kevin might be standoffish after his vision the night before, but he looked refreshed. He made a bed for me in the backseat of the van and I slept most of the rest of the way home.

Picking me up after work, Kevin gave me a lingering kiss. I asked what he'd been up to and he told me he'd hung out with my family and helped give Dad a sponge bath. He said this like it was the most natural thing in the world.

My dad talked a lot about how he missed basic human contact since being hooked up to a machine, and I wondered if Kevin saw the sponge bath as his chance to lay hands on my dad and work a miracle. To him it may have been a humble romantic gesture, like making me a cake, or a straightforward medical one for the child of a locally famous physician, but I knew in my gut he had no right to touch my dad like that. It wasn't his job to set the House of Bob in order. I was tired of him trying to make my problems go away. My problems were all I had.

"I don't care if he thinks he's the Prophet. You can't break up with him," Mom told me through a mouthful of Kevin's brownies that night. "These brownies are the only thing I can eat." She was in bed with Dad and the crumb she now stuck to her thumb was among the last of her stash. Evidently, she was still pissed at me for freaking her out when I'd called from the motel in Wyoming. "Listen," she said, swallowing dryly, "if he starts going off about any of that woo-woo crap again, you just tell him your mom is from Idaho. I can smell bullshit a mile away."

"Really?" I told her, "because you're eating some right now."

Dad nodded down at his cuff so he could talk. "No, Bob. I'm not deflating you so you can agree with him," Mom said. She started to sing "Oh Why, Oh Why, Did I Ever Leave Wyoming?" I'm not sure that song has ever sounded sadder. As Mom licked her thumb, rounding the chorus, I held one of Dad's puffy, kinked fingers and told him I was sorry. I wasn't crying but my throat hurt and it was hard to get out the words.

No harm, no foul, Dad mouthed. He was just glad I was OK.

I was too chickenshit to confront Kevin about the sponge bath. I didn't know what there was to confront him about: he was the one who'd told me about it in the first place, not with shame or pride, but in a tone of offhanded care. I didn't want him rubbing my legs and explaining it all away, telling me he was only trying to help.

I stopped returning Kevin's calls and texts, but I didn't break up with him. My friends Katie and John and I were going to a bluegrass festival in Telluride that June and I didn't want to end things with Kevin and then leave my parents to fend for themselves, defenseless to the man's charms and baked goods. He must have sensed I was pulling away because I came home from work the night before the road trip to find a John Legend CD on my bed and a letter covered in beautiful handwriting, full of romantic platitudes and heartfelt one-liners. (Kevin had been teaching himself calligraphy.)

"It was obvious from the day we met we would either be a total bust or one of the great love stories," Kevin wrote. That was his life—extremes of risk and reward. "There are plenty of obstacles in our way.

The worst has to be getting your bull-shit meter past the Degeunets."
I stumbled over this sentence. I still do. Was he saying the Degeunets
were bullshit or that I needed to trust him? Who hyphenates bullshit?
The letter concluded, "Call me if I can take care of anything on the
home-front while you are gone. As I said, it's my great pleasure to be
an extra pair of hands for you, and there is literally no limit to what I
would do. Love, Kevin."

I took that neatly folded piece of paper to my dad's room down the
hall and waved it around his hospital bed like it was on fire, making a
scene so I couldn't take any of it back later on, when Kevin's fantasies
were convenient once again. Part of me had wanted to live in a world
full of ghosts and angels, a world where I might get a Fulbright and fly
off to Poland with my cleaning lady. A world where nothing was wrong
with me and I was marching confidently in a golden army. I may not
have bought everything Kevin had told me, but I had wanted to believe.

The Tuesday after I got back from Telluride, I met Kevin at a public
park, conveniently located close to home and crowded with tennis
players and kids running around. The downside was that the park
was built into the foothills of the Wasatch Mountains, with steep and
winding sidewalks. Mild of a climb as it was, and on such a pleasant
evening, we may as well have been scouting locations for Hitchcock. I
was out of breath for most of our walk, pulling myself up the cement
stairs using the handrail, not daring to look up from my feet. I didn't
think he'd push me but if he did I probably wouldn't get back up again.

Kevin was dressed more youthfully than ever before, more like me,
not in his usual paisley button-down but in a silkscreen T-shirt from
Urban Outfitters. I tried to play the dying dad card, saying that I had
to go through this awful thing alone, but Kevin protested, repeating
what he'd said in the letter. He was happy to be an extra set of hands.
There is literally no limit to what I would do.

Kevin, a majordomo to the end.

"You haven't been honest with me about a lot of things," I
blurted out.

My guess is that this wasn't the first time someone Kevin loved was questioning his credibility. His wife, his business partners in Phoenix. It was like I'd drawn the air out of him with a syringe, his jazzy new clothes and summer tan suddenly ridiculous.

We turned to head back down the steep stairs. Kevin stopped me. "Wait," he said. He produced a piece of paper from his back pocket, sheepishly cleared his throat, and began going through a list of claims he'd made, turning our relationship postmortem into a game show, like he was starring in an FPS skit. This was as strange and out of the blue as it sounds, stranger in a lot of ways than giving my dad a sponge bath. His voice went high when what he'd said was true and bottomed out when he admitted a falsehood, a kind of vocal exercise. Studied at Yale—*TRUE*! Went to culinary school—*TRUE*! Was married—*TRUE*! Bought a Prius—*FALSE*. Bought an apartment—*FALSE*. Buying those paintings—*WANT TO*.

He looked up from his cheat sheet. "Really like you," he said, the music going out of his voice. "*True.*" The word caught in his throat. Hands trembling, he fumbled the piece of paper back in his pocket. "So, can I make it up to you?" he asked softly. He took a big breath. "Do I have a shot?"

No, I told him, he did not. "Just be more honest with the next guy."

Kevin's life wasn't one of risks and rewards, as he'd claimed. It was one of decency and delusion. Hearing his earnest, melodic confession was a little like catching Elizabeth Smart's kidnapper only to have him declared incompetent to stand trial: the outcome was the same, but the sense of satisfaction was sidelong at best. Nothing about angels or prophesies? No Monsieur Degeunet? It was hard to tell if Kevin was still trying to con me. I didn't know if he would end up with paintings of aspen trees or a loft downtown, a Prius or a church of beer-guzzling followers, but I did know I wouldn't be one of them. My brain had been damaged at birth but I wasn't that dumb.

It was starting to get dark. Dragonflies were dipping into drinking fountains and dogs sprang away from the families that called them, getting in one last lap. Kevin asked if he could hug me in the parking lot and I let him hold me for a minute, let myself smell his cologne and sweat one last time, before I lifted my leg into the Lexus and drove back down the hill to the respirator and the sick parents I didn't know how I'd live without.

It was only later that I saw what a small trace Kevin had left in the three months we dated: a few photos from a walk with the fam in Liberty Park, a single email about making me a cake. Just the other day, I was sorting through a bookshelf at my condo in Austin and Kevin's calligraphy love letter fell out of *The Wizard of Oz*. A waterlogged paperback above it held my long-lost, and now expired, passport. The universe was trying to tell me something, probably that I should stop hiding stuff in books.

When we broke up, I worried Kevin might stalk me, but in reality I've been the stalker. Over the years, I've tried to google him with little success. Someone with his name is an officer in a coin collecting club in Utah. Another Kevin is a dentist on the Fort Hall Reservation in southeastern Idaho. I can picture him leaning over an open mouth with a drill, wiggling crowns and bridges, trying to fix the problems in other people's heads rather than his own. Anything is possible. Kevin's brewing beer in Hampstead or meditating under a tree in his parents' backyard next to Wasatch Jr. High. My mom says the problem with dating a bald guy is that as soon as you stop going out, you see him everywhere. That, at least, is true.

AN UNUSUAL EVENT FOR YOUR SOCIAL CALENDAR

We wrote Dad's obituary under the gazebo as a family: bickering, chewing ice, eating cold Domino's, and passing my MacBook back and forth over Dad in his electric wheelchair.

Outside the dim caverns of our house, in the backyard, it was still summer, eighty degrees and pleasant in the shade. It was hard to believe it had only been three months since I'd parted ways with Kevin. It had proven to be both a short season and half a lifetime for Dad, who was aging like a fruit fly. It felt like we all were.

The pool was sloshing with golden dog hair and fallen raspberries, the patio furniture covered in bird poop and little cottonwood pods that stuck to my socks when I limped inside to flush a gallon of Dad's warm urine down the toilet. We were way past modesty.

Dad and I talked all the time about how much longer he wanted to keep going. Initially, he had said he'd die when he could no longer talk. Later, he set a date for the first day of fall, his favorite time of year. Dad's ten months on a respirator had been as full of epochs and adventures as his beloved *Lord of the Rings* trilogy. I'd bitched during every minute of them. Now I was sad they were behind us. I'd never felt closer to my family than when we were caring for Dad and I knew it couldn't stay that way, that we wouldn't want it to.

Some of the people we'd met in Dad's ALS support group had lived for years with the disease, their symptoms progressing at a snail's pace. With their limp arms, golf shirts, and slip-ons, they looked like they might just be super laid back or retired. They talked about mowing the lawn and wending their way through the new 432-page Lou Gehrig biography, *Luckiest Man*. A guy in a wheelchair named Marty had made it so long with ALS he was going on the Atkins diet to lose weight. But Dad's case proved heartbreakingly aggressive. The Lou Gehrig we knew wasn't waving his baseball cap at the crowd at Yankee Stadium, saying how lucky he felt. He was a ghost wielding a bat, taking swing after swing at us.

Dad was tan-limbed from all our walks, and sweaty, his blue eyes clear and alert, his lips chapped like mine had been on Accutane. Lou Gehrig's disease had wasted away the muscles in his chest and shoulders, made quick work of his diaphragm, hands, arms, and legs. Only his mind was still intact. Dad's fingers were curled atop a Tommy Hilfiger pillow on his lap, as if ready to peck out a substitute ending if only given the chance.

As far as revising history went, our view of the tennis court from the gazebo wasn't all that promising. The court was a wreck without Dad's stewardship. Covered in cracks and dog poop, anthills, and boxelder bugs galore, it was more like a sundial than a tennis court, shadows keeping track of time. A dozen years had passed since Dad had broken his neck in Hawaii. Much of that time we had filled with tennis, though perhaps it's more apt to say that tennis filled the cracks where self-doubt would have resided.

It amazed me to think of us out there, a man with a broken neck going toe to toe and tendon to tendon with his son. In all that time, shambling after balls, burning holes through my right tennis shoes, I can't remember feeling disabled. I felt like an athlete. Dad did that for me. I imagined some alternate dimension where we were still playing, switching sides so I didn't have to serve into the sun, redoing second serves, strapping on jetpacks. It was a nice thought.

Dad's favorite baseball cap, from the 2007 Boston Marathon, was pulled low on his brow so he didn't have to watch the dogs dig up the lawn. It was a great hat: blaze orange with a unicorn on it. I read online that the Boston Athletic Association chose a unicorn for its mascot back in 1887 to represent the mythic and ideal, something that can be chased but never captured.

Dad was going to wear that hat, along with a running outfit, in the casket at Larkin Mortuary for the viewing. That's how he wanted to be remembered: as a runner. I imagined his corpse covered in toxic makeup and mortician's wax, his nose hairs plucked one last time, cotton balls and spirit gum sealing shut the hole in his throat.

Then he was going to be cremated, his ashes scattered over his favorite ski run in Sun Valley, the road up Millcreek Canyon, and the slippery shore of Camano Island, where he used to spend summers as a kid.

Danny scrolled through what Mom and I had come up with so far, a pretzel hanging from his mouth and a grubby fingernail circling the lip of a half-empty Corona. Did we have to say Dad was paralyzed and on a respirator, he wanted to know, why not just really go for it and say he shit in diapers, too?

"Adult briefs," I corrected.

Dad clicked his tongue and emphatically mouthed a few words, nodding down at the little balloon attached to his trach so he could say something.

"See," I said to Danny. "He likes it how it is. Euphemisms in obits are dumb. They make everything sound like a drug overdose."

"Drug overdose?" Danny said. "This is Dad's obituary, not Mom's."

"Fart off," Mom said. "He's my husband and I'll put what I want."

I didn't write obits at the *Record* but I knew enough, on this most important advance job, to spare Dad common blunders: the God talk, the misuse of semicolons, the first person. Still, disputes arose. Jokes turned spiteful. "Though he loved journalism, his true love was family, especially his son Greg, who was far and away his favorite . . . in spite of being gay."

Thanks, Danny.

Striking a more inspirational tone, Mom wrote "Marathon Man" under Dad's full name. It had a nice ring to it, but (not to be nitpicky) had anyone ever called him that? If we were going with a nickname how about just "Bob"? And did Mom's fifteen-year battle with non-Hodgkin's lymphoma really deserve prime real estate?

Mom's hair had grown in from her latest round of chemo, though she weighed ninety pounds and looked half dead herself, her scalp a patchwork of scars and slick red bald spots where Alice had stitched her back together. Mom was bundled into a gray hoodie despite the warm weather. Her fentanyl patches left her loopy and the loopier she got, the more precisely she embellished. My parents had celebrated their thirtieth wedding anniversary in July. Mom kept rounding that number up by one. "I want that extra year, damn it!" she said.

Dad rolled his eyes. *Come on Deb*, he mouthed.

And then there were the balloons. Mom claimed, in the obituary's second paragraph, that friends and neighbors had released two thousand of them upon Dad's passing. We were already writing about Dad in the past tense. He would be long gone by the time the obit ran in the *Trib* and *Deseret News*, the balloons let loose or not.

"But two thousand? That's a fuckin' shitload of balloons," Tiffany pointed out diplomatically, squinting at my dirty laptop screen from over Dad's shoulder. She looked exhausted. "Are you sure it's not going to be like two hundred?"

Reclaiming my computer, I read aloud the five hundred words it had taken to render Dad's fifty-five years on earth. Mom had written in conclusion, "Our love goes with you, Bob, as you run marathons in the sky. You will be missed, but never forgotten. Remember to never, never, never give up."

"Dad's an atheist, though," I said after a second. "He's not going to be running anywhere."

After the whole Kevin snafu, I'd tamped down my spiritual side.

Mom and Dad locked eyes and Dad mouthed something only Mom understood for sure. She stood, stretched, and planted a kiss on Dad's dry mouth, hugging just his head as she cried. She must have jostled Dad's tubes because the alarm on his respirator went crazy, as usual.

Lately Dad had started saying, "Energy can't be created or destroyed." He'd also started saying, "When in doubt, err on the side of death," so take your pick: believer or nihilist. Either way, Dad would be unplugging in two days, ending the heroic measures that were keeping him alive. In the email blast that had gone out to his friends, Dad, in his best impression of Herman Munster, described the unplugging as "an unusual event for your social calendar."

Of all the visitors who turned up at the house the next morning, Dad's ski buddies were the worst, jangling car keys, picking dog hair off their fleeces, never knowing how to say goodbye. The Day Before the Day Of, we called it, like one of those incoherent end-of-the-world movies. The guys stroked their beards and elongated their pinched faces. "Some midlife crisis you're having there, Bob." If they weren't whisked out of the stuffy room they would become as choked up as Dad. I love how men cry, even hippie skiers, like they have something in their eyes. Better to help them along. "OK, well, he has to take a dump so see you at the viewing."

I rubbed his back as he sat on the commode and blasted Dolly Parton's version of "I Will Always Love You." Kevin had been good for a couple CDs at least.

I'm not sure how much Dad slept that night, but in the morning when he opened his eyes we were all standing over him like creeps, rubbing his arms and feet and softly saying, "Hey." Mom kept trying to feed me Klonopin to calm me down. I told her to fuck off. I didn't want to be as messed up as she'd been for the past year. Her survival had turned into a sad irony. "The wrong parent is dying," I told Dad loudly, as payback for Mom's attempt to drug me.

A wet-haired hospice nurse named Sunny came over around one and started an IV in Dad's stomach, or maybe the morphine drip was through his G-tube. It was hard to tell. "You probably feel like killing yourselves right about now," Sunny sympathized.

It wasn't like unplugging a lamp. It took a couple hours for the bag of morphine to trickle into Dad's system, so we loaded the drugs into a black backpack and piled him into the elevator for one last stroll around the neighborhood. We didn't bother putting sunscreen on him. Danny said it was good to die a little burned. We kept joking that Sunny had given Dad a placebo. He'd wake up and still have Lou Gehrig's, still be stuck with us. Dad tried to smile but his expression came out as a sneer. He kept saying he couldn't feel anything.

"Quit bragging," Danny told him, flicking Dad's hat. It was one of his running hats, a 26.2 patch sewn above the bill to represent the length of a marathon.

We were in the homestretch of our own grueling marathon, the final point-two. It wasn't long before we were back upstairs, lugging chairs from the kitchen, like we were putting on a play. Mom and the little girls climbed into bed with Dad. His eyelids were getting heavy. Dr. Bromberg waited in the back of the room, ready to ease Dad off the respirator after he lost consciousness. "If there is an afterlife, you better fucking contact me," I told Dad, pushing up the brim of his damp cap so I could put a hand on his forehead.

At the last minute, he told us to switch his hats, from 26.2 to Boston Marathon: he wanted to go out wearing that orange unicorn, not just have it on in the casket. After some commotion, the hat was found on the knob of the closet and passed from hand to hand until it made its way onto his head. He looked boyish and sweet in that baseball cap, like he was just drifting off for an afternoon nap, preparing to run marathons in the sky.

There was time for a last round of family photos. I handed my camera to my godfather Gary and huddled around Dad's hospital bed with my brother and sisters and mom, tugging sadly on the rim of Dad's ear to make it stick out for posterity. His eyes only half open, Dad drowsily mouthed what I took to be *bye, Greggo,* but he could have been saying anything. He could have been saying *Quit pulling my ear.* After a few somber pictures, Danny tossed a Kleenex over Dad's eyes and we all laughed, relieved, as Dad's fake smile became a real one, the first I'd seen all day. The Kleenex sat on his big nose, not fluttering, until Tiffany plucked it away. And just like that, there was Dad blinking up at us again, wearing an expression that looked a lot like wonder. *Not yet.*

Robert Wendell Marshall
"Marathon Man"
(1952–2008)

Robert Wendell Marshall passed away Monday afternoon at his home in Holladay surrounded by friends and family. He died after a two-year struggle with Lou Gehrig's Disease that left him paralyzed and on a respirator. He was 55.

Friends and neighbors released 2,000 balloons at his passing.

They remember Bob as a father, husband, newspaper publisher, and marathoner who put those he loved above all else.

He is survived by five children: Tiffany, 27, Danny, 26, Greg, 23, Michelle, 18, Mona, 17, and wife, Debi, to whom he was married for 30 years.

They were a closely-knit family who spent their happiest times traveling to favorite spots in Europe and Hawaii.

His parents Wendell P. and Barbara J. Marshall of Pocatello, Idaho, precede him in death.

Bob graced the lives of those he knew with compassion, strength, and giving. He coached his kids' little-league softball and basketball teams, took his kids to Utah Jazz games, volunteered at their schools and cared for his wife, who has battled non-Hodgkin's Lymphoma for 15 years.

He owned eight community newspapers and business journals in Utah, Idaho, and the Pacific Northwest.

He was publisher of the *Pekin Daily Times* in Illinois and president of the Kiwanis Club and Chamber of Commerce there.

Though he loved journalism, his true love was family. He also excelled at downhill skiing and running.

He began running marathons five years ago at the age of 50 and completed the Salt Lake and St. George Marathons twice, and the Chicago Marathon.

Four days after completing the Chicago Marathon in October 2006, he was diagnosed with Lou Gehrig's Disease, also known as ALS, a degenerative neurological disorder.

In spite of the devastating news, Bob completed the Boston Marathon that April with his running buddies. He was featured on the *CBS Evening News with Katie Couric* as well as local telecasts and newspapers for this feat.

He will be remembered for his grace, dignity, and determination.

Our love goes with you, Bob, as you run marathons in the sky. You will be missed, but never forgotten. Remember to never, never, never give up.

APRÈS BOB

In the muddle after Dad died, my French photo albums went missing. I only had my own negligence to blame and was lucky, days later, to unearth a few strips of negatives in my dresser.

The weird thing about the unprinted negatives was that they didn't tell the sad-sack story I thought I remembered from the summer before ninth grade, when I was fourteen, but one of a boy in a yellow shirt lighting votive candles and trying on hats in gift shops. It was jarring seeing my dad upright and alive in the frames, making goofy faces in front of man-made lakes, his blue backpack flung over one shoulder, hair just starting to thin.

Pathetic, really, that it took my dad dying to see that we weren't in a popularity contest. I'd spent the entire France trip worrying Bob was too good for me, that he would leave me in favor of Arnaud, Gene, and Ewg: a French teacher, a bus driver, and a tour guide. What I didn't understand was that he was doing it all for me. He had no crushing desire to tour France on a bus; he just wanted to give his nerdy gay son an adventure, and maybe have one of his own.

Dad accompanying me to France had never been just a matter of me not having a sense of direction or being slow to put on my shoes, either. There was no way Mom was letting her disabled teenage son traipse around France without some backup. Dad had climbed battlements and beaches with me, held out his hand like a valet to make sure I got down the narrow steps of Mont Saint-Michel and off the bus at Versailles. After he'd sabotaged my artsy picture of barbed wire and ocean at Normandy, he'd helped me out of the foxhole.

It was nothing we ever talked about, nothing that had to be said, but if I got tired of standing on a tour, I'd lace my fingers together and hang off his shoulder, hips jutting. If the metro was full, Dad found me a seat. If Nazis were afoot, Dad told me to hang tight.

On every steep and slick surface, during every death march, the Neckless Wonder had been there, staying back just enough I never quite realized he'd catch me if I fell.

One of the surviving negatives from our trip, which I remember labeling *Boob et Gregoire* in the album, pictures Dad and me in front of the Eiffel Tower. I'm sure I'll have the negatives printed again, though I have to admit there's something satisfying about squinting at this root-beer-colored square of film, studying it like an insect's wing. Dad and I are in ponchos, hands on each other's shoulders. Despite my dishwater hair and fuzzy eyebrows, I really do look like his son. He may be broad and handsome whereas I am squirrelly and acne-riddled, but we're clearly related. Paris drizzles behind us. You can just make out the clock on the Eiffel Tower counting down the millennium, but the smiles on our faces, those are too small to see.

MORE HAM

My older siblings and I gave speeches at Dad's funeral. Mona's eulogy took the form of an interpretive dance. She sat next to her ballet teacher in the pews, dashing to the back of the church when it was time for her costume change, and returned in a white dress with an artfully shredded skirt and a white leotard, like a contestant on her favorite TV show, *So You Think You Can Dance*.

The thing is, Mona really *can* dance.

Danny, my uncle Eric, and a cousin moved a table full of flowers aside on the altar and the first piano chords of a muffled indie pop ballad came on. Pastor Erin, the solemn and berobed minister of the United Church of Christ, sat as neutral as onlooking royalty at the back of the altar. Mona wouldn't stop referring to this mild woman of the cloth as a slut for believing in a higher power that clearly didn't exist.

On the makeshift stage, Mona didn't look that different from any other girl of seventeen, tumbling and kicking her long legs. She had compressed the choreography from one of her competition solos for this smaller performance space, her movements shy yet explosive, the powerful pre-flight practice flaps of a pelican. I worried not that Mona might stop but that she might soar, Kung Fu–style, an errant heel or taloned toe striking Pastor Erin in some soft, holy part. My little sister grieved wordlessly and with her whole body, or else not at all.

I'd seen her cry exactly once during Dad's two-year battle with ALS, when Dr. Bromberg unplugged the respirator. I suspect she may only have cried then because the rest of us were. More likely than not, Mona was mimicking emotion as much as feeling it, but it was her off-the-wall humor and sweetness that had helped see us through, the way she laughed hysterically at my brother's fart jokes or being shit on by a bird during a family walk, the way she danced around my dad's life-support equipment like it was nothing. Sometimes I wanted to shake her. Other times, hug her.

Mona's straightened brown hair swung and splashed around the smile she'd been trained to keep frozen on her face while performing, even at her own dad's funeral. She could roll her ankle doing a relevé and her lips wouldn't budge.

The music stopped and Mona sprang up from the floor, head down, hair covering her face as she slouched to the altar steps and back into the pews, no chest-heaving pose held for applause or bow to distract from the divine hush. It was just like Mom to let Mona turn Dad's glum send-off into a high school talent show, for that somehow to feel right. Seeing Mona dance, I cried along with everyone else. I didn't know what we were going to do with her.

Moe was fifteen, in eighth grade, when Dad received his death sentence. Before his illness, my little sister had lived a largely normal life. She repeated kindergarten on account of being such a pale, frail, premature squirt, but with a helicopter mom to micromanage her she more than squeaked by in school, enjoying a handful of carefully overseen friendships, crushes, and hairstyles. I'm partially to blame for Moe's introduction to dance. Her first go at what can loosely be defined as "choreography" came from Up With Kids. But, to my relief, Moe proved to be too shy for singing and acting. What she loved was movement.

If you'd stuck your head in her classroom in elementary school, you would have seen a lovable geek who was usually dancing next to her desk rather than sitting in it. It got to the point where she didn't talk about anything *but* dance, usually an inch from my face as spit bubbles gathered at the corners of her mouth.

Dad was the only one of us who could get her to change the subject or stop moving, and that was by telling her he had danced for the New York City Ballet. I'm not sure how this father–daughter gag started—Moe doubtful but not entirely disbelieving, my Dad playfully insistent, bending his knees, circling his arms above him—only that they revisited it every time they talked to each other for years, both with ludicrous grins on their faces. The rest of us didn't find it all that funny. We were danced out.

The illusion that everything was totally fine with Moe started slipping like the glasses down her nose once Lou Gehrig ascended from hell to assume center stage. Without Mom to do her hair and dress her every morning and Dad to check her math homework and cut her food for her at dinner, Moe was like an eight-year-old who'd gone to sleep and woken up a full-fledged teenager, the victim of a body swap she couldn't undo. When a child of eight eats with her hands and sleeps in her parents' bed, it's no biggie. When a fifteen-year-old does it, eyebrows shoot up. If we were at a restaurant, Moe would turn to one of us to order for her. Her voice went phlegmy and soft when she attempted to talk to strangers, and her body awareness wasn't great for a maturing young woman. "Do you not see that half your pubes are hanging out of your swimsuit?" Mom would ask as Moe sprawled out next to the crowded pool at the club.

Kids at school met Moe's enthusiasm for dance and the color pink, her bumbling, in-your-face social style, with *doy*s. They bullied her badly enough that by the time she hit tenth grade, and the end of Dad's life, she'd become mousy outside of the house. Except onstage. Dance gave her a routine and a set of social cues she couldn't mess up. Ballet, modern, tap, hip-hop—Moe took all kinds of classes. All the better if they were across town from each other and Tiffany or I had to drive her, both of us threatening to dry-heave if she didn't get her dirty feet off the dashboard.

Moe took the slogans on her dance gear literally: BLOOD, SWEAT, DANCE; DANCE IS LIFE. THE REST IS JUST DETAILS. Far from a disaster, my sister had the chorus girl's fatal flaw of being more interesting to watch than anyone around her, a showy mix of freak talents and accidentally outré reinterpretations that left fallen scenery and disheveled costumes in her wake. In ensembles that accommodated kids of many shapes, sizes, and freckle patterns, Moe had a better ballet bod than most, her features delicate to the point of underdeveloped until she curled her lips, thrust her chin forward, and showed the world her big ole teeth.

If her teachers ever thought to put her up front and let her lead the charge, they'd have turned a distraction into a showstopper. They never did.

In practical terms, Moe's love of dance meant one thing: *The Nutcracker*.

For those lucky enough to have been spared this acid trip of a ballet, or to have repressed the memory from childhood, it's basically the board game Candy Land set to department store music and turned into a multi-hour Christmas recital.

The story follows a girl named Clara whose toy Nutcracker comes to life on Christmas Eve and whisks her off to the land of sugar plums and snow.

If you haven't seen *The Nutcracker*, you've probably heard it. Tchaikovsky's confectionary suite is hard to avoid any day between Halloween and the new year. Choreographer George Balanchine is famous for bringing audiences the most beloved adaptation of the ballet. Since it premiered in 1954, his masterpiece has been endlessly repackaged to fit any budget, cast, or climate. Such is its genius. I once visited Key West for Thanksgiving and met a woman who was staging a *Nutcracker* in which the leading man wore a conch shell and did battle not with the Mouse King but with an enormous rooster.

The roles Moe nabbed in a local ballet studio's version of *The Nutcracker* every year were never that imaginative. She played every off-brand part, every part that wasn't Clara or the Sugar Plum Fairy: a Rag Doll, a Poinsettia, an Icicle, an Elf.

I remember one year she auditioned for *The Nutcracker* at Ballet West, a storied professional dance company in downtown Salt Lake, and made the first Party Girl cut but not the second. She came home in tears that turned to honking laughter when she told us how an instructor, a local dance legend in her eighties, had done a cartwheel into the splits for the nervous auditionees. "That's one way to pass the time," my dad said. "I cartwheeled into the splits at least twice a day when I danced for the New York City Ballet."

"I'm going to cartwheel into the splits *three* times a day when I dance for the New York City Ballet," Moe replied, and burst out laughing.

No amount of discouragement or sabotage persuaded Moe to sit it out. If Moe's icicle costume went missing, Mom would rip the plastic fruit off a Marzipan's tutu and push her on stage. If the costume lady forgot Moe's toy soldier outfit, as happened not once but twice in a single season, my mom would strip out of her black turtleneck and velour tracksuit in the quick-change area backstage and pull Mona into them. "Go dance your little *perdi* off!" she'd say, issuing a swat to Moe's rear.

That first Christmas without Dad, Moe's dance teacher, the same lady who had sat with her in the pews at the funeral, cast Moe as a pig in her production of *The Nutcracker* and tried to cut her from the show entirely for missing too many rehearsals.

Moe hadn't wanted to miss the rehearsals, of course. We'd had to ground her from dance the week of Dad's death. It was a punishment she accepted only because she was too scared to drive herself. Mom stopped by the studio and chewed the dance teacher a new asshole as Moe and I sang carols in the car. Wonder of wonders, Moe's role wasn't cut after all. Mom had saved at least one Christmas pig from slaughter. As was so often the case in our family, pain turned into amusement, a funny story: Moe played a pig. She had a part outside the pig pen, too, this one in Clara's living room after the Christmas Eve party in Act One.

The dance was cute and, for once, Moe wasn't stashed in the back corner, leaping nearly offstage. The tallest kid up there by a foot, my sister wasn't hard to spot. Moe, an old-for-her-grade sophomore in high school, was in a number surrounded by first and second graders.

Three months after Dad's death—what felt like three years—had left me impatient to move on with my life. It didn't help that Moe occasionally reverted to her toddler self, when we'd called her Monster Moe. Like every other human being, her existence was more than quirky asides. There was a bratty slant to her behavior. Without Dad around, Moe was acting out a lot more, lamenting his loss however she could, rebelling by getting weirder. As long as she could stick to her routine of school and dance, she was a blast to be around. But any deviation could lead to a tailspin. If she wasn't feeling well and had to go to the doctor, you could expect a days-long tantrum that could turn violent—biting, kicking, screaming—most of it in Mom's direction. If she opened a Christmas card and had to touch money, a phobia of hers, she'd shriek and run upstairs for a shower.

During this rocky time, there was no bigger deviation from how things used to be than my mom becoming romantically involved with Alice. In the wake of Dad's death, Mom mailed her former surgeon a suicide note. A purple-haired angel wearing a Human Rights Campaign baseball cap and a fanny pack, Alice didn't show up so much as she materialized one weekend and held Mom, sobbing and shivering in bed, for three days. On the fourth day, Alice somewhat ruefully admitted she'd had a wet dream. Despite raising two boys and having been married to a man for thirty years, Mom claimed not to know what a wet dream was.

This is where I usually stop her retelling of the story.

"Mom," I say. "You know what a wet dream is."

"I do now," Mom says back.

Alice lived and worked in Delaware but after Mom's cry for help she started making frequent trips to Salt Lake. One long weekend led to another, and soon the two were spending a lot of time together. I'd poke my head into my mom's room and there would be Alice in bed, playing movies on her laptop, my mom asleep with a pillow over her head. It was like they were already married.

Tiffany, Danny, and Michelle had all moved out by then. Because Moe and I were the only kids left at home, we were around to witness the intimacy and urgency of Mom and Alice's unlikely reconnection. I was relieved Mom wanted to keep living, relieved that if I found her collapsed on the floor of her bathroom, yogurt dribbling from her mouth and two fentanyl patches slapped onto her back, I'd have someone to call.

It went deeper, though. Mom had always said the only reason she kept battling cancer was to be there for us five kids. It gave me a pleasing jolt to think of her enjoying an identity outside of motherhood, an identity that had nothing to do with us.

I don't think I ever saw them kiss in those days, but Alice would come downstairs and make Moe and me enormous postcoital breakfasts of scrambled eggs with chorizo, ham, and cheddar cheese, wearing a silly grin that said, "I just fucked your mom."

Mom would wander out of her bedroom in the late morning, hair standing at attention around the red, silver-dollar bald spot on her scalp she'd acquired from skin cancer, a robe wrapped tightly around her. Her grin said, "It's true, I just got fucked."

"They slept naked," Moe would report to me, poking my side, a wicked smile spread across her face. "I went in there to get a hairbrush and they were *naked*."

I'd outgrown the hopeful notion that everyone was secretly gay, but I couldn't resist dreaming of a utopian world in which I was not the only gay person in my family, a world in which I could grill Danny with belittling questions at family dinners. "I know you say you're *attracted* to women but don't you find men beautiful? Are you telling me that if a gorgeous guy walked in here right now you wouldn't let him fuck you?"

Unfortunately, Moe saw Alice's arrival on the scene not as a sapphic deus ex machina but as a threat. This wasn't *Touched by an Angel*. It was *Touched by a Lesbian*. Alice wasn't saving my mom's life; she was taking Mom away from us.

Moe developed a new obsession: hating Alice. She found Alice revolting, disgusting, a total bitch, an asshole, an animal, a pig. "She's a lesbian!" Moe would moan, half smiling and half totally serious, trying to get under our mom's skin. "It's disgusting. She's trying to turn Mom into a lesbian."

"But Mona, I'm gay," I'd tell her. "It's the same thing."

"Two guys is fine but two girls is disgusting."

"I keep telling you shitheads I'm not a lesbian," Mom would say. "Alice doesn't think I am either. I fell in love with the person. I could never meet another guy as great as your dad."

When Alice visited Utah, she would sleep on my dad's side of the bed, which was nearest to the door in case there was a break-in—protecting her not from a rapist but from Moe, who could usually be seen outside Mom's bedroom door on her back. At first, you'd think she was stretching, maybe pretending to do the backstroke. Only when you got closer would you register that she was trying to kick down the door with her powerful dancer's legs.

"What? Alice is a bitch," Moe would say. "They're having sex. It's gross."

It would always seem like Moe was about to laugh, like this acting out was an elaborate ruse. I imagined her jumping up from the floor, becoming a completely different person. "I'm messing with you, dude," she'd say. "I'm just happy Mom is alive and not slowly committing suicide with opioids in patch form. And if she's gay now, a few months after Dad's tragic death? Great. He would want her to find peace and companionship."

It never happened.

Mom's door had a splinter running down the middle from Moe trying to beat it down.

What Moe needed was a father figure. Sadly, I made a terrible one. Rather than finding serenity in my dad's example, I felt less sure of my own future than ever. I was twenty-four and still working at the *Park Record*. When Dad was my age, he was just four years away from what would turn out to be the midway point of his foreshortened life, and he didn't waste it driving his little sister to dance and sitting through the wretched *Nutcracker*.

Living in an infuriatingly outdoorsy state, where the predominant idea of fun is hiking from one yurt to another, wakeboarding or rock climbing or riding your bike a hundred miles to work, I felt stranded and sheltered in ways I hadn't when Dad was around. I didn't trust myself to tackle the great outdoors in his absence and sensed a growing distance from my treasured high school chums who worked in ski shops and hip restaurants and didn't have dead dads. It was like mine had taken the fresh air and sunshine with him. I was burned out from being a caregiver and worried, as the dutiful gay son, that I'd be the one stuck caring for Mom and Moe in our increasingly cave-like house. For as much as I loved them, I didn't want to be their stooge and errand boy.

Greedy for the world, sure it was passing me by, I was exasperated by Moe's reliance on dance. Instead of seeing how the classes and rehearsals kept Moe strong and stable, how her hunched posture turned regal onstage and she really didn't stop smiling, I recalled my own breakup with acting, the time as a teenager when the costumes and makeup of the stage, the corny showtunes and stiffly delivered lines had come to seem childish to me, a kind of trap for a kid with a limp. I kept expecting Moe to outgrow dance, to have her munchkin moment.

The irony of this smacks me square in the forehead now, like a cherry launched from a spoon. I wanted out of Little Girl Land at the very moment my sister needed it the most. Every show, it was the same guilt trip. "You have to come see Moe dance," Mom would beg. "She has no one else. We're it."

"Did you ask your other three children who also live in Utah if they'll be attending?"

"They have their own lives," Mom said.

"I have my own life!" I protested.

"I know, sweetie. Look, do you need me to spell it out for you? Your brother's probably drunk in his loft, Mitch just had a baby, and I'm too scared of Tiffany to ask her to do anything for me right now."

"Because she'll tell you to sober up?"

"Just get in the fucking car."

So there I sat on a December night in a theater in downtown Salt Lake as my gangly seventeen-year-old sister invaded Clara's living room with a bunch of mice-children ten-plus years her junior. In that moment, it would have been more pleasant to recall Dad getting wheeled through our own living room on a mortician's stretcher than face the reality before me: Moe had more than a little catching up to do. There was a difference between being a little mousy and being a mouse.

The stage was going blurry. I held my breath.

"Are you crying?" Mom asked. The flowers she had heaped on her lap to give Moe after the show rustled in their cellophane. I wiped my eyes and let out a sob. A lady a row up turned to shush us. Without adjusting her volume, Mom said, "Are you crying because Moe is doing such a great job and it's remarkable to see her dance?" She didn't have to revise her hypothesis aloud. *Are you crying because Moe is a teenager and she's rolling around the stage with seven-year-olds?*

"She's an honors student," I gasped. "Why is she up there with little kids?"

Around the time my dad had been diagnosed with ALS, an aunt of ours had floated the possibility that Moe had Asperger's syndrome. It was the first any of us had heard of it. All the language that's so commonplace now about the autism spectrum and neurodiversity was completely foreign to us in the late 2000s. We didn't know there was a spectrum and "autistic" brought to mind Dustin Hoffman in *Rain Man*. And there was this: in all her doctor visits, Moe had never been diagnosed with anything of the sort.

In a house where the rain clouds of cancer—and then ALS— never lifted, my parents weren't exactly forthright about my own diagnosis, treating innocent inquiries about my leg like they were so explosive they could blow up in all our faces and eradicate my sense of self. Trips to Dr. Stevens never provided much clarity, the appointments brief and filled with paperwork, more about symptoms and treatment than underlining causes and always, always Mom lurking.

Following the same script they'd used for my tight tendons, my parents deflected attention from Moe's difference. She was just premature, immature, a little delayed. It was like pulling a string on a doll, Mom chirping out the well-worn yet vivid catchphrases we'd grown up hearing about Moe's rocky start. *Three-and-a-half months early*, she'd say. *Weighed less than a can of Campbell's Soup*, she'd say. *The size of a Barbie but blue. Brain hemorrhages. Dead intestines. Ruptured appendix. Hearing loss. One functioning kidney.*

All of it was true. I'd witnessed it as a terrified six-year-old hoisted up to hospital glass. What I hadn't seen was how much these words obscured, how they explained almost nothing about the essential Moeness of Moe.

During the ALS years, our cranky non-Mormon neighbor, Ralph, admitted to being bewildered that Moe was not in special ed. Watching her clap and high kick next to Dad's respirator, he remarked, "You're telling me that kid is in normal school?"

"Straight A's," I said, pissed at his rudeness. I'd tried to think of age as just a number for Moe, to not compare her to other kids. That was until I saw her doing forward rolls and giving her all with baby mice in *The Nutcracker*.

Post Dad-Just-Died *Nutcracker*, I tried to talk to my mom and Moe about seeking help. We'd ignored her needs for long enough. It bugged me that my little sister felt the need to slick her hair into a headache-inducing bun, wear contacts, and let Mom beat her face with a powder puff backstage to do what she loved. It had taken me years to talk about my tight tendons without despairing. I didn't want Moe to follow in my plodding footsteps. I wanted her to meet with a counselor and an occupational therapist. We could buy Moe Pee-wee Herman–size forks and grippers for her keys, get her a pair of super cool nerd glasses, not to mention the accommodations she deserved, like extra time on the ACT and the AP exams she'd take at the end of her junior year.

"If nothing else, being disabled will make for a killer college essay," I tried.

Why I chose to undertake this conversation in the car in a crowded mall parking lot in December I can't remember. Moe got a mad glint in her eyes and I knew we were headed for trouble. "Fuck you, Greg, you have social anxiety," she said, her voice full of hurt. "You need therapy." It was the meanest thing she could think to say, and accurate.

After trying to channel my mellow Dad, I got frustrated and started channeling myself: a bitter, exhausted older brother. I was tired of Moe beating Mom up, hearing screams and sobs anytime I walked through the door. "We just need to find out what the fuck is wrong with you, Moe, and deal with it," I snapped. "You're not a little girl anymore."

I was coming to see Moe's journey with disability as a mirror image of my own, the same but backwards. I had long searched for words to make my mind and body make sense to me, even if they turned out to not be altogether accurate: hemiplegia, hemiparesis. I wanted to know everything about my leg. I thought saying Asperger's or "on the spectrum" would be a good first step for my sister, a way to give Moe an easy, albeit incomplete, answer if people asked what was up.

There were also safety concerns. Moe had been doing jumping jacks in the kitchen at three that morning, nearly burning down the house while making fudge. Mom countered that I'd only noticed the jumping jacks because I was smoking pot with my friends in the basement directly beneath the kitchen. She was right. Every jumping jack had sounded like a battering ram to our paranoid ears.

"I don't need to hear about how Moe must feel trapped in her body, Greg," Mom said. "We don't need you to fix us. We just need you to love us." To Mom, "diagnosis" was just another kind of label she didn't want to smack on her kids. Moe was better off without one.

I can see now that these battles with Mom over Moe's well-being were proxy wars for control of my own body and the ways, out of denial, love, and magical thinking, Mom and Dad had worked to impede my understanding of it. After all, what I was just coming to realize about my sister, Mom had been grappling with for years. I was late to a party I didn't want to attend.

Making matters more insulting, Mom had developed the annoying habit of framing Moe's life as the inspirational sequel to mine, the same basic story retread for a new era.

"If you ever doubt yourself, just look at Greg," Mom would say. "He wasn't even supposed to walk and now look at him. Just look!"

Moe's life was a sequel to mine in another way. In the defiant stance Mom took toward what was wrong with Moe, in her willingness to rewrite medical history and bank on clichés and the power of belief to carry us through, I not only heard echoes of how my family had

downplayed my tight tendons. I also finally got how doing so had been
as much for their benefit as for my own. It was easier to not reckon with
our troubling bodies, to just try to make us pass. Pointing this out made
me feel both like a protective big brother and a complete douchebag.
The more I tried to intervene on Moe's behalf, the more Mom tried to
frame it as the ultimate betrayal. "That girl used to worship you," Mom
would tell me. "But you broke her heart."

After my failed intervention in the mall parking lot, I was too ashamed to
try to level with Moe as an adult anymore. I resolved to stop trying to be
a crummy stand-in for Dad and decided to start sarcastically egging Moe
on. *Decided* is probably too strong a word. With Dad gone, I regressed
to what I'd always done at home: voices. The one I used to address Moe
was part former child star of *Barney* and part Gail, my old boss at Don't
Amend. It bubbled out of me like cheap champagne. I responded to Moe's
obsessive dance talk by giving it right back to her, not with acrimony or
anger but with over-the-top enthusiasm, razzing her in a keyed-up, sibilant
Utah-drama-coach of a voice that made us both laugh in spite of ourselves.
     The thing is, I knew where she was coming from. I may have packed
it in early to avoid a spotlight on my leg, but there was still an Up With
Kids cast member doing jazz hands inside me. The trick with Moe was
not to bury my inner theater kid but to free him.
     Say Moe shattered a glass on the kitchen floor and leapt right over
it. Instead of yelling at her in my mean big brother voice, I'd squeal in
a relentlessly chipper falsetto that she was doing absolutely *awesome
awesome AWESOME* leaping and holding her leg over her head, but
if she could unwrap her tongue from her front teeth and sweep the
dangerous pool of shards she'd created into a dustpan that would be
super-duper, baby cakes!
     It was either camp it up or slap her across the face.
     Your average high schooler would be horrified at her gay brother
offering bromides about shooting for the stars, saying she was awesome,
calling her a big *dill*. Moe loved it. I did too, this special shared language.
It meant: I see you. It meant: let's not take this all too seriously.

Once I laid off Moe, a wonderful thing happened. We became each other's biggest fans. We couldn't walk by one another in the kitchen without bursting into song or attempting a round of "Down by the Banks of the Hanky Panky." Our interactions turned into dance routines and clapping choirs. Moe didn't want me to fix her. She just wanted me to perform with her.

Asperger's or not, I had to respect Moe's determination to be a great ballerina: she anticipated going on pointe the way most teenagers anticipated getting fake IDs. She dreamed of the *barre* the way I dreamed of better gay bars in Salt Lake (or any gay bars). Moe became her own taskmaster, shouting incoherent French phrases in the kitchen. "Posse into relevé!" you'd hear her cry as she slapped her tiny, scarred abs with an eight count. Moe may have had some of her intestines taken out at birth but the girl had guts. She even danced when she watched TV, spinning her glitter-speckled finger to show the rest of her body what to do. "Come on, Mona, focus," she'd say. "Get your ass in gear."

I figured we were off the hook *Nutcracker*-wise once Moe was in college at the University of Utah, living in the honors dorm. She had auditioned to be a dance major—first in ballet and then in modern—and been rejected from both programs. She settled on studying psychology and spent her days volunteering in labs and participating in experiments. Too old for most children's dance studios in town, Moe found a Chilean *danseur* who specialized in late bloomers and old maids, aka any unattached young woman over the age of nineteen in Mormon country. His name was Cristóbal but everyone in Utah said it like a first and last name, *Chris Stobel*.

My mom bought Moe a used Subaru—if she wanted to go to dance, she'd have to start driving herself. Moe put the dents and speeding tickets I'd racked up to shame. A cop once pulled her over for driving without her headlights on *at night*. Moe couldn't figure out how to roll down her window so she went ahead and opened the driver's side door to talk to him. The officer shined a light in her face and asked if she had come from a party. Had she been drinking or smoking *reefer*? Did she know what reefer was?

Moe's eyes were red from wearing gunky contacts all day, though she was in tights and a leotard, so she had a plausible case to make for the truth. The officer breathalyzed her and made her stand on one foot, walk a straight line, touch her nose. Moe passed every part of the sobriety test like it was a dance she'd done a million times. The officer asked, with new worry in his voice, if she was all right in the head. Who knows what she told him, but the cop showed her how to turn on her headlights and let her off with a warning. Then he followed her all the way to her dorm. "That fucker!" she told me later, a smile on her face. "Why was he following me?"

Danny and I, dickhead brothers that we were, called Moe Mrs. Magoo for her misadventures behind the wheel. Moe was always wandering cheerfully into trouble, the lenses of her glasses badly smudged, and finding her way out of it. It was like if you took a brainy psych major and gave her a weed brownie every day of her life. "Just think of her as being too high to function right now," my high school friend Iris advised, passing me a bowl in the backyard. "Sort of like you are."

Cristóbal's *Nutcracker* was entertaining because his boyfriend, a local drag queen, played Mother Ginger. Meanwhile, Cristóbal partnered with the Snow Queen for one of the ballet's climactic numbers. He'd cram his shapely, middle-aged body into white tights and squash his sizable manhood under a dance belt the ruffled texture of a greasy paper plate.

"See, that's why I quit acting," I'd stage-whisper to Mom.

"Because of your giant balls?" Mom stage-whispered back.

One of Moe's arms didn't extend all the way, so she often performed in elbow-length gloves and regularly carried a prop—a flute, a fan, a mask on a stick, a rifle—or stuck both hands into a muff. I'd sit in the dark of the theater, the fattest, gayest novel I could find on my lap, and imagine Moe a very old woman, her ballet bun gone silver, that breast-hiding slouch from her teens now the result of aging. She'd hop around the stage from one knee replacement to the other playing a stale piece of marzipan. At ninety, she'd still be working on her turnout. I could picture the newspaper headline, too: HOW MY LITTLE SISTER OVERCAME OSTEOPOROSIS TO TUMBLE OUT OF MOTHER GINGER'S DRESS FOR THE MILLIONTH TIME.

In spite of the terrific brother–sister act we'd developed at home, my conflicted feelings about Moe's addiction to dance only grew stronger. I didn't want my extraordinary sister to spend her life surrounded by bitches, smelling like feet, lost in another, prettier girl's dream, the screwball comedian in the background. I wanted her to sneak out the backstage door and go smoke a cigarette with the lady who was always losing her costumes. It's one thing to stick around year after year when you're the star. The prima ballerina. It's another, I figured, if you were Moe. If you were Moe, you did it for the joy. That's the part that concerned me. *Dance like no one is watching,* read one of the stenciled canvases in her room. Moe really did. The way I saw it, people like my sister and me had one major role in life: to make sure no one *was* watching. Our job was to disappear.

One of my many blind spots as an older brother was my inability to see Moe's progress as a ballerina. Somewhere in all this, she was becoming a fine dancer. Cristóbal took a real interest in my sister and trained her so well she started auditioning for summer dance intensives. Her dance bag was always soaked because she couldn't screw the cap on a bottle of water. She also struggled with putting a lid on the superglue she used to reinforce her pointe shoes and fused them to the floor during one audition. But once she got going Moe moved with precision and tenacity.

She kept auditioning for these dance intensives, and she kept getting into them. Mom and Moe would spend summers in Boise, Boston, and Orlando. Mom would move Moe into the dorms and check into a nearby hotel, on hand to help with hair and makeup.

I held down my newspaper job for a year after my dad died, and then bounced from Los Angeles to Austin to get an MFA. I kept writing.

Moe moved home from her dorm and kept dancing. I still fielded my mom's upset phone calls reporting Moe's rages like minor earthquakes, but advising was easier from afar, now that I wasn't in the middle of them myself.

Our big family house in Holladay was lonely, and a lot to manage, with just Mom and Moe living there. As if determined to disprove Moe's disses, Alice would fly in on weekends and get to work using her surgeon's brain to pack up parts of the house or drive my mom all over the valley trying to track down replacement pointe shoes.

"Alice is pretty nice for being a bitch, isn't she, Moe?" we'd tease.

Never underestimate a lesbian. One is probably doing something nice for you right now. But even a lesbian put to work all weekend couldn't replace the full-time handyman Dad had been. My brother called our house a museum of the nineties, cluttered with fat TVs and dusty remnants of an old life. A menagerie was more like it, once the dog shit started piling up from the two rambunctious golden retrievers that only got walked when I was in town. Mom also had an ancient "chemo kitty," Brighton, so named for her tendency to curl up on Mom's head like a ushanka after treatment. Brighton was so good at keeping to herself she got trapped in our pool shed for two weeks without anyone noticing. The gutters were filled with twigs and leaves and the furniture was covered in more dog hair than ever. "I'm worried that I'll get sick and Moe will be stuck caring for me," Mom said. "And then I'll die and she'll have no life."

Moe got her chance at a life the spring of her junior year of college: she auditioned for the trainee program at the Joffrey School of Ballet in New York.

"Trainee for what?" I asked.

"For the professional company, or Broadway," Moe said, her voice phlegmy with the thrill of it. "Trainees audition all the time for Broadway shows."

I imagined a gang of anorexic bunheads who had aged out of behavioral boot camps or escaped from conversion therapy. I suspected such a school was well out of Moe's reach. The nicey-nice Mormons back home were too mean for Moe. You're telling me she could hang with a bunch of dancers in New York?

I kept my phone nearby that afternoon, ready to console her when the inevitable rejection came. Hours after the audition, she called me sobbing and laughing from the emergency room. She had broken her thumb in the middle of the tryout. "What a fucking disaster," she said.

To make matters worse, Moe twisted her ankle during an adult dance class a few days later. Not long after that she called again. "What bone did you break today?" I asked.

"What?" she said. I could hear the smile in her voice. "None."

Moe had done it. In spite of her injury, she'd been accepted into Joffrey's trainee program. Mom and Moe were moving to New York. She could finish her last year of college at the U by earning credits online.

"Shouldn't you at least get off your crutches and out of the thumb cast first?" I asked. I'll admit I thought this was all happening a little fast.

There was still the house and the dogs to think about, but rather than let that stop them, my mom started making calls. Brighton would be fine as long as we left the bathroom faucet dripping and a neighbor kid would check on the dogs every morning and night.

"Mom, that can't be your solution," I said. "Berkeley and Mazie are members of our family. Leaving them alone for basically the entire day is just not going to work."

"It is going to work," my mom said, "because Moe and I can't stay in this house living like this for one more second. If you want the dogs so bad, come and get them."

Well, in that case, I was sure they'd be fine.

By August, Moe had moved into a dorm in Brooklyn Heights and my mom had taken up residence in the Brooklyn Bridge Marriott a few blocks away, where she would stay, off and on, for the next two years. She rode the subway into Manhattan with Moe no fewer than twenty times before she let her no-sense-of-direction daughter do it alone, and even then Moe wasn't really alone because my mom would trail her or hide outside the studio, jumping out of the bushes if she noticed anything amiss. "Hey, ding-ding," she'd shout, "you're going the wrong way."

I was terrified for Moe at first. We have similar brains. I may know to roll down the window if a cop pulls me over, but I also know what it's like to not fully trust your mind. A break in routine can feel catastrophic or lead instantly to panic for me, too. Simple directions can be baffling. I have to take pictures of where I park to find my car, and it's bright yellow. Street addresses, subway signs—they may as well be advanced calculus. It seemed cruel to drop Moe in the middle of New York and tell her to find her way.

"Here's the deal, Moeham," Mom would say whenever I was around. "Greg and your other siblings think we're too stupid and weird to live in a big city. They don't think we can do this. We have to prove them wrong."

"We will," Moe would reply, dancing around like always.

I visited them for the first time in the fall of 2013. Let's just say I was impressed. While I wistfully sang the Liza Minnelli song about vagabond shoes longing to stray, Moe led me on the subway to her fire hazard of a dance studio in the West Village and to her favorite smoothie shop. Her goofy style of sundresses and galoshes, headbands and tights, big pink purses and big pink sunglasses would have gotten her sent to a psych ward back in Salt Lake, but in New York this hodgepodge fashion was unremarkable. Mom was always telling us that before she died, she needed to know that Moe could stand up for herself. If a teacher stuck Moe in the back of a class or, worse, didn't offer her any corrections at all, Mom encouraged my timid-in-public sister to "reach down deep, deep within yourself and find your inner bitch."

This always made Moe laugh. New York was having the opposite effect on her. Though she couldn't resist bashing Alice a couple times in passing, I could tell her heart wasn't in it. Moe no longer picked at her face or sucked on her hair like she had at home. Her eyelashes, which she used to pluck out, were starting to grow back for the first time in memory. She was content, and she didn't have a single rage during my stay.

My mom embraced the freedom of living in a big city, too, and talked openly about being in a relationship with a woman. She didn't come out to me like I'd come out to her, but visiting the Cloisters one afternoon, she told me her water aerobics class had started calling her Frankie.

"Wait, who's Frankie?" I asked.

"Me!" Mom said. "*I'm* Frankie."

Between sips of iced tea, Mom explained that Grandma Rosie and Grandpa Joe had wanted to name her Francis and call her Frankie for short but the nuns at the orphanage in Boise had already christened her Debi on account of her acting, in spite of being parentless, like a little debutante. Because my Basque grandparents didn't dare contradict a bunch of nuns, Debi stuck.

Now all these years later, Mom was ready for a fresh start.

"Deb is dead," Mom said. "Deb has just kind of had enough. I mean, doesn't Frankie sound like someone who's full of life and having fun?"

Mom traded in her Mormon-friendly Coldwater Creek blazers and capris for an Adidas windbreaker, black leggings, and sparkly gold platform boots. The concierge at the Marriott liked my mom so much that when Mom complained about her thinning hair, the result of aging, scalp biopsies, and epic doses of chemo over the years, the lady took her to her favorite wig shop in Harlem.

"I was African American in a previous life," Mom told me on the subway, gloating because a guy on the street had asked if she was Puerto Rican. "I don't like white people. White people aren't nice to each other. I'm too much for them." She took a sip of her iced tea and pulled her bangs down when I signaled that they were riding a little high and you could see the dark netting underneath. "Isn't it great? It's warmer than a hat!"

I doubted this poor concierge could stand my mom, but when I met her she came out from behind the desk in the lobby and gave my mom a hug before turning sternly to me. "We need to get Frankie into an apartment," she said. "She's spending way too much money on that room."

It was only October and Moe was already doing eight hours of *Nut-cracker* rehearsals a day. She passed on stories about how her Russian instructor, Era, had been in a coma for a year following a serious car accident, how she'd danced for the Bolshoi, and, even in her fifties with the accident and all her injuries, she could lunge and spin around the room. "But can she do a cartwheel into splits?" I asked.

Moe started meeting up with a lanky boy in her dorm who helped her with makeup, taught her to twerk, and called her sis. She began saying *yass queen* and *werk* and got invited to real drag shows as opposed to the ones I put on in our kitchen back in Holladay. Her inner bitch must have been proud. Mine was. Moe had made her first gay friend.

"Other than you," Moe said, patting me gently on the back.

"And Frankie," I added.

More of a New Yorker every day, my little sister developed a funny bowlegged walk. She still goobered her phone and computer to death every six months; lost her credit card; had her dance bag stolen; broke her glasses; lit the communal microwave on fire; fainted and came to on the sidewalk to a ring of concerned Jewish octogenarians offering her black-and-white cookies; got kicked in the face in class, an injury that required lip stitches; sliced her thumb with a butter knife; went to sleep with her dorm door wide open and her purse in the hall, leading the kids on her floor to assume she'd been attacked; and burned through a year's supply of contacts in a month. But aside from these minor hiccups, anyone could see that New York was the place for Moe. She was a different person there, more outgoing, no longer scared to leave the house because of her awful driving. She even lost her virginity courtesy of a sleazy Russian guy who lived down the hall from her. He was majoring in computer programming at NYU and went by the name Dmitri Gamma.

"What's his real name?" I asked.

"What do you mean?" Moe asked.

"I don't know, Dmitri Gamma just doesn't sound like a real name."

A Russian dude with a fake name cribbed either from a Eurotrash DJ or *The Matrix* wasn't the person I would have chosen to take my little sister's virginity, but really, who would have been? And it's not like Moe was complaining—not until she found out Dmitri Gamma had a long-distance girlfriend and an infant son. Rather than get discouraged, Moe joined a dating app and started seeing guys more like her.

"Being here isn't about dance," Mom said. "It's about life."

"No, it's about dance," Moe said, clutching me. "Greg and I are going to be on Broadway. Can't you just see us under the lights?"

I told Moe I'd write her one-woman show if she'd star in it.

Anything but *The Nutcracker*.

"The *Nut* Cracker." Moe barked out a laugh and poked me in the stomach. "Get it?"

Moe completed her online courses that spring and flew home to walk at the University of Utah's commencement. For pictures after the ceremony, she put on her beaten-up pointe shoes and posed with her diploma, cap, and gown. She had graduated summa cum laude with a degree in psychology, a major she'd chosen for the sole purpose of telling us that Asperger's didn't exist anymore as an official diagnosis. Moe beamed when she said this, like Asperger's was a deadly form of cancer she'd beaten. It turned out she was right. The syndrome had disappeared from the latest edition of the DSM, having been so widely applied as to become meaningless, clinically speaking. It didn't help that the Austrian physician it was named after, Hans Asperger, was revealed to be a Nazi who shepherded weird kids to their deaths. What sounds like a technicality felt like a major victory for Moe. She had managed to plié through her teens and early twenties without ever being labeled an Aspie outside our family. Now she never would be.

I was conflicted about Moe wiping away her diagnosis. In one way, I envied her autonomy and headstrongness. No label or set of assumptions would encumber her as she moved through the world. On the other hand, she'd always be othered, always be Moe, whether or not she had the language to describe herself. By going it alone, as I had, she would find no community through her difference. Selfishly, I knew I was losing out on having the kind of connection with my little sister I'd briefly shared with Dad. It might have been one of the reasons

I'd pushed so hard for her to seek help in the first place. Now I saw that she needed to come out in her own time, when she was ready.

In August, my mom sold the big house in Salt Lake to our Mormon neighbors, a clan known in my potty-mouthed family as "the whores up the street." They'd earned this label not because they were prostitutes but because their daughter had tormented Moe when they were girls. Mom took their money, undiminished by realtor fees, and rented a two-bedroom apartment closer to the hospital where she gets chemo and IVIG, planning to split her time between Salt Lake and New York. She set up Moe's room as it had been at the house, everything pink and covered with dance trophies and inspirational sayings. Stubborn as ever, Moe didn't come back for any of it. At first, she said she didn't have a home, and then she revised her statement to something truer: "New York is my home now."

Before we knew it, it was *Nutcracker* season again. I visited New York the week before Christmas so I could see Moe dance. She was supposed to be a Snowflake, but they cut her after the last dress rehearsal. Fortunately, Moe had two other parts: a Caroler and a Russian. Mom and I walked around Rockefeller Plaza and saw *Aladdin* on Broadway. Moe remained stuck in the land of sugar plums and snow. She didn't have any costume malfunctions that year, just walking pneumonia. Being ill didn't stop her; though, by her final outing, she was as exhausted by the whole enterprise as we were.

Mom and I skipped Act One entirely that day in favor of to-go salads at Dean & DeLuca and then we wandered back to the theater. There was a peaceful protest in Washington Square Park following the acquittal of the cop who killed Eric Garner and, because of the congestion, we had to hustle to make it back to the theater in time.

We were still unwinding our scarves and settling into our seats when the house lights dimmed and the familiar jump of Tchaikovsky's strings told us Moe would soon come flying in from the wings in her peasant blouse and black skirt. She looked wan under her makeup, her Cheshire grin painted on with effort. The choreography was rapid, every half-second a new lunge, squat, or kick. My leg went stiff under me, my foot cramping in my tennis shoe.

The normies onstage, not to mention their families in the audience, would have no idea what it had taken Moe to make it to her seventeenth *Nutcracker*. No idea, no interest. They'd only remember her if her costume fell off, if she leapt so high she smacked her head into a light. She'd be the ghostly rapscallion in the back of a hundred cast selfies, the one untagged girl with the giant red-lipped smile. Some things Moe would never know, either, like how I danced with her from my seat every time she was up there, my bad leg tensing to every jeté. Moe, who looked up to me even when I didn't deserve it.

You see *The Nutcracker* enough times and your mind starts to wander. You start imagining things turning out different. A dad leaps from his hospital bed and cartwheels into the splits. A star sister with a smile as big as her heart never gets cut from a dance or put in the back or told to play a pig. A brother with a limp keeps acting anyway, even though you can definitely see his nuts in tights. You sit there long enough and it's like you become the dream. All seventeen *Nutcrackers* play at once, a show belonging not to Balanchine but entirely to Moe: Moe the Icicle, Moe the Poinsettia, the Hurricane, the Rag Doll, the Rat, the Toy Soldier, and finally the Bolshevik. I'd been so worried my little sister would never grow up, I'd failed to see that she had. Her life wasn't a sequel to mine. It was a ballet. Here she was, dancing in New York just like her dad.

The pneumonia *Nutcracker* turned out to be Moe's last. That spring, she was accepted into a master's program in early childhood development at Columbia's Teachers College. Mom grudgingly decamped from the Marriott in Brooklyn to a building with a doorman on the Upper West Side. For the first winter in a long time, Moe was not trapped in a snow globe of a ballet but in a preschool, student-teaching special needs kids in Harlem. We spent that Christmas as a family in New York. Moe decorated the tree with dry Swiffer pads instead of ornaments and we didn't go to a single *Nutcracker*. Thank God.

COREY

Even if it hadn't been next to the Rite Aid where I bought my lice shampoo, the Out of the Closet on Sunset Boulevard would have been hard to miss. The thrift store was attached to an AIDS Healthcare Foundation Pharmacy. Strapped to the roof of the building, a fifteen-foot inflatable muscle man flexed his biceps. FREE HIV TESTS read the sash across his chest.

The counselor who administered the test handed me the certificate verifying I was negative—my clean bill of health—and shook a basket of free condoms at me. The wrappers were red with the word *Love* written across them in white letters, like Valentines. "Remember, use lots of lube," he said, as if I were limping because I hadn't thought to.

What can you see about me that I can't? I remember wondering.

Corey pulled up as I was coming home. We'd been messaging on gay.com for the past week and I was disappointed to see he wasn't worse looking. A big lug of a guy with flouncy brown hair, he didn't appear to be missing any digits, and when he took off his Ray-Bans both eyes tracked me darting into his field of vision. I had liked that his profile was un-Hollywood: no sizzle reels, shirtless selfies, or YouTube videos with adorable dogs. I'd thought I might have a chance.

I felt bad for the guys I met online. Based on how I presented myself, it'd be reasonable to expect a shaggy blond camp counselor ready to scramble up a boulder. It wasn't a lie, exactly, just not the complete picture. While I loved to jog in the Hollywood Hills with my roommate Katie, and while I *did* resemble a camp counselor, the able avatar I created online would fall apart the second I stepped toward these internet beaus, no matter how flat I tried to walk, how earnestly I attempted to roll from heel to toe or swing my right arm. My limp made me the damaged goods people warned you about on the web.

The alternative, I figured, was to add "super minor case of tight tendons" to my profile and end up with an even sadder inbox. I took my chances instead.

I showed Corey the Band-Aid where the counselor had pricked my finger and told him he better get tested soon, in case this was going somewhere. Corey laughed and said he'd just gotten tested, too.

"And?" I asked.

He smiled an easy smile and I made out a toothpick-size gap between his two front teeth. His chin was weak, his voice deep and charmingly doltish, like a surfer's. "Negative," he declared. "And by the way, hi."

A wave of relief larger than I'd like to admit whooshed through me. Growing up, I'd been taught to think of LA as a cesspool of crime and HIV. Two nights before leaving Salt Lake, I went to a Bret Easton Ellis movie that took place in LA in the glamorous 1980s. The film featured Kim Basinger injecting drugs into Billy Bob Thornton's penis and ended with a chick in a gold bikini roasting on the beach as she died of AIDS.

It was obvious: moving to a bigger city meant bigger risks.

I was totally going to be the girl in the gold bikini.

"Don't worry, babe," my friend Iris had told me. "You're not that thin."

Corey offered to drive and I hoisted myself into his truck, casually lifting in my right leg after me, my usual arsenal of excuses at the ready. For the first few minutes of the drive I was glad he didn't ask about it, and then I started to get annoyed. What's your deal, buddy, I wanted to say. Didn't you notice my limp? Are you some kind of asshole?

The truth hit me with a pleasurable pang: *He's a little nervous.*

Corey had a decal from the parochial school he'd attended in his rear window and a school picture of his little brother Miles on his dashboard. "That's some fro," I said, pointing to the orb of curls engulfing Miles's cherubic face.

It was all the invitation Corey needed to spend the rest of the date, at a Mexican restaurant in Silver Lake, bragging about Miles's college prospects and SAT scores. "He's smart in school and dumb in life," Corey said, not without pride.

Corey didn't use the term Asperger's, not at first, though it was easy enough to piece together given what my family had gone through with Moe. I recognized many of Miles's proclivities, as described by Corey: an endearing if overpowering inability to go with the flow of a conversation or speak at an appropriate volume, the trouble making friends and clumsiness with social cues, the detachment that could read as bratty or immature, the obsessions that were endearing on paper but could be relentless in person. They were both terrible drivers, both honors students, both spoiled little shits, both kids who'd been cheated of better childhoods.

"And they'd both be super pissed off if they heard us talking like this about them," I said with a nervous laugh.

Mostly, I identified with how much Corey adored his younger sibling. That was the main thing. In our different ways, Corey and I had been thrust into dad roles in our twenties when we should have been chasing daddies ourselves. Far from perfect, we'd earned the right to diagnose our siblings on first dates, damn it, to vent and brag.

Miles and Moe were just one year apart in age. "If it doesn't work out with us, maybe we'll set them up," I said. "Or even if it does."

The waitress brought out our beers on a tray. Picking at the label on mine, I apologized for being so in Corey's face about getting tested earlier. I'd just watched my dad slowly die of ALS. Plus, my mom had cancer. At that time, she was still back in Utah with weird, wonderful Moe.

"Anyway, that's why I'm a total hypochondriac," I said.

My leg tightened under the table and I had to work to keep from flinching. In addition to tight tendons, I have what my brother refers to as *verbal diarrhea*. I say something harmless like "I'm a total hypochondriac" and then find myself bringing up pertinent if unflattering anecdotes such as the time I caught crabs on my dad's farewell cruise on the Mediterranean.

"The thing is," I whispered to Corey across our two top, "I hadn't had sex for *months*."

"It sounds like you're not a hypochondriac," Corey said, picking up my confidential tone. "*It sounds like you had crabs.*"

But where'd they come from, these immaculate crabs? It couldn't possibly have been the theater major with the cute accordion bong I'd hooked up with a few months before college graduation. No, like many before me, I blamed a pair of chinos I'd tried on at a Banana Republic outlet days before our flight to Barcelona.

Probably because of what I still insisted were the mysterious circumstances of my first outbreak, I remained paranoid about crabs for years, periodically shaving my body hair and lathering my crotch stubble with specialty shampoos.

This habit followed me to Los Angeles.

"And how are the crabs now?" Corey asked, scratching a spot behind his ear.

"Gone," I said. I didn't add that I kept a nit comb and shampoo under the bathroom sink just in case of a recurrence.

When Corey didn't slip away to the bathroom, never to return, I thought I just might invite him over.

I was living in a turquoise house on Harold Way with Danny and Katie, my best friend from college. The three of us had moved to Los Angeles together to make it as writers: Danny kept up a raucous blog about his life and was going to screenwriting school at USC; a journalism major like me, Katie worked as a personal assistant out of a famous media mogul's Brentwood mansion; and I stayed home and edited the two short stories I'd written in college. (I hadn't yet moved to Texas and was still applying to MFA programs.) As a side project Katie and I were also adapting, on spec, one of Roald Dahl's adult stories, "The Great Switcheroo." We had a recycling bin filled with bottles of Two Buck Chuck to prove it.

Our street, like our lives, was what you might call "showbiz-adjacent." Harold Way was sandwiched between Sunset and Hollywood Boulevards. A derelict motel sat at the end of the block, the sort that could plausibly be closed off for both premium cable shoots and the sleazy activities they depicted. News choppers circled low. Harold Way was where many a police chase came to an end.

Why did it feel so much like home? Our landlady, Maripat, had raised the funds to buy this crumbling block of Hollywood by playing a nun in a one-woman show. Red-faced and usually wearing a Hawaiian shirt, Bermuda shorts, and rubber boots, Maripat lived three doors down from us with her girlfriend Glinda and a gang of Chihuahuas named after Chicago mobsters. She wrote emails in all caps and, like a nun, threatened to line us up and slap us across the face whenever we left our security door flapping open at night. It had been installed backwards, so coming or going made you feel like you were in a behavioral psychology experiment. When the plumbing backed up, Maripat shouted in our front lawn, "*You tell Katie to stop flushing her tampons down the toilet.*"

A pot of coffee a day plus the shared-bathroom sitch turned me into the bungalow's outdoor water feature, forever whizzing into some ivy off the back patio. A rocking chair sat on the front porch and a lemon tree dropped its bounty onto the hood of my dad's hulking Lexus at the back of our skinny driveway. Around the corner from a Roscoe's Chicken and Waffles, Harold Way always smelled deliciously of fried chicken and hashish, except for the time someone down the block ran over a skunk.

Katie's godmother, Maripat's long-suffering sister, was an interior designer. She had decorated our house, stringing our single bathroom with Christmas lights, sponge painting the living room purple with gold stenciling. A candy-colored acrylic chandelier hung in the kitchen, where you'd also find a pallet of Diet Coke and an overflowing trash can filled with the brown paper towels I used as coffee filters. A glorious midlife crisis of a place, we called it the Bungalow.

Corey entered our stanky lair with low-key aplomb. I was more attuned to fibs and fabrications after Kevin, and it took me the second half of that first date to determine that much of what Corey had told me about himself wasn't true. This is not a testament to my skepticism or detective work. Whereas Kevin's lies had been grandiose, Corey's lies were lazy—he was a couch potato of a liar. There wasn't even any guile to them. The first fib was that he had gone to Berkeley. In an unlucky break for Corey, it just so happened that Danny had also gone to Berkeley. Naturally, when the two met over drinks at our kitchen table, the subject came up. Danny asked where on campus Corey had lived. "Where did I live?" Corey said. He took a quick swig, looking up at the colorful chandelier as if he might divine the answer there. "Sort of all over."

I'd only visited my brother a few times in college. Most of one homecoming weekend I'd spent blacked out in a side room in his frat that had been filled with packing peanuts. But even I could recall a handful of street names and major landmarks. Corey had never heard of Noah's Bagels, Zachary's Pizza, Telegraph Avenue—places I knew just from being alive.

"Telegraph, yeah, that sounds right," Corey said. "I lived there. Around there."

At the end of the night, Danny and I rolled aside the gate at the front of our driveway so Corey could back out. "Your boyfriend is full of shit," Danny said, giving him a friendly wave. "But he's probably just trying to impress you." It only occurred to me later that this is exactly what my dad had thought about the motivation behind Kevin's lies.

We watched Corey's brake lights blink at the end of the block and disappear around the corner. The palm readers, payday lenders, and weed dispensaries on Gower would be open for business now, neon signs lighting up their windows.

Someone trying to impress *me*? I liked the sound of that.

Walking home from 24 Hour Fitness a few days after our first date, I got a call from Corey telling me he had been fired from his job as a construction site manager. He'd already tied his mattress to the flatbed of his truck, planning to leave behind his Santa Monica apartment, and his annoying roommates, to move back in with his mom and Miles about forty-five minutes down the 405 in Orange County. It was for the best, anyway. Miles was a senior in high school. He had a lot to figure out about his future and it'd be good to have Corey around.

I hit the WALK button to cross Gower. "That happened fast."

"I was subletting," he said. "Hey, aren't you going to tell me you're sorry I had a rough day?" He let a bit of irritation creep into his voice.

"Of course," I said. "That really sucks. Can I help you move?"

"Nope, all good," he said, "but I'd like to take you out. Do I get a second date?"

"I can't turn you down now," I said.

Corey came over and made out with me in the driveway for a good two minutes. Things were looking up. For starters, he'd already gotten rehired at his old job at a fuel dock in Newport Beach and for another—here he pulled a red T-shirt out of his backpack and tossed it to me—he was the newest part-time deckhand on the Balboa Island Ferry. "Look on the back," he said proudly. "See how it says CREW? They only give these shirts to actual crew members. I stole one for you."

Sure, it was a little fishy Corey had lost his job, found two new ones, and moved within days of meeting me, but I was struck by the modesty of his invention, if that's what it was: this "Berkeley" grad had gone from being a construction worker in Santa Monica to a gas station attendant in Newport Beach. Big whoop. We were in a recession. I never even got a response to the job applications I filled out.

Until I did. Sort of.

On a Wednesday night in March, about a month after meeting Corey, I received an email from the director of the Michener Center for Writers in Austin. All the coffee had paid off. The promise of a funded, three-year fellowship lay before me. My writing career—if that's what I was now embarking upon—was taking me to Texas. I'd be moving by the middle of July.

Corey turned down my offer to celebrate at Disneyland with Katie. He was disappointed I'd be skipping town; he was also happy for me. It took the pressure off. We figured we should enjoy each other for whatever time we had left, not worry about our relationship status. We didn't have sex, not for that first month of seeing each other. I had a swimsuit rash and an appointment at a free STD clinic on Melrose: I wanted to make sure the rash wasn't herpes. Plus, I wasn't ready to take off my jeans and explain the surgical scars on the backs of my legs and have my flaccid penis poked at. My limp didn't bother him, but I was scared Corey would pull a Tyler Townsend and not want to see me anymore if he found out I'd never topped anyone, ever, and that I doubted I could. I wasn't letting the topping genie out of the bottle of Cetaphil this time.

Corey proved worth the wait. One of the great lays of my life, he was so hung he was bashful about it. Gentle with my stiff legs, he displayed the kind of patience with my temperamental parts I pledged to practice with his jumbo ones. The subject of me topping never came up, though he'd boyishly offer to blow me when he got drunk. Sober, Corey was squeamish about anything that smacked of passivity. *He* was the top. "Masc." A dude's dude. Give him a beer or four, though, and he'd camp it up, rolling his eyes and lisping, a giant grin on his face. It felt good to let Corey inside the tight coil of my body, to give up control. I'd be so relaxed when he left I'd walk into walls as I made my way up the stairs to Katie's attic bedroom to tell her all about it. There was JBFed and then there was JBCed: Just Been Coreyed.

Still—we weren't exclusive. I went on dates with a guy whose WASP roots stretched back to the *Mayflower* and who enjoyed John Irving novels as much as I did. And I gleefully hooked up with the guy who hosted me during my program visit in Austin that spring. (What can I say? His condo complex had a sauna.) But I was happiest with down-to-earth Corey. He was the first guy I ever knew who called me handsome to my face. "Hey, handsome," he'd say, and I'd stand there blushing, astonished at how good it felt.

"You know what you're getting with a guy like Corey," Danny said, brushing pretzel crumbs from his lap. "His ancestors weren't butt fucking on the *Mayflower*, I'll tell you that. Life with him means hanging out on a fart-stained couch."

Danny meant this as a compliment. Corey was great at hanging out on our couch.

When we weren't boning, we'd go on dates to the Getty or the La Brea Tar Pits. We'd walk around Hollywood Forever, tossing bits of granola bars to the cemetery's peacocks and taking turns posing with the tombstones that, anywhere else, would have been roadside attractions: the granite replica of the Atlas missile, the bronze statue of Johnny Ramone humping his electric guitar. Corey teased me when I left a stone on Estelle Getty's grave. "*The Golden Girls*, seriously?"

Hiking in Griffith Park, he playfully flipped off my camera and snuck kisses during a laser show at the observatory. He'd make me laugh when he told stories of playing tricks on his dad, of bleaching his hair as a teenager and earning badges as an Indian Guide, the YMCA's version of the Boy Scouts.

Corey was as sketchy as he could be sweet. A lot of our relationship was don't ask, don't tell. He'd stand me up and then text the next morning about how he'd hit his head in his dad's garage and sustained a concussion. I'd offer to meet him somewhere in Orange County and save him the drive to Hollywood and he'd turn me down. After a night of being standoffish, he almost passed out at a Dr. Dog concert at the Palladium and had to go take a seat in an armchair in the lobby. "What is up with you?" I shouted over the music. "Why are you being weird?"

Corey mentioned once or twice that his dad was Jewish, mostly as a way of putting him down. I'd find out later from Miles that their mom identifies as Native Californian, descending from the Indigenous inhabitants of the state. It was a heritage Corey openly rebelled against. If he said the word "Mexican," it was usually with the word "dirty" in front of it, even if we were out in public—at the ArcLight, say, as the lights dimmed.

The only time I ever saw Corey really lose it was when he tried to use chopsticks at a pho place in Silver Lake. I remember him throwing them down and banging the table with his open palm so hard I jumped in my seat.

"Hey, it's not like I'm great with them either," I offered, holding up my spoon.

Corey's dad had accidentally backed over his right hand when he was five or six and he couldn't spread his fingers or make a fist. I'd hardly noticed the thick white scar that ran between his thumb and index finger, but he carried the trauma of the accident with him all these years later. Corey's parents divorced when he was fifteen and, in a fit of anger, Corey had accused his dad of turning him gay. That's how Corey had come out of the closet, not with tears and hugs and his mom giving off-color advice about hooking up with boys and girls to see which he liked best, as mine had, but with a shouted accusation. *Honestly, you should feel butthurt that I'm a fag, Dad. I wouldn't be out there packing fudge if not for you.* It was hard not to laugh at the story the way Corey told it, using his dad's prejudice against him, but I could also tell there was real pain there.

Now that I was leaving Los Angeles for grad school, I gave up any pretense of finding work and spent my days reading literary fiction and AIDS memoirs on our back patio, library books and coffee mugs piling up around me.

It had been a dozen years since I'd sat in Mrs. Palmer's seventh-grade Life Science class and met her friend Dennis. I'd educated myself a good deal on HIV/AIDS since then. Except for my Croatian fling with Tyler Townsend, I'd consistently used condoms. What hadn't changed was my fear.

I had a habit of turning anxiety about my disability and my parents' terminal illnesses into hypochondria, and not just about AIDS. AIDS was just my most long-standing concern. I'd write Iris emails about terrible palpitations in my left pec, imagining the fasciculation that had foretold Dad's demise, or rehash the fear I'd had since college that my hair was falling out, or report that I had a painful sore in my mouth. "If you're worried, go to a doctor so you can stop thinking about it and know for sure," Iris replied. "I don't think you have it. Any of it. I don't think you're a balding ALS victim with mouth cancer, but if you ever are, I will love you, and push your wheelchair. I will also go with you to the doctor if you want."

With Corey, I tried to turn my hypochondria into humor. Not good humor, mind you, but AIDS humor. After hooking up one afternoon, I joked that a birthmark on his thigh was a lesion he was trying to cover with makeup. I'd read about an actor doing that very thing in a tell-all memoir on my nightstand. "You're a jerk," Corey mumbled.

This reaction in itself was surprising. I'd expected Corey to laugh.

I spent the rest of the night walking back my stupid joke.

But yeah, I wanted him to buy firming cream for the bags under his eyes and told him he needed to see a dermatologist about the acne on his legs. He claimed he already had seen a doctor about the outbreak: it was from not toweling off properly after the shower.

And maybe his semen would be less watery if he started working out?

"Eat a dick," he told me.

"OK," I said with a shrug.

In his driver's license picture, taken just a few years earlier, Corey was downright chubby. Only in retrospect would I recognize the wrinkled flab on his stomach as a sign of catastrophic weight loss, as if the fat had been lipo-ed off rather than slowly burned away through diet and exercise. Far from alarmed at his recent downsizing, I made fun of him for being a former fatty. He put his hands on my butt and pulled me toward him. "You don't seem to mind when I'm doing you," he said. It was true: I didn't even have to touch myself to come against the flab of his belly.

Corey wanted to follow me to Texas, but he had his brother and mom to look after in the OC. I felt relieved he couldn't move with me, and then guilty for feeling relieved. I'd only just started being confident enough about my lame body to date in LA. This was my big adventure. I wanted it to be mine. I wanted to play the field. But would Corey be willing to drive with me to Texas?

When he made the bumpy descent into Salt Lake, the starting point for our road trip, I took him home and introduced him to my mom and Moe, who hadn't yet moved to New York. Moe was seemingly already practicing for it, doing ballet arms in front of the TV like a broken clock, a look of grim determination on her face. First position, second position, fifth. *First second fifth!*

"I don't think my brother has what your sister has," Corey said.

"It's a spectrum, dickwad," I said. "Miles is just as weird as Moe."

"Can't argue with that," Corey said, laughing.

Later, when I was ninety percent sure Mom and Moe had gone to bed, I pulled Corey outside by his busted hand and had him make love to me on a lawn chair by the pool in the backyard as I looked up at the starless purple night. I'd always wanted to do that.

On our drive south, we got caught in a lightning storm in Arizona. Stuck on the freeway because of a flash flood warning, we watched patrolmen pile sandbags along the road and poke the beams of their flashlights into the cars in front of us. I gave up on our audiobook. It was Kazuo Ishiguro's *Never Let Me Go* and Corey would not stop imitating the monotone British actress doing the reading. "Have it your way," I said. I turned off the car and we watched lightning cross the sky like we were at a drive-in movie. I gave Corey a blowjob but he gagged at the suggestion of returning the favor. "I hate swallowing," he said.

Corey got me settled in this new city with its bats and cockroaches and terrifying frontage roads. He built my IKEA bookshelf, desk, and chairs. Sometimes he got cranky but he was mostly a good sport. He picked out an expensive couch at Crate & Barrel and then guilted me into buying it by making fun of me in front of the saleslady. "You're getting that couch," he said. "You should own one nice thing."

It was red, mid-century modern, and I still have it.

Corey cleaned the bugs out of my light fixtures, hung curtains, and drove me to two Costcos across town from one another to buy a TV. We walked to a place playing live music on South Congress one night and I tried to make him race me down the street. All he would do was call after me that I was being a dick. He wouldn't swim in Barton Springs or eat at Whataburger. He hated Whataburger. He wouldn't even try tacos. "I have a sensitive stomach," he said. Friends ask me now what Corey *did* eat, if not burgers or tacos, and I tell them the truth: I can't remember. What I do remember is renting *Dirty Harry* and *Once Upon a Time in the West* from the Blockbuster on South Congress and watching them on the crushed oatmeal carpet of my unfurnished living room. We had so much sex Corey said he felt like his dick was broken.

One of our last nights together, lying on my recently delivered mattress on the floor of my bedroom, Corey told me he loved me.

"I love you too," I replied. "I love you like a brother."

Corey rolled off the mattress and said he would sleep downstairs.

After fifteen minutes or so, I got up and found him drinking a bottle of water in the kitchen. The anger was gone, replaced by a sadness he'd never let me see before. I didn't realize until then how much he cared about me.

He told me how lucky I was to get to move to Austin and start a new life.

"You can visit," I tried. "You'll have your own bathroom."

My new place had three.

"I love you," he tried again, looking me full in the eyes.

"I know," I said, feeling my scalp prickle. "I love you too."

It was the easy thing to say. I wish now we'd had it out, cried, screamed. Things might have turned out differently. I would have asked him why he lied about dumb stuff like where he'd gone to college, why he had kept me away from his friends, why he'd never introduced me to Miles. Individually, none of these things were a big deal, but taken as a whole they'd held me back from going all in. Instead, we just started kissing. Next thing I knew I was lying on the floor with my foot in his lap and he was spreading my bunched toes. In the shower, I asked him if he would say yes if I proposed. He looked down at his large, pale feet. "Probably."

When you're twenty-five, such a remarkable turn of events is possible: over the course of a single night, even a single hour, you can go from loving someone like a brother to getting a foot massage to floating a marriage proposal.

Corey stayed with me for two weeks. At the end of our time together, I gave him an orange Longhorns cap and kissed him good-bye at the airport. He told me he loved me and I thought he might cry. I hurried out my own *I love you*. He looked cute in his new hat, hair flopping over his ears. "No one's being shipped off to war," I said. "No one's *dying*. We can always Skype."

Those early days as a Michener were filled with fiction workshops, screenwriting classes, after-class beers at Crown & Anchor, and talking to Corey. We'd Skype and chat at the same time, typing long strings of gibberish to each other when the screen froze or we got disconnected.

I was stoked to see that Corey was experiencing a personal renaissance. He was taking night classes in Long Beach to become a high school history teacher or a psychiatrist. "You should see the looks people give me when I tell them I went to Berkeley," Corey said.

I'll bet, I thought.

Corey joined a gym, went running, cut his shag, lost even more weight. He seemed to be coming out of a years-long funk. "Now all we have to do is get rid of those bags under your eyes," I said. "Let's raid the MAC counter."

Corey and I Skyped less as the fall wore on. I assumed it was coming from my end. I was dating the writer with the sauna who'd hosted me during my program visit. We spent one Saturday reading naked on the rocks of Hippie Hollow and arguing about what he should call the spaceship in his Mars novel. My vote, for reasons I've now forgotten, was DietCoke.com.

"The writer's giving me a bedframe," I reported to Corey.

"I'm gonna beat that guy up," Corey said, kidding but not.

Corey sent a card for my twenty-sixth birthday in October. *You have changed my life for the better. Love, Corey.* He called on my birthday, too, but I was at a café on Lake Austin with the writer. I Skyped with him the next day to scold him for not singing to my voicemail. I felt bad for not answering.

"Do you want me to sing to you right now?" he asked. "I will if you want me to."

"No," I said.

A smile spread across his pixelated cheeks. "Do you want me to?"

The writer broke up with me a week after my birthday. Among other things, he did not appreciate me calling his spaceship DietCoke.com. I started to think maybe Corey really was the one for me: loyal, epically endowed, handsome as hell. Maybe he should move to Austin so we could make a go of it, this time without the prospect of an impending departure to cap our intimacy. "Let's at least spend New Year's together," I told him, tilting my laptop down so he could see the Crate & Barrel couch he'd picked out, finally delivered to my living room. "You'd look good in a tux."

"I would," he agreed through a cough. It wasn't a racking cough or a hacking cough, a dry cough or a wet cough. Just an everyday, regular old cough. The next time I tried to Skype with him he said his computer was broken.

In mid-October, the Michener Center gave us free passes to the Austin Film Festival and I took full advantage, going to movie after movie. I had just come out of a Friday night screening of *I Love You Phillip Morris* at the Arbor when I got a call from Corey's best friend, Daphne. Corey talked about her sometimes, but we'd never spoken. My dad's Lexus was still splattered with bugs from the drive to Texas and, finding it in the lot, I hesitated at the thought of leaning against it. The lights above were crowded with bugs, too.

Daphne told me that, the night before, Corey had been admitted to the intensive care ward of a hospital in Orange County and treated for pneumonia. They had intubated him and pumped a quart and a half of fluid from beneath his lungs and said he was going to be fine. She'd brought him car magazines and yelled at him for being an idiot and not taking care of himself. "He didn't want me to call you, but I figure if my boyfriend was in the hospital I would want to know," she said. I had the urge to correct Daphne, tell her Corey and I weren't technically together, but I settled for saying thanks and to keep me posted.

It was weird, though, him not wanting me to know he was sick.

I went to a movie at the Alamo Drafthouse on Sixth Street the next day with my new classmate, Mary. Mary was from Jackson, Mississippi, in her early thirties, divorced. She already had an agent and a published story collection. She'd been in *McSweeney's*. I thought of her as a lady.

In the middle of the movie, I got a call from Corey's phone and excused myself to the lobby, expecting to hear a pneumonia-weakened wheeze.

"Hi!" I said. "Corey! How are you feeling?"

"This isn't Corey. This is Miles. Corey's brother."

"What's that?" I pressed the phone to the side of my face and folded my other ear shut to hear better. "It's sort of loud in here. I can't understand you."

I went out to the sidewalk and, when that was even louder, back inside to the lobby. Eventually, I found a nook near the front door where I could just make out Miles's words on the other end of the line. Like Daphne, I'd never spoken to him besides shouted hellos during my phone conversations with Corey, never seen him except for that picture Corey kept in his truck. Miles would say "Hi Greg!" in the background and Corey would relay the message. "Miles says hi."

"Corey is gone," Miles said. He sounded clinical, more grown-up than you'd imagine possible from a college freshman who had just lost his only sibling.

"What do you mean he's gone?" I asked.

"He's gone," Miles repeated matter-of-factly. "I'm looking at him right now."

The incongruity of this statement made my leg go rigid: Corey was gone but also present. Miles was in the room with him, right then, watching him not breathe.

At the end of the call, I went back into the darkened theater and took my seat on the aisle. The movie dragged on for another hour with bad jokes about rednecks and musical numbers with fiddle and banjo. I kept the screen in my periphery, turning my face away from Mary, feeling, as I picked at the Philly cheese steak I'd ordered, like one of those people who does weird things after committing a crime. Corey was dead. What else was there to do but settle my check and wait for the credits?

I must have been curt with Mary because as we left the Drafthouse and came out into the bright afternoon, she wanted to know, in her soft Southern cadence, if I was mad at her. "Things are about to get very short story-ish," I said, starting to cry.

"We should get you home," Mary said.

On the walk back to my car, I told Mary what a terrible person I was, how I insisted to Corey that we weren't together after my move to Austin, how I dated other people while I was dating Corey. "We just seemed so casual," I said.

"You're young," she said. "You can't blame yourself for not being ready."

Once I was settled back at home, Miles called again and asked if I was sitting down. Instinctively, I got up and paced around the red couch, Corey's couch. I sensed what Miles was going to say before he said it: Corey had succumbed to PCP, pneumocystis pneumonia. At the time of his death, he had a T-cell count of twenty-two and what Miles described as "full-blown AIDS." I found an unopened envelope on the coffee table and wrote "22" and "full-blown AIDS" on the back of it and circled them again and again in pen.

I don't know why we always call it *full-blown*, like the virus is a scared pufferfish.

"How are you holding up?" I asked.

"Not very well." Miles's voice trembled a little. "You?"

"Same," I said.

I still don't know if Corey got tested when I met him, or ever. What I do know is that he lied to my face about it half a dozen times. He'd roll on a condom and come inside me or let me swallow his cum without so much as a heads-up.

Miles's tone remained steady as he relayed what the doctors were telling him and his mom. Judging from Corey's state of physical collapse at the time of his death, he had contracted HIV in his late teens and fought the disease for years without seeking treatment or, apparently, telling anyone close to him he was sick, an especially baffling thing to do considering he had been out to his family for a decade. The doctors said Corey would have needed to come in four or five years earlier to have a real shot at prolonging his life. Corey had been doomed from the day we met. He was always going to leave me before I left him.

After hanging up with Miles, I found Corey's Jet Blue itinerary in my email. He'd flown back to Long Beach on Friday, August 13. That made it seventy days since we'd had sex, almost enough time for me to be through the window period. Thank you, Mrs. Palmer.

Not for the first time since my move, I missed Harold Way, and not for any of the normal nostalgic reasons but for its proximity to the Out of the Closet on Sunset. It was open Saturdays. No testing center in Austin could say the same, at least none that I could find, and all the thrift stores were just thrift stores.

Out of reasonable options, I called Mary and asked her to drive me to the emergency room. The nurse who took my blood pressure whispered that I'd be better off going home. "They don't test people when they come in off the street like this," she said. "All you'll get is a bill."

In retrospect, I must have looked pretty bad.

The nurse turned out to be right. Texas law says you can't reveal a positive test result to a patient without providing the opportunity for counseling. Since the ER couldn't offer anything like that on a Saturday evening, they couldn't test me. The attending physician tried to explain all this but it remained murky in my mind for years. She discharged me with instructions to follow up with the health department or my family doctor for an HIV test *without fail* and to not have sex until I got the results. We all assumed I had it.

Mary and I prowled East Sixth Street looking for a testing center on wheels. The good nurse had said she thought there was such a thing, a bloodmobile for STDs, and that they rolled it out on weekends.

Walking up to food trucks, I'd ask, "Is there an AIDS van around here?"

"Sorry man," one guy said. "We do brisket."

We must have made a funny pair, inching along the busy street in Mary's white Accord. As if we needed to look more like lost out-of-towners, Mary's car had a Mississippi license plate in back and a pink Patty Peck dealership plate in front. It was like driving around in the Flannery O'Connor mobile.

Sunday was agony, not knowing if I was positive, not knowing if my whole life would be different from here on out. I sobbed and wandered around my condo naked, hating my body, missing Corey, hating Corey, staring at my face in the mirror. I tried to write. I tried to remember if the condom ever broke. I prayed to Dennis like he was a Jedi ghost, waving at me from my youth. As far as I could recall we'd always used one. Even when we'd had sex in my mom's backyard? I dunno, I thought so. It's not like Corey had resisted the idea. He hadn't been fanatical about it either, hadn't made extra sure.

How could Corey not treat a treatable disease? How could he abandon Miles? I wanted to spit in his face. I wanted to ask him why he'd never told me, though of course I knew: it was the same reason I didn't mention my leg in dating profiles.

I felt like an idiot for not calling him out on all his fibs, for thinking I could move away from home and live the life of a normal person without contracting a deadly disease. I let dark fantasies overtake me. My tongue was covered in thrush. My lymph nodes were swollen. My groin was spotted in what must have been Kaposi's sarcoma. My legs were stiff with edema. I remembered a time in May when I had a sore on my lip, another time when I cut myself shaving. Had he used the razor? I'd come to Austin with a stye on one of my eyelids and had such an upset stomach the week after Corey left I'd gone to an urgent care on South Lamar and gotten tested for parasites, *E. coli*, salmonella, and shigella. It had all come back negative and the next week my stomach had settled down and I'd forgotten about it.

Determined not to panic my mom, I decided to consult Alice. They were now a couple of years into a long-distance relationship, seeing each other on weekends and taking tropical vacations. They wore each other's engagement rings and if Mom had treatment, Alice would rearrange her clinic and surgical schedule to fly out for it. I should have guessed they'd be together.

"Hi Greg," Alice said when I called. "Your mom's right here. Let me get her."

Before I could stop her, Alice passed the phone to my mom and I broke down.

Mom was surprisingly calm. She told me she'd devote all her time and money to helping me stay healthy. They'd clear out the guest room in her and Alice's apartment in Delaware. I could move in and get treatment under her care.

My crying let up a little. "You've officially moved in together?"

"I'm on the lease," Mom said. "That's not my point, honey."

"Mom, I don't care if you're on the lease. I'm not quitting grad school," I said. "That is not happening. You realize I get a stipend, don't you? They're paying me to be here."

"I know Corey loved you," Mom said. "You could see it in the way he looked at you."

"I know." I was shaking so hard I could barely hold the phone. "I'm not going out like Corey." I tried to find the resolve in my voice. "Not without a fight."

"No, you're not," Mom said.

We talked for maybe fifteen more minutes before Mom concluded, with a clarity that startled me, "It isn't fair you can get a disease just from having sex, is it?"

After we hung up I blew my nose and took a picture of a spot on my hip and texted it to Alice. *Is this a lesion?* I asked.

Lesions are late-stage symptoms sweetie, Alice wrote back. *You're not late stage.*

Once I'd told Mom about Corey, I figured I should call my siblings.

"I can't lose you, not after Dad," Danny said, choking up. "You're my best friend."

"I'd cut off Corey's balls if he wasn't dead," Tiffany wept.

Meanwhile, Katie and I pledged, through laughter spiked with tears, to finish our "Switcheroo" script. "It's our *masterpiece*, dude," she said.

Since we'd lived together the entire time I dated Corey, Katie had hung out with him almost as much as I had. She had memories of the time before Corey, too, when I would barge into the living room after a night at Akbar, covered in hickeys and asking if you could get HIV from precum. "I doubt the condom ever broke, dude," Katie said. "I'm pretty sure you would have freaked out about it."

"What about all the times I blew him?" I asked.

"I googled it," Katie said. "He would have had to come directly in your eyeball."

Mary and I arrived at a free testing center on Cesar Chavez that Monday morning. A church van pulled up next to Mary's car in the lot and a group of women filed out wearing tank tops and sweatpants. A few had smudged magenta eyeshadow and glitter on their cheeks. From the look of it, they'd had a rough weekend too.

"We better get you in there or we could be here a while," Mary said.

I complained to the counselor about the runaround trying to get a test. The ER doctor I'd seen on Saturday, the one who had turned me away, had accidentally referred me to a treatment center, not a testing center, a mistake that had cost Mary and me an hour of waiting in the wrong place that morning. I suppose I wanted to air my grievances before I lost the capacity, while I could still play the role of concerned citizen rather than pissed off antibody-positive gay man, as if the disease would taint my opinions as well as my immune system.

The counselor had me swab my cheek and asked about my sex life, whether or not I injected drugs. "Some of these questions don't apply," she said.

"He lied to my face," I told her. "He told me he got tested and that he was negative. Is there any chance he just didn't know? He didn't look like a walking AIDS patient. He was pretty healthy and strong. He had bags under his eyes and he was losing weight, but I congratulated him on it."

"He probably knew," the counselor told me.

By the time I was finished dumping out my feelings, the test was ready. I held my cheeks in my hands, my body not numb but tingling, like I'd been hit.

This is it, I thought. *This is my life.*

The counselor warned that the results were preliminary. The window period for a third-generation antibody test, which is what I'd just taken, could be anywhere from three to six months from last contact. That word seemed weird to me, *contact*, like Corey was the disease and not the carrier.

I returned to the waiting room with swollen eyes and the certificate with the test results. They were on a half-page piece of paper. I was negative. The counselor had filled in the blanks for me, like it was a worksheet in high school:

"In the next week, I will: *talk to friends and family about my results.*"

"You were sure in there a long time," Mary said, nervously pulling out her earbuds. I gave her the certificate to read and she stood up and hugged me. "Your shit is clean!" she cried, her ladylike demeanor dropping away with her nerves.

The women in the waiting room cheered.

Corey's mom, Anita, called between classes that week to ask me to come to Corey's memorial. It was going to be on a boat. I recognized her garbled tone from my mom's grief-fueled benders after my dad died. "We have to keep him alive. In our hearts," Anita added, after a long pause.

I parked myself on a patch of dirt under an oak tree on campus and ran my hands over its lumpy roots, looking out at a bunch of carefree kids in flip-flops migrating across the lawn to class. It was weird that I wasn't one of them anymore. "I knew something was wrong, but I didn't know what," she said.

Anita was glad to hear that I was OK. She sounded hurt when I asked if she had been in touch with Corey's other partners. "Other partners?" she asked. There had only been me.

I emailed her some pictures I'd taken of Corey, though it was hard to find ones where he wasn't sticking out his tongue or gagging or giving the camera the bird. Corey fake-smiling in front of a pen of flamingos at the Los Angeles Zoo. Corey squinting on a bench next to a plaque encouraging patrons to "Join the Wild Beast Society." And there were the ones I took around the house: Corey brushing his teeth in the bathroom, my head on his shoulder. Corey pulling the comforter over his head in bed. Corey kissing me in our colorful kitchen, his eyes squeezed shut, looking rapturous. I kept those for myself.

"Thank you for being Corey's friend and everything," Anita wrote in reply. "I miss him so much, I am in a real fog, but it will take some time. Like you, I am sure." She'd sent a link to his four-line obituary in the *Daily Pilot*. It didn't mention anything about AIDS and was written like an E. E. Cummings poem, with weird spacing and line breaks. Besides his friend Daphne, I was the only one outside the family they'd told. "We want to keep things private," Anita explained. "Corey was a very private person."

I flew to Los Angeles the Thursday before Corey's funeral and crashed on the couch at Harold Way. Katie and Danny told me about how the guy who was renting my old room, a former Marine turned cinematographer, had come into the living room to find them crying the day Corey died. When they'd explained why, he'd gone back into his room and flipped the mattress, like a homophobic Hulk. He had scrubbed every inch of our house, tossed my lice shampoo from under the bathroom sink, even done the dishes. Katie had visited her psychic on Gower, who said I was going to be OK. Danny had gone to Out of the Closet and gotten tested.

"I wasn't aware you were bottoming for Corey," I said.

"I know, I'm nuts," Danny said. "We're all total hypochondriacs."

The truth is, we'd all had that reaction: throwing out toothbrushes, razors, eyedrops, and tubes of Neosporin. Mom had flown to Austin, slept on my red couch, and sterilized my condo with Lysol wipes. I'm ashamed to admit I even threw out the birthday card Corey had sent me.

Following in my brother's footsteps, I returned to Out of the Closet the next morning. It had only been twelve days since I had tested negative in Austin, twelve days since the waiting room full of women with glitter on their cheeks cheered.

"Wow, this is a lot of testing," Jonah, the counselor, said. I'd wanted it to be the same guy who'd given me the *Love* condoms last winter, but it wasn't. This was Hollywood. People came and went. "I can test you again but the result is going to be the same."

"I'd appreciate it," I said, pulling out a crumpled twenty dollar bill to bribe him. "Here's my donation, and I'm planning on buying some shirts."

If I was positive, I wasn't going to Corey's funeral. I was angry enough as it was.

I hoped I wasn't shaking as I ran the swab along the inside of my cheek.

"Total déjà vu, your situation and mine," Jonah said. "My ex lied to me about getting tested, too. It took him months to come clean. I thought he was going to tell me he was back with his wife." Jonah let out a theatrical sigh, took the swab back from me. "I don't know how positives find me. It's not like I talk to them at parties and they say they're positive and we go home together."

"It's because you have a good aura," I told him, pointing to the Virgin Mary inked on the underside of his wrist.

"Oh, my crazy self," he said, swatting away my compliment.

The morning of Corey's funeral I was a plank on the couch, already feeling too sore and exhausted to move. I woke my brother up riffling through his dresser for socks and we got into a fight. I told Danny he couldn't blog about Corey's funeral and he told me he could blog about whatever the fuck he wanted. His room smelled like a bar.

"I don't want to go to your gay boyfriend's AIDS funeral anyway," he said.

"Yeah, this must be a really hard day for you," I said.

Danny sat up in bed, not saying anything for a few seconds. When he finally spoke his voice was soft, hand over his heart. "Can we not fight? Today is shitty enough already."

While Danny elected to stay home and get drunk, Katie took the day off from her new magazine job to attend the funeral with me. We got there early, looking like goons in our sunglasses, and killed time with cheap French roast coffee and croissants filled with Nutella, debating whether or not we should go to Disneyland or the Nixon Library after the memorial, as if the experience wouldn't leave us totally wrung out.

Miles was the first person to walk up to us on the pier, hugging me before I even introduced myself. He planted an ear against my chest to listen to my heart.

He was the same cherubic nerd I'd seen in his school picture, a miniature Eugene Levy with curls and retro black glasses bracketing his brown eyes. Corey had bought those glasses for him. If Miles had sounded detached on the phone, in person he was full of quiet composure, a state all the more remarkable given the disarray of the rest of his family. He reminded me, just a bit, of a benevolent teddy bear.

"Corey had the best time on your road trip," Anita said, hugging a purple shawl tightly around herself. "The best time." If Anita was barely holding it together, Corey's dad was rocking the laid-back California vibe: silver soul patch, short-sleeve shirt, wraparound sunglasses. I couldn't shake the feeling that this was what Corey would have looked like had he made it to the fiefdom of his mid-fifties—red and jowly from a lifetime of working on the water. Corey's dad was passing around a Ziploc bag of childhood pictures—I recognized one from Corey's gay.com profile—and I suddenly had the urge to accidentally run his hand over with a truck. Instead, I just teared up and said the pictures were nice.

The boat where the service was held was named *Salty Snail*. It was normally used for whale spotting tours, not funerals. Corey's co-workers at the dock had pulled some strings. We didn't even have to take off our shoes.

Daphne was already on the boat. I assumed she knew Corey's family but she'd met Anita and Miles for the first time in the hospital waiting room the weekend he died, when she'd brought him magazines and told him he was an idiot. As far as I could tell, I was the only boyfriend, Katie and I two of only a handful of friends among the dozen people in attendance. It startled me to see how small Corey's world was, small and *not dealing with his death*. It wasn't like my dad's funeral. No one sang Neil Young songs or made awful jokes or offered fierce rocking hugs or interpretive dances. It says something that the nineteen-year-old on the spectrum was the most emotionally in-tune person aboard.

I don't usually go in for the "celebration of life" thing. If a funeral isn't a mega bummer, something's up. But I will say it's hard to stay sad on a boat. Leaving the trashy shore behind, we made our way through an obstacle course of buoys and into the spectacular open water. The captain let us cruise around for a while, the sun on our faces, spume spraying our shades, not a whale in sight, and then he found a patch of smooth blue ocean and cut the engine. I took a deep breath for the first time that day and accepted one of the yellow roses Corey's stepmom was passing out.

As the boat gently rocked, Miles ducked into the captain's deck, a wad of damp pages in one hand. A voice wavering between bass and nasal in that unmistakably teenage fashion came over the speakers. In his eulogy, Miles quoted Emerson with undergraduate solemnity and talked about how Corey had helped move him into his dorm and had checked in with him every night during his first months of school. It was not that different from what he'd done for me in Austin. "That part of my life is over," Miles concluded with a finality that should have been illegal for someone his age.

I tottered at the back of the boat, the smell of gasoline still stinging my nostrils, devising a plan for how I would smuggle Miles back to

Texas. It had occurred to me on the ride out beyond the harbor that Corey wasn't the only one light in the friend department. Besides his spindly abuela, Miles didn't have a single friend on that boat, no one from high school or college backing him up with a flask or a joint. Now I couldn't stand the thought of leaving him behind. "If anyone wants to share a few words, please come up," Miles was saying. Painful seconds passed in which no one made a move toward the captain's deck, not Anita or Corey's dad, not Daphne or me. This wasn't cool.

I poked Katie's leg with the stem of my rose. "I'll hold your rose, go," I said, and Katie gamely gripped the railing and strode up to the microphone in her calf-length boots and Joe Biden aviators. Most of her impromptu speech was snatched away by the wind, but she got in a good line about how Corey was excellent at "hanging out."

Battling a bout of inappropriate laughter, shoulders shaking, I handed Katie back her rose, too emotionally pinched off to cry. Miles reassumed the mic. "Now we'll scatter Corey's ashes," he reported.

I'd known this was coming but it still seemed sudden, indicative of a desire to get things over with. My dad had been dead two years and we still hadn't scattered his ashes.

Miles hung up the mic and descended the deck, heading sternward with his parents. The engine sputtered to life and the breeze picked up, the boat's wake spreading its white wings behind us. I remember the urn was lined with a plastic bag that Miles and his parents hoisted over the back of the boat and emptied like a wastebasket, letting Corey's ashes spill into the harbor, the wind for once, thank God, at his back. I composed myself with a single sniff and threw my rose in with the others.

In college, we called it going on tour when a guy came out of the closet and slept with anyone he could get his hands on. Seeing those childhood pictures of Corey that day, it was hard not to think of the angry teenager he had grown into, blaming his dad for making him gay, bleaching his hair, and then going on tour with his broken hand and beautiful dick. To think the simple act of having sex had made him sick. It wasn't fair.

*   *   *

With Anita's go-ahead, we carried Miles off to lunch at a restaurant in the harbor—Katie, Daphne, and I—watching from our table by the window as a batch of tourists deposited their shoes in a laundry basket and boarded *Salty Snail*. Even though we were the same age, Daphne gave off the sardonic vibes of an older sister. It was clear we would have gotten along if Corey had let us meet each other earlier.

"I think he was worried we'd all become friends and leave him behind," she said sadly, taking little stabs at her Cobb salad. "He wanted to keep us apart, the jerk."

Without realizing it, we honored Corey in the small way we could that day. We hung out and kept hanging out. An hour passed without anyone noticing. Afternoon sun sparkling off the water, the four of us walked the pier, a goth funeral procession somehow less miserable than the sendoff we'd just endured. We talked about *Waiting for Godot*, Quentin Tarantino, and comic books, anything to avoid saying goodbye. Corey hadn't mentioned Miles even liking comic books, but everything else about him was just as described, this short, sweet savant. We hugged and I let Miles climb into his car to collect his mom only if he promised to call.

"And if you think of it, send me the names of some comics." I hoped this might give us something to talk about in the off chance he did reach out.

I came home from the memorial to an email from Miles. Subject line: *Comics Reading List*. "So you asked for a comics reading list and while I could think of hundreds of cartoonists who I consider essential, I'll start you on ten of them. Ten Great Cartoonists, in No Particular Order."

Returning to my life as a Michener, I went to readings and wrote short stories and screenplays and put together a photo essay about my dad. Comics were a big part of my life, too. I spent the rest of that fall and winter placing holds at the public library, scavenging through the university stacks. On the phone with Miles past midnight, I might find myself scribbling down an artist's name to look up later. Miles talked about things like diagrammatic space and minimal line drawing, who it was blasphemous not to like and who was unmitigated filth. The kid had an astounding vocabulary and, it must be noted, some quirky phone habits.

If he called and I couldn't pick up, if I were, say, in class or hauling groceries up the stairs to my condo, he would try me ten or eleven times in a row, try until I dug my buzzing flip phone out of my pocket and answered. To my frantic "Is everything OK?" he would offer a casual, "Hey, Greg. Yup, everything's fine. How's it going?"

He was just checking in.

I put my few moth-eaten sweaters away that spring, made dating profiles, and met a twenty-two-year-old Cuban guy. He'd lost a testicle in college to an untreated hernia and replaced it with a prosthetic twice the size and hardness of his remaining ball. The jawbreaker, I called it. I vowed to protect his last surviving testicle, softly kissing it before bed, but my affection was misplaced. We parted ways because I was tired of standing at a Broken Social Scene concert and started to bicker that maybe Broken Social Scene wasn't the greatest band of all time, as he'd claimed. That was it. That was all it took to walk home three blocks apart from one another. I opened my front door and found the key I'd given him waiting for me on the arm of my couch. "He didn't even have the ball to break up with me," I told Mary, still feeling rawer about Corey than I cared to let on.

The constant in my life was Miles buzzing away on my phone. The theme of those days: Love the caller, hate the calls. I thought about not answering, just being done, but then I'd picture someone blocking Moe's number, how she'd just keep trying and trying. My disastrous attempt to help her address her disability made me that much more skittish about scaring away Miles. I just couldn't find the language to say, "Your brother told me you're on the spectrum. Is that what's going on? What the fuck is wrong with you, little genius man?" I knew even nudges toward self-revelation could feel like I was calling him out. Miles didn't need me to diagnose him any more than Moe did. He just needed me to listen. Still, the whole thing was intense. My phone would buzz and buzz, go to voicemail, then spring back to life like an unkillable cockroach you thought you'd squashed. I remember slumping on the kitchen floor with a Snickers bar and watching my phone skitter next to me, letting it ring and ring, trying not to cry. "Hi, Miles. Everything OK?"

The guy I dated after the Cuban came up with a solution. Rather than telling me to blow Miles off, this new guy, Lucas, suggested we set up a time to talk each week and stick to it. Make it part of the routine, text if anything came up. It worked. All those months of turmoil and stress and it was as simple as that. My phone would ring right at ten every Tuesday night and I made sure to answer. My own need for routine satisfied, I started to look forward to Miles's analytical announcer voice on the other end of the line. We talked about movies, comic books, art, the classes we were taking, comic books again. We talked on Corey's birthday, Christmas, the anniversary of his death. But mostly, we talked on Tuesdays at ten.

I'll admit I had a lot of questions, though I tried not to put Miles on the spot. Every time he confirmed another one of Corey's whoppers, my right leg would seize up and I'd hobble around my living room feeling stupid all over again, then just sad. There had never been any roommates in Santa Monica or a job as a construction site manager. Corey had lived in his mom's house with Miles the whole time we'd dated, picking up shifts at the dock. Nor did he go to the fancy religious academy whose decal he'd stuck in his truck window. Miles had. After coming out, Corey had gotten into some fights and been sent to a remedial high school in Orange County. He'd barely earned a diploma, let alone gone to Berkeley. His brotherly advice when Miles started college was "Don't give them a reason to hate you."

The trouble with fabulists is that once you doubt one thing they tell you, you come to doubt everything else: the three-month trek in Australia, the road trip to Bonnaroo. It's not even clear if Corey's dad ran over his hand with his truck. Daphne remembers him injuring the hand on a plumbing job. That one I deserved. I couldn't expect Corey to be honest about his impaired appendage when I wasn't all that forthcoming about mine. Maybe his hand was as mysterious as my leg. Cast out from his high school and a lot of his old life, Corey may have let his imagination run away with him. At some point it stopped being worth untangling the lies. What mattered was the truth at the heart of Corey's life: his little brother.

In a switcheroo worthy of Roald Dahl, it's Miles, not his older brother, with whom I've developed a long-distance friendship. I knew Corey for eight months. I've talked to Miles on the phone for more than a dozen years now. If it hadn't been for him, I probably would have come to reduce Corey to a cautionary tale from my twenties: The Jerk Who Lied About AIDS. Instead, I've gotten to know, posthumously, the loving big brother who pitched in for school supplies, the guy who may not have thought he was smart enough to go to college but made sure his brother got there. I'm reminded of the man who changed my life for the better.

The risk of talking about the dead is that we romanticize them. On the other hand, what's wrong with a little romance? Let me remember watching Clint Eastwood movies on the floor of my unfurnished living room with the only other person I knew in an entire city lying next to me, my arm going to sleep under him.

I like to think the certainty Miles and I would talk in those first years freed him to live his life, to draw and play Dungeons & Dragons, to switch his major from engineering to art and seek out other comic book lovers. I know it helped me. We still talk a couple times a year, sometimes for hours, though now Miles is in his thirties with a job at a wedding cake shop and a girlfriend. Baking has replaced comics as his obsession. Other stuff has changed, too, but you'll have to ask him about that. It's fair to say the kid is baffling, brilliant, ever-evolving, getting older by the day, just like I am. It's also fair to say he's not a kid anymore. More and more when I call, he offers a friendly hello and excuses himself, promising we'll catch up when he's not in the middle of something. I tell him not to worry. I'm just checking in.

"Life is long," I tell him. I say it into the phone like a wish, hoping he'll agree.

OUR CAMELOT, WITH CHICKENS

Lucas and I got married during a thunderstorm on a farm in east Austin. I remember the weirdest stuff about it—my mom speaking chicken to the chickens, the wedding planner's fedora, the stolen bottle of vodka (thanks Mitch)—and none of the stuff I should remember. I couldn't tell you which Adele song my mom and I danced to, but I'll never forget sipping my gin and tonic with satisfaction, a sweaty arm around Lucas, as the moochers from the food truck on the property (not our guests) came out of the fancy porta-potty our parents had paid for and doused themselves with Febreze they thought was free bug spray.

The farm came with a vintage airstream trailer named Miss Bliss. It was supposed to be a retreat for Lucas and me, but both our families piled in before the ceremony to get out of the heat, rendering the trailer some granny-chic version of a clown car, the doily-covered windows steaming with the swelter of soon-to-be in-laws, not lovemaking.

Not that I blame them. Miss Bliss had the only AC on the farm. It was late September and so hot and humid I had to change my shirt four times over the course of the day and night to keep from walking around drenched.

"Four times? More like seven," Lucas says now.

I drank and sweated and danced and sweated some more. We didn't have a wedding, I tell people. We had a shamanic experience. What I mean is: It was very hot.

"Don't rewrite history," Lucas says. "We had a great wedding. You cried the entire time."

"That's my point," I say. "I was severely dehydrated."

I hadn't wanted to walk down the aisle. It's not that I didn't want to get married or that I balked at the idea of my mom giving me away. I just couldn't stand the thought of limping in front of all our guests, the zippers on the sides of my stealthily orthopedic boots tinkling. *Step-drag. Step-drag.* I knew walking down the aisle was traditional, but screw tradition. There was nothing traditional about two thirtysomething dudes tying the knot on a chicken farm anyway.

A wedding is full of people meeting you for the first time. If I weren't careful, the day would devolve into me answering friendly questions about my leg. I didn't want to have to explain myself or make anyone feel embarrassed. "You looked stiff as a board coming down the aisle, buddy!" "Those must be some uncomfortable dress shoes! Got rocks in them?"

"What you saw was an involuntary spasm," I imagined saying. "Which is something I know about from Google. I have a disability, you ableist fuck. Thank you so much for the bath towels. They're the worst thing on our registry. Enjoy Austin!"

I had been visiting my mom in Salt Lake the morning the Supreme Court ruled on *Obergefell v. Hodges*, the 5–4 decision that made same-sex marriage legal in all fifty states. By the time I texted Lucas and figured out how to work Mom's DirecTV in the living room, President Obama was singing "Amazing Grace" at a Methodist church in Charleston, a eulogy that didn't have anything to do with marriage but one that was tangled up, for me, with grace in a larger sense: the grace of a dad who'd told his son it would all turn out OK.

Mom came out of her room with my dad's wedding band for me to try on. It was a little small. Once it was thoroughly stuck on my finger, removable only with Windex, Mom informed me that she put it on every now and then. "I wanted to wear it every day but I just couldn't. Too many sex dreams."

"Great to know," I replied, trying harder to pull it off.

Less than a month after the Supreme Court decision, on the hottest day of the year so far, Lucas and I spent the night at the Driskill in downtown Austin, where President Bush once planned his cabinet. We'd already talked through what was going to happen but we could afford a little romance. Surrounded by oil portraits of cowboys and crossed revolvers, we made history of our own kind. I sat in a chair and Lucas got on his knees and proposed. I said yes.

Initially, I hadn't wanted a big wedding. I had wanted to go away and come back and just be married. Scribble vows on bar napkins, utter them on courthouse steps, seal them with a kiss. That idea lasted the length of one phone call with my mom. One minute of one phone call. Her reaction to our engagement that night was so huge it felt like grief. She cried for a long time and ran out to the balcony of her apartment in Salt Lake to howl up at the night, trying to get Dad's attention as he jogged in the sky. *We did it, Bob. We raised our son. He's getting married.*

My path to matrimony hadn't been smooth. I lost Corey to AIDS seven months before meeting Lucas on OKCupid and I was still so traumatized by the experience I had convinced myself, high on a friend's super-strong weed on a trip to Utah, that Lucas was too good to be true. Was he really who he said he was? I mean, look at my track record.

No longer content to have guys jerk me off and then jerk me around, I'd called Lucas, who was back in Texas, and asked him point-blank what was up. Instead of being scared away by my paranoia and inability to handle any drug more potent than caffeine, he picked me up from the airport and told me to open the glove compartment, where I found, in a tidy stack, every piece of government-issued ID he owned: social security card, passport, voter registration.

The message was clear. The man was who he said he was, and so much more.

Lucas is from a family of psychologists and was unflappable when it came to hearing about all that had gone down in my life: Kevin and Corey, cancer and ALS. "It's all so recent!" Lucas said, grilling steaks at his place on Mary Street one evening.

It's funny I had questioned his identity because, of the two of us, *I* was the one living like a serial killer. On one of our first dates, I invited Lucas over to kill a cockroach I had trapped under a mason jar. That was how I was managing at the time: with cockroaches trapped under jars. I was on my mom's Costco account and my cupboards were flung open, as if ransacked, and stuffed with stacks of Cup Noodles and Chef Boyardee. I kept a box of Snickers bars in the fridge for lunch. I was devoted to buying in bulk.

Thankfully, Lucas thought the idea of an adult having a cupboard full of Chef Boyardee was sidesplitting rather than creepy or sad. After the cockroach had been dispatched and the Boyardee slurped, we ended up making out on the couch. He told me years later he'd noticed I wasn't hard but took it as a challenge to be a better kisser.

Lucas was lean and tall with square glasses and twinkling green eyes. I studied him in a way I wouldn't have before Corey, suspicious of how he turned from unassuming Clark Kent into Semitic Superman when he took off his specs. The closer I looked, the better. That worried me, but I kept looking.

Lucas had cute, furry shoulders that jumped when he laughed, freckles and little red angioma (benign, hereditary, non-contagious, I checked) on his chest and back, early-onset crow's feet, and a kind smile full of mismatched teeth. His feet were as arched as a dancer's or an evil stepsister's, and I'd never seen more muscular calves. (His balletic turnout blew Moe's mind.) When we went night swimming together in Barton Springs, he'd turn on his back and kick, like an otter. He'd worn a bar between his legs as a one- or two-year-old and he walked just a little bit on his toes.

There was no getting around it: the guy was my type.

Life with Lucas was fun. It still is. The alarm on his phone, a jingle repeating the phrase *Good morning*, made me laugh. Lucas taught seventh-grade English and history at an all-girls school, and though he often spoke in the wry tone of someone sipping the world's driest martini he usually had a nursery rhyme or old summer camp song stuck in his head. "Wherever You Go, There's Always Someone Jewish" was our hit single of summer 2011. His favorite adjective, for reasons that are still inexplicable to me, was *jolly*. "You jolly fool!" he'd say. He was so ticklish he could barely bring himself to hug. Touching was a chore for him. "No soft touch!" he'd cry in bed. "No soft touch!"

Oh, yes, soft touch. Soft touch for sure.

As for my own physical shortcomings, Lucas didn't notice my leg until I pointed it out on our third date. "You limp?" he asked. I found his apparent absentmindedness charming.

Lucas may not have found everything I did charming, but he didn't break up with me when I brought a Tupperware container of raw almonds to the Arbor rather than paying for popcorn. I started to fall for him when he agreed to walk out of *The Tree of Life* with Mary and me. He let me pluck his ears—I referred to the thatches of hair sprouting on either side of his head as his Princess Leia buns—and he was unfazed by the condom wrappers that crinkled underfoot when I at last let us graduate from making out on the couch to making out in the bedroom.

Long, painful experience had taught me to keep my jeans on during those make-out sessions and to put off sex for as long as possible under the guise of taking things slow. I could still hear my eighth-grade health teacher, Mrs. Shell, imploring me, in a coach's weary bark, to *keep buttons buttoned and zippers zipped* and to *stay vertical*. Staying vertical was the whole problem. I still had some serious ED. Most guys I was with eventually wanted to bottom and when I couldn't deliver, they would drift away. They never told me my lack of tumescence was the reason things didn't work out between us—but of course they didn't. They weren't monsters. They were just a bunch of disappointed buttholes.

"I'm a slob, not a slut," I told Lucas. "At least you know I practice safe sex."

"A lot of it," Lucas observed, peeling a condom wrapper off his foot.

"Practice" is the optimum word here because I had bought a box of Trojans in bulk and gotten a little carried away ripping them open and slipping them on, like a chaste teenager. I was practicing using condoms, not practicing safe sex, wanting to be prepared if a boner should ever accompany me in the presence of another human being.

The night we went up to my bedroom, I melodramatically confessed to Lucas I could never top him. My dick just didn't work like that.

"I didn't realize we were having sex this instant," Lucas quipped, pulling down his madras shorts. From the look of it he was ready to go whenever.

Lucas spent so much time at my condo that summer we pretty much lived together. Back at the adorable house he rented a few blocks away, the one with the backyard grill, his best friend/roommate—whose last name, get this, is Jolly—put a clothing rack in his bedroom and turned it into a closet.

One night I came back from class to discover Lucas had cleaned my condo from top to bottom, picked up the paper explosion in the office and the condom wrappers in the bedroom.

That's it, I thought. *I have to fuck this guy.*

That week we went into the county health clinic for a battery of STD tests, like a model couple. Our pipsqueak counselor had floppy bangs he kept pushing out of his face; Lucas was sure he was wearing a wig. The counselor asked us to evaluate our HIV risk on a scale of one to ten. I said seven. Lucas said one.

"One?" the counselor asked.

"It's been a while," Lucas deadpanned.

In the end he compromised. "You know what?" Lucas said. "Add a point-five just to be safe."

The evaluation sheet the counselor gave Lucas after the appointment went under a koala magnet on the fridge, like an IOU for a cute picture of us. Under the "goals" section at the bottom, the counselor had written in the following for Lucas: "My new partner and I will continue to use condoms for anal sex and continue to talk about STDs."

If only Lucas knew what he was signing up for. Being in a monogamous relationship didn't turn off my hypochondria. STDs were still all I talked about. STDs and my mom.

On the first day of Christmas break that year, Lucas moved in officially. He spent the rest of the holiday with my family in Salt Lake. I was a little nervous bringing him home. My family isn't a family. It's a way of life, and a chaotic one at that. I shouldn't have worried. Within a day, Lucas was crammed into a folding chair watching Moe play a candy cane in Cristóbal's off-brand *Nutcracker*, and a day after that he was jingling down the stairs in a Santa Claus costume my mom had rented to entertain my nieces and nephews.

Santa Lucas wore cowboy boots and a fake white beard over his real one that made him so ticklish he had to keep pulling at it.

"A Jewish Santa!" mused Mitch's husband.

Lucas hadn't grown up celebrating Christmas and didn't know the first thing about it: the names of the reindeer, say, or whether Mrs. Claus was Santa's wife or his mother. I was happy to educate him, knowing he'd love the songs. "Round *yon* virgin," I'd say, "not young virgin. Like, 'See that virgin over yonder? Go gather round her.'"

When it came to exchanging gifts, Lucas gave me a pair of expensive tweezers with my name inscribed on them, both a tribute to my skills plucking his ears and an indictment of them. *Greg Marshall*, TWEEZER-MAN. "Don't you get it?" Lucas said. "Tweezerman is the name of the brand and that's your name. You're Tweezerman!"

I had to admit it was a genius gift. In return, I gave him a Norelco nose hair trimmer.

"What's up with you two and plucking hairs?" Danny asked, popping a pimple on Moe's back as she screamed.

"If you ever break up with him, we're taking him and not you," my mom told me before we left for the airport after the new year.

Two Christmases later, in 2013, we were once again in Salt Lake when a district court overturned Prop 3, the constitutional amendment banning same-sex marriage, the one I'd fought against for Don't Amend the summer after freshman year of college. For a few weeks, before a higher court put a stay on the order, gay couples could tie the knot in Utah. In less than a decade, Don't Amend had gone from fringe to status quo. I thought about my dad telling me at the end of that discouraging summer that I'd find someone special and that we'd get married. That everything would turn out Gina Jones. Even platitudes sound prophetic when they come from your dying dad, especially when they take years to become reality.

It was too early for marriage talk with Lucas. We'd been together only two years and I was still waiting for his schizophrenic break or for his wife to turn up on our doorstep, something. There was just no way someone this untroubled could like me. When we fought, I had to tell Lucas to be more of an asshole, like my mom used to do to my dad. We concluded that a Yuletide courthouse wedding was out but a dress rehearsal wouldn't hurt. I pulled out my yellow XXL Don't Amend shirt from the closet and made Lucas take a selfie of us kissing in front of the Temple. "Merry Equality Christmas!" I posted on Facebook. It got eight likes. Equality Christmas never became a thing, no matter how hard I tried to make it one.

I had always told myself that if I didn't have tight tendons I'd have no problem getting any guy I wanted. It turned out I just needed Lucas. Flings and one-night stands were the opposite of enjoyable. It took the patience and trust of a long-term partner, experimenting with different positions, to figure out what put the least strain on my legs, and my ego. We didn't have a bad sex life, Lucas and I, just one with constraints.

Occasionally I tried to top, piling more pillows under my ass than *The Princess and the Pea*. I'd end up feeling like buttered linguini, my trembling right leg straight out in front, my left leg bent, a finger doing the work the rest of me couldn't. I was like the world's most incompetent proctologist, a doorbell ditcher who'd lost the will to run, one who just kept pressing and pressing. "Is that your dick?" Lucas would say from on top of me. "Is *that* your dick?"

Sex is more delicious and complicated than being a top or bottom, a pitcher or a catcher, and I learned to enjoy playing ball, even if I couldn't compete in every position. At the same time, I'm a guy. I suspected that if I could top, even just once, I would stop worrying about it.

This is where my mom's Viagra comes in.

Shortly after my dad died, she had gone on a trip with Moe and Tiffany to Costa Rica and visited a local pharmacy, the kind where you didn't need a prescription to get painkillers. I'm not sure if it was the language barrier or what, but she'd gotten nervous at the last minute and accidentally scored Viagra instead of Vicodin.

Years later, she presented the sorry story to me as a joke, playing it for laughs. I saw it more as a bawdy fairy tale about a drooping, uncut beanstalk, the Jack in the story a gay man named Greg, his magic beans arriving not via witch but via widow.

"Doesn't that just figure? I got the one drug I have no interest in using," Mom said.

"I'll take the Viagra, Mom," I said. "Really."

"Don't be silly, honey. You are your father's son. You don't need Viagra."

Mom deflected and demurred and "lost" the Viagra for months in her jumbled medicine cabinet. "It's expired. I need to ask Alice if it'd be OK to give to you," she finally admitted.

"So ask her," I said. "Or I can give her a call."

"Hi Greg," Alice shouted in the background, busted. I knew I'd been on speakerphone. To be fair, Alice was probably tired of having a phone thrust in her face, answering urgent questions about my privates. She told me once she never would have imagined her life with my mom would involve so many dick pics. "I don't think expired Viagra would do anything bad. The worst that'll happen is that it won't work."

The crushed four-pack arrived a week later with a greeting card that swept aside Mom's previous reservations. *Thought you boys would have fun with these. I can't use them. Ha!* The price sticker was still on the box. Mom had shelled out 22,500 colónes, or about forty dollars, for these powder-blue, fifty-milligram pills, each shaped like a diamond. I put the box on the alarm clock on my nightstand and waited for the right time.

That March, Lucas and I went to a Renaissance festival about an hour outside of town. Sherwood Forest Faire, it's called, off the whimsically named Old Potato Road.

It was one of those days when you feel dumb with love and vitamin D. We gnawed on turkey legs, sipped mead, threw knives, and even hyper-ticklish Lucas put on chainmail. When we got home, without saying anything, I punched out one of the boner pills and swallowed it down with an unromantic slurp of LaCroix. I figured it was a day for trying new things. It had been a decade since I'd lost my virginity in college, and here I was trying to lose it all over again, this time with nothing to hide.

Taking off his glasses, Lucas squinted at the long-past expiration date on the box. November 2009. *Five years ago.* "Where'd your mom get these again?" he asked.

"Who cares, too late," I said. I stripped off my clothes and lay atop the comforter, like I was about to be sucked into a UFO.

Seconds passed, then minutes. I felt my heartbeat in my extremities and saw myself rise like a slowly inflating air dancer at a car dealership. We dizzily propped a pillow under my rear and scrolled to a Dave Matthews playlist. Lucas climbed on top. It took about an hour of trying. Then it was all me. I lasted about thirty halting, exhilarating seconds.

Afterward, I cried.

It wasn't perfect. The first time never is.

You may be wondering why I didn't just go to the doctor for Viagra if I wanted it so badly, but if I had been the sort of twenty-nine-year-old to go to the doctor for Viagra I probably would have been the sort to know I had cerebral palsy all along rather than finding out about it while applying for health insurance that fall. I suppose it was all mixed up with my leg, being terrified of illness and fallibility, avoiding any doctor who wasn't a dermatologist or a cheery technician swabbing my throat for STDs I never had.

Mom did not handle getting caught lying to me about CP for nearly thirty years with a ton of magnanimity. (Remember the beginning of the book when she cursed my dead dad for making her handle this alone?) I knew that whatever I wanted to find out about my leg was up to me. In the days after that first marathon phone call in the fall of 2014, I made an appointment with a primary care physician at a community clinic in Austin, noting on my intake papers that I had cerebral palsy, drops of sweat splashing onto the page. The doctor was Southern and genteel with a gray goatee, like Colonel Sanders, and a propensity to sweat as much as I did. The heat and sweat and slowly churning desk fan gave our daytime confab a hard-boiled feel. He looked at me, wiped his brow, looked at my chart, looked back at me. "You have cerebral palsy?"

"I do."

I half expected Frankie to jump out at me with a butcher knife, maybe take out the Colonel too, sobbing as she sliced at us, "*I don't! Believe! In labels!*" The doctor wrote me a referral for an orthopedic surgeon and helped me down from the exam table, the paper under me sticking to my damp butt and legs like I'd had an accident. He scheduled a follow-up to check on my blood pressure.

I can't say visiting the orthopedic surgeon did much to lower it. In cowboy boots and a snap-button shirt, he looked like he might be shooting a Chevy commercial. He tried to rotate my rigid right foot, moving it around like a stuck stick shift. "Sure is tight!" He spoke slowly and asked if I'd gone to college in that small-talky way of doctors. "Northwestern, wow! You must be real smart." He had me walk for him in the hall and told me how lucky I was and to come back when I had hurt myself. "Whether it's your knee or your hip we'll fix ya right up. Can't do much for you now, though. You're walking pretty good."

"How'd it go?" Lucas asked when I got home.

"It was worthless," I said, lobbing my keys onto the couch. "I can see why my mom lied to me about my leg. It's not like any of these doctors can do anything about it."

The growing pains related to my leg made me feel all the luckier to have ended up with Lucas. Our relationship has always smacked of serendipity. We know couples who waited years, decades even, to get legally married, with all the tax breaks and protections and nice dishes that come with it. My mom and Alice couldn't have gotten married in Utah or Delaware back in the day, not even if they'd really wanted to. We were keenly aware that we had the kind of opportunities our forefathers and gay moms didn't. As we were getting off the flight home from Costa Rica for Tiffany's wedding, a woman stopped us out of the blue to say she hadn't seen two people so in love in a long time. "Enjoy each other," she said. We do. We know our luck.

We were going to get married at the moment and in the manner of our choosing, and I complained about it all: the catering misfires that sent us scrambling for the bathroom, the upset phone calls and

Facebook messages from family friends who were or weren't invited, who would or wouldn't come. We had to devise a regular plan *and* a rain plan and put down deposits on both. Life bent toward convention. People who were scared of Zika or too chickenhearted to come to a gay wedding sent along beautiful geode bookends and hideous hot-pink champagne flutes with their regrets.

When it came to walking down the aisle, I was the biggest chicken of all. I planned to just wait for Lucas under the ancient pecan tree where we would recite our vows. The chandelier hanging from its branches would provide the only drama we needed.

"You little shit," my mom said when I made my proclamation at the rehearsal. Mom poked me with her water bottle. "I didn't survive a bazillion chemos and outlive your father so you could stand under a tree."

With everyone in the wedding party fanning themselves and threatening to pass out in the heat, I finally caved. "Fine," I told my mom, snatching her hand. "Let's do it."

Scraping my foot down the dirt aisle on our walkthrough, I tried to count the number of steps to the pecan tree but lost track when Mom dropped to her knees, wrapped her arms around my legs, and started fake sobbing. "I won't give him up. I won't!" Then, with considerably less alacrity, she climbed back onto her feet and brushed herself off. "I'll give you up," she told me, "but it'll just be pretend."

The phrase "in sickness and in health" kept kicking around my brain. At thirty-one, I was still young but my body would not age gracefully. I knew that. My back would only get sorer and more hunched, my hamstrings and shoulders tighter. My muscles would shrink and stiffen. My balance would deteriorate with my posture. I'd tire faster, be plagued with knee and hip problems in a losing battle with gravity.

Already, I'd made small adjustments. I'd given up running on the treadmill because of a gargantuan wart on the pad of my right big toe, the result of smacking with each step. Hesitantly, I'd traded in the runner's high I craved, and my dad's old Asics, for the lesser joys of the elliptical and the rowing machine. I couldn't go around

beating up my legs for sport anymore. A fall down the steps outside
our condo left me with a bruised tailbone and hobbling around on
a CVS cane for a couple of weeks. I learned to watch my step and
check to make sure my foot had clearance at the top of every flight,
like an amateur Euclid.

None of these coming attractions of aging were revelatory, exactly.
What was new was that I wouldn't make the passage alone. Lucas had
taught me to find tranquility in my body and appreciate it for more
than its hour of daily exercise, to notice it rather than always trying to
fix it. Now when I pictured my bald, sagging future self, I could also
picture my arm in Lucas's, his crow's feet no longer premature, his horn-
rimmed Groucho glasses no longer the ironic look of an overworked
teacher, his curly hair as white as baby powder. I'd walk through life
on my own two feet but I'd be joined in matrimony. At the end of the
aisle, I'd have Lucas.

We skipped the bachelor party but in the hotel the night before the
wedding Tiffany slipped a bubblegum-colored sash over me. BACH-
ELORETTE, it read in sparkly rhinestones, except Tiffany had picked
out the ETTE, casting it in stubble. My sash had a five o'clock shadow.

When the big day finally arrived, we felt good. Hillary was ahead in
the polls. Justice Scalia, the staunchest opponent to marriage equality,
had died at a ranch forty-five minutes south of us and was rolling over
in his grave, a tidbit my future father-in-law would note over cracks
of thunder in his toast later on. Forget the old ways. We were making
new ones. Miss Bliss had a sign in it: MR. & MRS. . . . AND THEY LIVED
HAPPILY EVER AFTER! We stuck our pointer fingers in there to make it
MR. and MR. S. That's "s" for Sodomy!

It was sunny while we took pre-ceremony pictures and so hot I
was ready to call the whole thing off. My mom could get weird about
being with a woman around our relatives and I kept pulling Alice into
family shots before Mom could leave her out. Ever hopeful of her own
prospects at tying the knot with a Marshall, Alice had worn a MARRY
US! T-shirt to our casual rehearsal dinner the night before and posted up

unsubtly beside my mom. Today, she was in a classy pressed white shirt and pearls, like she was the one getting hitched, camcorder strapped to her palm to capture any romantic twist.

By the time guests started arriving the sky had turned to a dim whitish blue. When they got drinks at the bar and ambled to the pews around the pecan tree, it was thundering.

We lined up to walk down the aisle.

The sleeves of my suit jacket were a little too long and I kept fussing with them, thinking they made my hands look boyish, like I was dressed up for a play.

Lucas and I had bought our suits off the rack at Macy's. It hadn't occurred to us to have them altered. They were even the same size, which made no sense because Lucas was a good three inches taller and an inch or two slimmer.

"You're bigger in back," the saleslady had told me, making a scooping, butt-shaped motion with her hands. "It makes up for your shorter legs." It had never once occurred to me, in thirty-one years of questioning everything, to question the size of my ass. Thanks, marriage.

"Let's go," shouted my future father-in-law, pumping a stringy arm in a circle like a first-base coach. "It's about to start pouring."

The wedding planner put a hand on her fedora to keep it from blowing off. "We're waiting on the last party bus!"

"Screw the last party bus," screamed Tiffany, pulling down the hem of her cocktail dress. Even in the gloom it sparkled.

I chugged half my beer and set it next to a cactus.

I suppose it was a good sign it was the walk down the aisle and not the lifelong commitment I was about to make that freaked me out. My leg trembled under me but I figured it would hold. It had carried me this far. It could carry me a little bit farther. Lucas was just ahead of us, a parent on each arm. He reached up to scratch his mustache with a long, tapered finger. Lucas! The man I vowed to limp beside the rest of my days.

To think of that stormy, sweltering Texas wedding now. So many of the most important people in our lives were huddled together around an old tree, sports coats and shawls pulled over their heads, umbrellas opened, Lucas and I about to climb into the center of all that love. "It was our Camelot, with chickens," I tell anyone who asks. "It was there and then it was gone."

At the last minute, we had chosen to enter to "Here Comes the Sun." It was the song my mom and dad played at their wedding in 1978. I'd meant it as a tribute, but I think Mom was a little offended. We weren't paying tribute; we'd stolen their song.

Mom took my hand, squeezed it. Her nails were unpainted and bitten to the quick. She wasn't wearing the diamond engagement ring she'd picked out with Alice. Instead, she'd slid my dad's dull gold wedding band onto her middle finger, sex dreams be damned. A bit of subterfuge in front of Dad's family, yes, but it was the only way for him to walk down the aisle with us—one final conjuring trick from the Mother of Oz.

Mom will be gone someday, but not really. There are parts of us cancer can't kill, not even after 140 chemos, a number that will surely be out of date by the time you are reading this book and one that is probably approaching a Guinness World Record, and too many surgeries to count. Non-Hodgkin's lymphoma, viral meningitis, H. pylori, breast cancer, skin cancer, a troubling dependency on fentanyl, iced tea, and yogurt—none of it has taken Mom out. If she were just swollen lymph nodes, bones, chalky white pills, and sticky patches, she would have died thirty years ago, disappearing under an itchy wig like one of Roald Dahl's witches. I'd be writing about an evil stepmom instead. Probably, I wouldn't be writing at all.

The heart of the matter isn't the same as the whole truth. Columnist, greeting card writer, avenging angel, Mom disavowed cerebral palsy in the newspaper as a way of peeling the label off my leg and throwing that label in the trash.

For all the hours I spent pleasantly sipping a Coke in front of the TV as a kid, I spent even more time attempting to ride a bike without training wheels, pulling myself along lane lines during kickboard drills at swim practice, or reciting Hail Marys on the ski slopes as my little sisters glided past me down the mountain. One sock was always soaked, flopping off my foot. My lungs ached from running, my wrists from catching myself when I lost my balance. I lasted about forty-five minutes as a Boy Scout before going home to soak in the bathtub.

It could be fun wanting the world. I guess that's my silver lining.

Of course I'd walk down the aisle.

In the distance, the chandelier shook on its hundred-year-old bough, like someone upstairs was testing the plumbing. A drop or two of rain hit my face. Soon it'd be thundering and pouring in silver streaks and we'd be under the wedding tent I'd almost cheaped out on having us rent, sweating and drinking and dancing to the euphoric sounds of Whitney Houston and Sia.

"Your dad would have loved Lucas," Mom said, swinging my arm like she'd done when I was a kid just learning to walk. "I'm sorry they never met."

"Me too," I managed.

As Dad's legs had given out, the walks with him had become trickier. If Danny or Tiffany weren't around, I had to take the lead getting him into his wheelchair. Pulling Dad to a sitting position, hand on the back of his head, breathing tubes over my shoulder, I'd stand him up and pivot, and we'd both dip down to the seat, hoping I'd remembered to apply the brake.

Most of the time, I could transfer him no problem, but I did drop him once. On his knees, as the machines squawked, Dad held me in his gaze and mouthed the word *lift*. The tennis we'd played over the years, the conversations we'd shared, his relentless assurances that I'd find the right guy—it had been a kind of dance, the abstract movement of two people responding to each other. Lifting your dad off the floor is no less a dance. I couldn't have done it without him, without all the strength in his legs and mine.

Boob et Gregoire, Paris, June 1999

ACKNOWLEDGMENTS

Zack Knoll's belief in *Leg* changed not just the course of my writing life but also the narrative of failure I'd built for myself as a person with a disability: that someone like me, no matter what else I might accomplish, would never be good enough or smart enough to publish a book. Zack, you win the award for funniest track changes. Thank you for being younger and cooler than I am and for knowing that a book about a gay guy with a secret case of cerebral palsy and a messy family deserves a spot on the shelf. I hope *Leg* doesn't get banned, but if it does I suppose we'll know we've done our job.

Thank you to everyone at Abrams: Annalea Manalili, Margaret Moore, Melissa Wagner, Sarah Masterson Hally, Devin Grosz, Deb Wood, Andrew Gibeley, Kevin Callahan, Christian Westermann, Melanie Chang, Jamison Stoltz, Michael Sand, Michael Jacobs, Elisa Gonzales, and Lindy Humphreys.

Thank you to the other member of this dream team, Hannah Brattesani of the Friedrich Agency. Hannah, your stewardship, editorial guidance, and humor are a gift. I hope to be sending postcards back and forth about Budd, Chet, and Joe for years to come. *Leg* would not have been published without you.

Thanks to the Michener Center for Writers: Jim Magnuson, Marla Akin, Debbie Dewees. Hugest thanks of all to *my* favorite literary couple, Elizabeth McCracken and Edward Carey, who have encouraged me in countless ways in the decade since I graduated, sometimes while shucking oysters and pouring champagne.

Thank you to MacDowell and Yaddo for helping me rediscover a sense of joy in creation. I loved my time as a bon vivant in the winter of 2018.

Thank you to the National Endowment for the Arts for the enormous financial and psychological boost. It came not long before the pandemic and sustained me.

Thanks to the magazine editors who took a chance on my work, especially Colleen Kinder, Bobby Rae, Yi Shun Lai, Kelly Luce, and Chaya Bhuvaneswar.

Special thanks to *The Best American Essays* and Robert Atwan for patiently sorting through the mail random writers like me send you year after year. Shout-out to Leslie Jamison for changing my life by including me in the 2017 edition.

Thanks to my early readers who also happen to be three of my favorite writers: Katie O'Reilly, Mary Miller, and my brother Danny. I hope you enjoy reading my stuff half as much as I enjoy yours. If not, sorry for the years of suffering.

Thanks, Chloé Cooper Jones. Your irreducible work and friendship swung open doors in my mind that have been stuck for years. And thank you, Ryan O'Connell, trailblazer and fellow power top. In spite of being my most famous friend, you read my book the fastest.

I'm grateful to the many teachers I've had over the years: Anna Keesey, Sheila Donahue, Stuart Dybek, Allan Gurganus, Lane Fenrich, Jennifer Flitton, Kay Quealy, Charlotte Howe, Lyn Harrison, Justin Thompson, Nancy Ballard, and Jill Thackeray.

Thanks to the friends who cheered me on in the writing of *Leg*. Some of you are in the book and some of you aren't. It's a compliment both ways, I promise. Thanks Iris Moulton, Gretchen Schramm, Lizzy Karp, Natalie Knight, Libby Walker, Yalitza Ferreras, Sheree Greer, Beena Kamlani, Kamila Forson, Mary Adkins, Lee Pinkas, Julia Hill, Lazaro Camarillo, Grace Preston, Christina Child, Barbara Vujanović, Scott Guild, Parini Shroff (book twin!), Destiny Birdsong, Juleen Johnson, Julia Wertz, Fiona Doyle, Amy Waldman, Lewis Hyde, Carrie Laben, Monica Macansantos, Chad Nichols, Elizabeth Pinborough, Maud Newton, Koji Nakano, and Haruko Tanaka. Ghosts see ghosts. Thanks to the Pod (Téa, Dan, Gully, etc.) and to the Briarcreek Boys.

Thanks Mercedes and Mango, Epplers, Barrells, and Howes.

Thanks to my godfather, Gary Neuenschwander of Wisconsin, for proofreading my college papers and for teaching me about punctuation, wit, and style.

Thank you to my four siblings—Tiffany, Danny, Mitch, and Moe—for showing me it's OK to take up space and live the life you want. No book, let alone the note at the back of one, could hope to capture all the nuances of our relationships or the agony of growing up Marshall. I hope my love for each of you shines through.

Thank you to my mom for teaching me to never, never, never give up. I know when you adopted that slogan you were talking about cancer, not your son's one-liners about your wigs and iced tea consumption. I'm proud of the way you have continued to heal and move forward after Dad's death. When I first started pitching some version of this book to agents they all assumed you were dead—and that was like eight years ago. I'm thankful for all the trips to physical therapy, singing "Barbara Ann." You gave me the courage (and the balls) to keep going.

Thanks, Alice. My mom wouldn't have made it without you.

Thanks, Dad. I'd say more but you're dead.

Thank you to my husband, Lucas Schaefer. I couldn't have written a word of this memoir without the safety and sanctuary of our marriage. I can't wait for your book to come out so we can afford real floor lamps. You're going to be a great dad. You already are one to our poop machine, Zeus.

Finally, thank you, reader. Maybe you loved this book so much you're still wiping the tears from your eyes, or maybe you thought, *Seriously? I could write something ten times better.* I hope you do. I hope your leg gets all the love it deserves. Remember to never, never, never give up.

ABOUT THE AUTHOR

GREG MARSHALL was raised in Salt Lake City, Utah. A National Endowment for the Arts Fellow in Prose, Greg is a graduate of the Michener Center for Writers. His work has appeared in *The Best American Essays* and has been supported by MacDowell and the Corporation of Yaddo. He lives in Austin, Texas, with his husband, Lucas, and their dog, Zeus. *Leg* is his first book.